To My Parents

The difference between the mathematical mind (*esprit de géométrie*) and the perceptive mind (*esprit de finesse*): the reason that mathematicians are not perceptive is that they do not see what is before them, and that, accustomed to the exact and plain principles of mathematics, and not reasoning till they have well inspected and arranged their principles, they are lost in matters of perception where the principles do not allow for such arrangement. . . . These principles are so fine and so numerous that a very delicate and very clear sense is needed to perceive them, and to judge rightly and justly when they are perceived, without for the most part being able to demonstrate them in order as in mathematics; because the principles are not known to us in the same way, and because it would be an endless matter to undertake it. We must see the matter at once, at one glance, and not by a process of reasoning, at least to a certain degree. . . . Mathematicians wish to treat matters of perception mathematically, and make themselves ridiculous . . . the mind . . . does it tacitly, naturally, and without technical rules.

—PASCAL, *Pensées*

Contents

Part III. Alternatives to the Traditional Assumptions

CONCLUSION: The Scope and Limits of Artificial Reason

Preface

In choosing to dissect artificial intelligence, Hubert Dreyfus has undertaken an inquiry of great public importance. This branch of science is seen by its practitioners as the basis for much more powerful versions of the computer technology that already pervades our society. As anyone can see who reads the daily press, many people are torn between hopes and fears aroused by digital computers, which they find mostly incomprehensible and whose import therefore they cannot judge. But, as science lays claim to public support, so the public has a claim on critical analyses of science.

Dreyfus serves all of us in venturing into an arcane technical field as a critical layman, a professional philosopher committed to questioning and analyzing the foundations of knowledge. Far, therefore, from shunning him as an unwelcome intruder or pelting him with acrimonious invective, artificial intelligence should welcome Dreyfus, draw on his correct insights, and set him right publicly, gently but ever so firmly, where misunderstandings or incomprehensions might flaw his logic. Dreyfus raises important and fundamental questions. One might therefore expect the targets of his criticisms to react with greater human intelligence than when they simply shouted loud in response to his earlier sallies. The issues deserve serious public debate. They are too scientific to be left to philosophers and too philosophical to be left to scientists.

Dreyfus sees agonizingly slow progress in all fundamental work on artificial intelligence. This he interprets as a sign of impenetrable barriers, rather than as the normal price for overcoming enormous technical and conceptual difficulties on the way to inevitable success. He sees artificial intelligence as limited by its assumption that the world is explicable in terms of elementary atomistic concepts, in a tradition traceable back to the Greeks. This insight challenges not only contemporary science and technology but also some of the foundations of Western philosophy. He puts in question the basic role that *rules* play in accepted ideas of what constitutes a satisfactory scientific explanation. Thereby he strikes at far more than the ability in principle of digital computers—bound as they are to follow rules—to exhibit intelligence of a kind which, according to his analysis, cannot be explained according to Kantian rules.

He is too modern to ask his questions from a viewpoint that assumes that man and mind are somehow set apart from the physical universe and therefore not within reach of science. Quite to the contrary, he states explicitly his assumption that "there is no reason why, in principle, one could not construct an artificial embodied agent if one used components sufficiently like those which make up a human being." Instead, he points out that his questions are "philosophically interesting only if we restrict ourselves to asking if one can make such a robot by using a digital computer." Curiously enough to this technologist, Dreyfus's own philosophical arguments lead him to see digital computers as limited not so much by being mindless, as by having no *body.*

This conclusion emerges from the contrast between the ability of human beings to "zero in" on relevant features of their environment while ignoring myriad irrelevancies and the enormous and admitted difficulty of artificial intelligence in determining what is relevant when the environment presented to a digital computer has not, in some way, been artificially constrained. The central statement of this theme is that "a person experiences the objects of the world as already interrelated and full of meaning. There is no justification for the assumption that we first experience isolated facts or snapshots of facts or momentary views of snapshots of isolated facts and *then* give them significance. This is the point that contemporary philosophers such as Heidegger and Wittgenstein are trying to make." The burden of artificial intelligence is indeed its apparent need to proceed—in futility—from the atom to the whole. People, on the other hand, effectively seem to perceive first a whole and only then, if necessary, analyze it into atoms. This, Dreyfus argues following Merleau-Ponty, is a consequence of our having bodies capable of an ongoing but unanalyzed mastery of their environment.

Either Dreyfus's position or that of artificial intelligence might some day be corroborated or destroyed by new evidence from artificial intelligence itself, from psychology, neurophysiology, or other related disciplines. Unless and until this happens, Dreyfus's work will stand for the layman as a lucid analysis of a difficult matter of great public moment. To the computer scientist concerned with progress in his specialty and with deeper understanding of the world, Dreyfus presents a profound challenge to the widespread idea that "knowledge consists of a large store of neutral data." Dreyfus clearly is not neutral.

—Anthony G. Oettinger
Aiken Computation Laboratory
Harvard University

Acknowledgments

The occasional acknowledgments scattered throughout the following pages only begin to reflect my indebtedness to a host of sympathetic and critical readers who not only weeded out mistakes but made many substantive suggestions. Without the help of Ned Block, Susan Carey Block, Burton Bloom, Stuart Dreyfus, John Haugeland, Terrance Malick, Anthony Oettinger, Seymour Papert, George Rey, Charles Taylor, and Samuel Todes, this book would have been published much sooner and been easier to read, but also easier to dismiss.

I am grateful to the American Council of Learned Societies, the National Science Foundation, and the RAND Corporation for supporting various stages of my research and writing, and to the Study Group on the Unity of Knowledge for enabling me to organize colloquia on several topics which subsequently found their way into the book.

I also want to thank Rena Lieb for debugging an early version of the manuscript, and especially Barbara Behrendt, who deciphered the first draft and helped in more ways than I can mention.

In making the changes which I hope improve the form and content of this revised edition I have been especially helped by Geneviève Boissier-Dreyfus and John Searle.

Introduction to the Revised Edition

What Computers Can't Do stirred up a controversy among all those interested in the possibility of formal models of man by arguing that, despite a decade of impressive print-outs and dire predictions of superintelligent robots, workers in artificial intelligence (AI) were, in 1967, facing serious difficulties which they tended to cover up with special-purpose solutions and rhetorical claims of generality. During the subsequent decade this critique has been more or less acknowledged. In the five-year period from 1967 to 1972 the *ad hoc* character of AI work was admitted and, indeed, elevated to a methodological principle. The study of artificially circumscribed gamelike domains was proclaimed a study of *micro-worlds* and was defended as a necessary first step toward broader and more flexible programs. Then, during the next five years (1972–1977) the micro-world "successes" were seen to be ungeneralizable, and in the best AI laboratories workers began to face the problem of representing the everyday general understanding which they had spent the first fifteen years of research trying to circumvent. Recently, even the wishful rhetoric characteristic of the field has been recognized and ridiculed by AI workers themselves.

My early outrage at the misleading names given to programs such as Newell, Shaw, and Simon's General Problem Solver (GPS) is now shared by M.I.T.'s Drew McDermott, who writes:

[I]n AI, our programs to a great degree are problems rather than solutions. If a researcher tries to write an "understanding" program, it isn't because he has thought of a better way of implementing this well-understood task, but because he hopes he can come closer to writing the *first* implementation. If he calls the main loop of his program "UNDERSTANDING", he is (until proven innocent) merely begging the question. He may mislead a lot of people, most prominently himself, and enrage a lot of others.[1]*§

McDermott also singled out overrated GPS:

Many instructive examples of wishful mnemonics by AI researchers come to mind once you see the point. Remember GPS? By now, "GPS" is a colorless term denoting a particularly stupid program to solve puzzles. But it originally meant "General Problem Solver", which caused everybody a lot of needless excitement and distraction. It should have been called LFGNS—"Local Feature-Guided Network Searcher".[2]

Even my earliest assessment that work in AI resembled alchemy more than science[3] has been accepted by Terry Winograd, formerly at M.I.T., now at Stanford:

In some ways, [AI] is akin to medieval alchemy. We are at the stage of pouring together different combinations of substances and seeing what happens, not yet having developed satisfactory theories. This analogy was proposed by Dreyfus (1965) as a condemnation of artificial intelligence, but its aptness need not imply his negative evaluation . . . it was the practical experience and curiosity of the alchemists which provided the wealth of data from which a scientific theory of chemistry could be developed.[4]

Winograd is right; as long as researchers in AI admit and learn from their failures their attempt to supply computers with human knowledge may in the end provide data for a totally different way of using computers to make intelligent artifacts. But until recently, admitting their failures so that others can learn from their mistakes—an essential part of any scientific field—has been virtually unknown in AI circles. McDermott reiterates my point that, as he puts it, ". . . AI as a field is starving for a few carefully documented failures." And he warns: "Remember, though, if we can't criticize ourselves, someone else will save us the trouble."[5] I take this as my cue to return for a critical look at the research of the past ten years.[6]*

What strikes me, and has struck other writers reviewing the history of the field,[7] is how my views and those of workers interested in the theoretical issues in AI have gradually converged. In recent years the attempt to produce special-purpose programs tailored to narrowly restricted domains, with the concomitant principle that this should be achieved in whatever way is most efficient regardless of whether such methods are used by human beings, has been abandoned by AI *theorists* and frankly and quite successfully taken over by self-styled AI *engineers,* with no interest in making generally intelligent machines. Among those still interested in the theoretical issue of using computers to produce the full range of human intelligent behavior there is now general agreement that, as I argue in this book, intelligence requires understanding, and understanding requires giving a computer the background of common sense that adult human beings have by virtue of having bodies, interacting skillfully with the material world, and being trained into a culture.

Given the epistemological assumptions dictated by the information-processing model (see Chapter 4) this precondition of intelligent behavior necessarily appears to AI workers as the need to find a formal representation in which all the knowledge and beliefs of an average adult human being can be made explicit and organized for flexible use. Almost everyone now (with one exception we will deal with later) agrees that representing and organizing commonsense knowledge is incredibly difficult, and that facing up to this problem constitutes the moment of truth for AI. Either a way of representing and organizing everyday human know-how must be found, or AI will be swamped by the welter of facts and beliefs that must be made explicit in order to try to inform a disembodied, utterly alien computer about everyday human life. With this recognition, which characterizes the most recent five-year phase of AI research, unfounded optimism has given way to somewhat self-critical caution.

AI research has thus passed from stagnation to crisis during the decade since I concluded my research for this book. If I were to rewrite the book today I would divide this decade into two phases and include them as Chapters 3 and 4 of Part I, so as to cover the full twenty years the field has been in existence. And I would modify the Conclusion to take into account the recent maturation of the field. But since the overall argument of the book is confirmed rather than contradicted by the latest developments, I would rather leave the original book intact—only reworking the material where a sentence or a paragraph has proved to be murky or misleading—while including what are, in effect, Chapters 3 and 4 and the new conclusion in this Introduction. The reader who wants to get a chronological sense of how research in artificial intelligence developed should skip ahead to Chapters 1 (Phase 1) and 2 (Phase 2), and then return to this critical survey of the past ten years. Moreover, since the arguments at the end of this Introduction presuppose and extend ideas which are more fully developed in the last half of the book, the conclusion of the Introduction to the Revised Edition might be best read after finishing Part III.

Phase III (1967–1972)
Manipulating Micro-Worlds

When *What Computers Can't Do* appeared in January 1972, making a case that after an exciting start which raised high hopes, work in artificial intelligence had been stagnating, reviewers within the field of AI were quick to point out that the research criticized was already dated and that my charge of stagnation did not take into account the "breakthroughs" which had occurred during the five years preceding the publication of my critique. Bruce Buchanan's reaction in *Computing Reviews* is typical:

One would hope that a criticism of a growing discipline would mention work in the most recent one-third of the years of activity. . . . To this reviewer, and other persons doing AI research, programs developed in the last five years seem to outperform programs written in the tool-building period of 1957–1967.

For example, it is dishonest to entitle the book a "critique" of AI when it dwells on the failure of early language translation programs (based primarily on syntactical analysis) without analyzing the recent work on understanding natural language (based on syntax, semantics, and context).[8]

If the point of these objections had been that my book did not take account of excellent programs such as M.I.T.'s MATHLAB (1970) for manipulating symbolic algebraic expressions, and Stanford's DENDRAL (1970) for inferring chemical structure from mass spectometry data, I would plead guilty. I would point out, however, that these programs, while solving hard technical problems and producing programs that compete with human experts, achieve success precisely because they are restricted to a narrow domain of facts, and thus exemplify what Edward Feigenbaum, the head of the DENDRAL project, has called "knowledge engineering."[9] They, thus, do not constitute, nor are they meant to constitute, progress toward producing general or generalizable techniques for achieving adaptable intelligent behavior.

Buchanan would presumably agree since the programs he mentions as giving the lie to my accusations of stagnation are not these engineering triumphs, but theoretically oriented projects such as Winograd's natural language understanding program, and the perception programs developed at M.I.T. and Stanford.[10] These, plus Patrick Winston's concept learning program, are the programs most often cited by those who claim that my book ignores a breakthrough which occurred around 1970. If these programs do constitute progress they roundly refute my charge of stagnation, so we must now take a detailed look at each of the programs, as well as a brief look at robot research, which was generating a great deal of excitement just as this book went to press (see p. 000).

Since by all accounts it is Winograd's natural language understanding program (SHRDLU—1971) which demonstrates what Papert and Minsky call "a major advance,"[11] we will turn to it first. SHRDLU simulates a robot arm which can move a set of variously shaped blocks and allows a person to engage in a dialogue with the computer, asking questions, making statements, issuing commands, about this simple world of movable blocks. The program is an integrated system which makes use of syntax, semantics, and facts about blocks. It is thus, as Winograd cautiously claims, "a computer program which 'understands' language in a limited domain, by including a model of the subject being talked about and a context of discourse. . . ."[12]* Furthermore, this program explores the new idea of representing this knowledge in the form of procedures. The resulting dialogue is strikingly natural. Here is a sample. (The sentences in capital letters are computer print-out. The parentheses contain Winograd's comments.)

1. pick up a big red block.

    OK.

    (The system answers "OK" when it carries out a command. In order to pick up the red block, it had to clear it off by finding a space for the green one and moving the green one away.)

2. grasp the pyramid.

    I DON'T UNDERSTAND WHICH PYRAMID YOU MEAN.

    (There are three pyramids in the scene, so the program does nothing.)

3. find a block which is taller than the one you are holding and put it into the box.

    (The system has to figure out what is meant by "one" and "it", as well as using deduction to decide which block it is holding.)

    BY "IT", I ASSUME YOU MEAN THE BLOCK WHICH IS TALLER THAN THE ONE I AM HOLDING.

    (Printed out to keep us informed.)

    OK.

    (The hand has to set down the red block to pick up the taller blue one.)

4. what does the box contain?

    THE BLUE PYRAMID AND THE BLUE BLOCK.

5. what is the pyramid supported by?

    (Earlier the system responded to "the pyramid" by saying "I don't understand which pyramid you mean". Now, it assumes that we mean the one just mentioned.)

    THE BOX.

    . . .

9. can the table pick up blocks?

    NO.

    (The semantic rules make this a nonsensical question which therefore must be false.)

10. can a pyramid be supported by a block?

YES.

(The deductive system finds an actual example, so it knows this is possible.)

11. can a pyramid support a pyramid?

I DON'T KNOW.

(The question makes sense, but there is no example in the scene, so there is no easy way to tell without being able to examine the robot's programs.)

12. stack up two pyramids.

I CAN'T.

(The robot tries and fails.)

13. the blue pyramid is mine.

I UNDERSTAND.

(This data is added to the data base.)

14. I own blocks which are not red, but I don't own anything which supports a pyramid.

I UNDERSTAND.

(Two new theorems are created for proving things about "owning".)

15. do I own the box?

NO.[13]

If being a major advance means being more general than its predecessors, then SHRDLU, since it no longer depends for its analysis of language on external constraints of the sort essential to Bobrow's STUDENT, is a major achievement. Winograd himself points out the superiority of his program over earlier language understanding programs:

. . . A program may succeed by carefully choosing the problem it will attack, so that some simple special-purpose solution will work. ELIZA (Weizenbaum, 1964) and STUDENT (Bobrow, 1967) are examples of programs which give impressive performances owing to a severe and careful restriction of the kind of understanding they try to achieve. If a model is to be of broader significance, it must be designed to cover a large range of the things we mean when we talk of understanding. The principles should derive from an attempt to deal with the basic cognitive structures.[14]

If, however, "a major advance" means that a step has been made in dealing with the basic cognitive structures needed to cover everyday understanding—that thanks to SHRDLU there is now reason to be optimistic about the possibility of AI—then no progress at all can be claimed. To justify this negative judgment we must first find out how the optimists of the early seventies were able to convince themselves that, with SHRDLU, AI was at last on the right track.

If one holds, as some AI workers such as Winograd do, that there are various kinds of understanding so that whether an entity has understanding or not is just a question of degree, it may seem that each new program has a bit more understanding than the last, and that progress consists in inching out on the understanding continuum. If, on the other hand, one holds that "understanding" is a concept that applies only to entities exactly like human beings, that would stack the deck and make AI impossible. But it is not up to either side in the debate to stipulate what "understanding" means. Before talking of *degrees* of "understanding," one must note that the term "understand" is part of an interrelated set of terms for talking about behavior such as "ask," "answer," "know," etc. And some of these terms—such as "answer," for example—simply *do* have an all-or-nothing character. If one is tempted to say that the DENDRAL program, for example, literally *understands* mass spectroscopy, then one must be prepared to say that when it is fed a problem and types out the answer it has literally been asked and answered a question, and this, in turn, involves, among other things, that it *knows* that it has answered. But whatever behavior is required for us to say of an entity that it "knows" something, it should be clear that the computer does not now come near to meeting these conditions, so it has not answered even a little. If one is sensitive to the central meaning of these interconnected intentional terms it follows that the claim that programs like SHRDLU have a little bit of understanding is at best metaphorical and at most outright misleading.

Workers in AI were certainly not trying to cover up the fact that it was SHRDLU's restricted domain which made apparent understanding possible. They even had a name for Winograd's method of restricting the domain of discourse. He was dealing with a micro-world. And in a 1970 internal memo at M.I.T., Minsky and Papert frankly note:

Each model—or "micro-world" as we shall call it—is very schematic; it talks about a fairyland in which things are so simplified that almost every statement about them would be literally false if asserted about the real world.[15]

But they immediately add:

Nevertheless, we feel that they [the micro-worlds] are so important that we are assigning a large portion of our effort toward developing a collection of these micro-worlds and finding how to use the suggestive and predictive powers of the models without being overcome by their incompatibility with literal truth.[16]

Given the admittedly artificial and arbitrary character of micro-worlds why do Papert and Minsky think they provide a promising line of research?

To find an answer we must follow Minsky and Papert's perceptive remarks on narrative and their less than perceptive conclusions:

. . . In a familiar fable, the wily Fox tricks the vain Crow into dropping the meat by asking it to sing. The usual test of understanding is the ability of the child to answer questions like:

"Did the Fox think the Crow had a lovely voice?"

The topic is sometimes classified as "natural language manipulation" or as "deductive logic", etc. These descriptions are badly chosen. For the real problem is not to understand English; it is to *understand* at all. To see this more clearly, observe that nothing is gained by presenting the story in simplified syntax: CROW ON TREE. CROW HAS MEAT. FOX SAYS "YOU HAVE A LOVELY VOICE. PLEASE SING." FOX GOBBLES MEAT. The difficulty in getting a machine to give the right answer does not at all depend on "disambiguating" the words (at least, not in the usual primitive sense of selecting one "meaning" out of a discrete set of "meanings"). And neither does the difficulty lie in the need for unusually powerful logical apparatus. The main problem is that no one has constructed the elements of a body of knowledge about such matters that is adequate for understanding the story. Let us see what is involved.

To begin with, there is never a unique solution to such problems, so we do not ask what the Understander *must* know. But he will surely gain by having the concept of FLATTERY. To provide this knowledge, we imagine a "micro-theory" of flattery—an extendible collection of facts or procedures that describe conditions under which one might expect to find flattery, what forms it takes, what its consequences are, and so on. How complex this theory is depends on what is presupposed. Thus it would be very difficult to describe flattery to our Understander if he (or it) does not already know that statements can be made for purposes other than to convey literally correct, factual information. It would be almost impossibly difficult if he does not even have some concept like PURPOSE or INTENTION.[17]

The surprising move here is the conclusion that there could be a circumscribed "micro-theory" of flattery—somehow intelligible apart from the rest of human life—while at the same time the account shows an understanding of flattery opening out into the rest of our everyday world, with its understanding of purposes and intentions.

What characterizes the period of the early seventies, and makes SHRDLU seem an advance toward general intelligence, is the very concept of a micro-world—a domain which can be analyzed in isolation. This concept implies that although each area of discourse seems to open out into the rest of human activities its endless ramifications are only apparent and will soon converge on a self-contained set of facts and relations. For example, in discussing the micro-world of bargaining, Papert and Minsky consider what a child needs to know to understand the following fragment of conversation:

Janet: "That isn't a very good ball you have. Give it to me and I'll give you my lollipop.[18]

And remark:

. . . we conjecture that, eventually, the required micro-theories can be made reasonably compact and easily stated (or, by the same token, *learned*) once we have found an adequate set of structural primitives for them. When one begins to catalogue what one needs for just a little of Janet's story, it seems at first to be endless:

Time	Things	Words
Space	People	Thoughts

Talking: Explaining. Asking. Ordering. Persuading. Pretending
Social relations: Giving. Buying. Bargaining. Begging. Asking. Presents. Steal-
                    ing . . .
Playing: Real and Unreal, Pretending
Owning: Part of, Belong to, Master of, Captor of
Eating: How does one compare the values of foods with the values of toys?
Liking: good, bad, useful, pretty, conformity
Living: Girl. Awake. Eats. Plays.
Intention: Want. Plan. Plot. Goal. Cause. Result. Prevent.
Emotions: Moods. Dispositions. Conventional expressions.
States: asleep. angry. at home.
Properties: grown-up. red-haired. called "Janet".
Story: Narrator. Plot. Principal actors.
People: Children. Bystanders.
Places: Houses. Outside.
Angry: State
          caused by: Insult
                       deprivation
                       assault
                       disobedience
                       frustration
                       spontaneous
Results   not cooperative
          lower threshold
          aggression
          loud voice
          irrational
          revenge
Etc.[19]

They conclude:

But [the list] is not endless. It is only large, and one needs a large set of concepts to organize it. After a while one will find it getting harder to add new concepts, and the new ones will begin to seem less indispensable.[20]

This totally unjustified belief that the seemingly endless reference to other human practices will converge so that simple micro-worlds can be studied in relative isolation reflects a naive transfer to AI of methods that have succeeded in the natural sciences. Winograd characteristically describes his work in terms borrowed from physical science:

We are concerned with developing a formalism, or "representation," with which to describe . . . knowledge. We seek the "atoms" and "particles" of which it is built, and the "forces" that act on it.[21]

It is true that physical theories about the universe can be built up by studying relatively simple and isolated systems and then making the model gradually more complex and integrating it with other domains of phenomena. This is possible because all the phenomena are presumably the result of the lawlike relations of a set of basic elements, what Papert and Minsky call "structural primitives." This belief in local success and gradual generalization was clearly also Winograd's hope at the time he developed SHRDLU.

The justification for our particular use of concepts in this system is that it is thereby enabled to engage in dialogs that simulate in many ways the behavior of a human language user. For a wider field of discourse, the conceptual structure would have to be expanded in its details, and perhaps in some aspects of its overall organization.[22]

Thus, for example, it might seem that one could "expand" SHRDLU's concept of owning, since in the above sample conversation SHRDLU seems to have a very simple "micro-theory" of owning blocks. But as Simon points out in an excellent analysis of SHRDLU's limitations, the program does not understand owning at all because it cannot deal with meanings. It has merely been given a set of primitives and their possible relationships. As Simon puts it:

The SHRDLU system deals with problems in a single blocks world, with a fixed representation. When it is instructed to "pick up a big red block", it needs only to associate the term "pick up" with a procedure for carrying out that process; identify, by applying appropriate tests associated with "big", "red", and "block", the argument for the procedure and use its problem-solving capabilities to carry out the procedure. In saying "it needs only", it is not my intention to demean the capabilities of SHRDLU. It is precisely because the program possesses stored programs expressing the intensions of the terms used in inquiries and instructions that its interpretation of those inquiries and instructions is relatively straightforward.[23]

In understanding, on the other hand, "the problem-understanding sub-system will have a more complicated task than just mapping the input language onto the intentions stored in a lexicon. It will also have to create a representation for the information it receives, and create meanings for the terms that are consistent with the representation."[24] So, for example, in the conversation concerning owning:

. . . although SHRDLU's answer to the question is quite correct, the system cannot be said to understand the meaning of "own" in any but a sophistic sense. SHRDLU's test of whether something is owned is simply whether it is tagged "owned". There is no intensional test of ownership, hence SHRDLU knows what it owns, but doesn't understand what it is to own something. SHRDLU would understand what it meant to own a box if it could, say, test its ownership by recalling how it had gained possession of the box, or by checking its possession of a receipt in payment for it; could respond differently to requests to move a box it owned from requests to move one it didn't own; and, in general, could perform those tests and actions that are generally associated with the determination and exercise of ownership in our law and culture.[25]

Moreover, even if it satisfied all these conditions it still wouldn't understand, unless it also understood that it (SHRDLU) couldn't own anything, since it isn't a part of the community in which owning makes sense. Given our cultural practices which constitute owning, a computer cannot own something any more than a table can.

This discussion of owning suggests that, just as it is misleading to call a program UNDERSTAND when the problem is to find out what understanding is, it is likewise misleading to call a set of facts and procedures concerning blocks a micro-*world,* when what is really at stake is the understanding of what a world is. A set of interrelated facts may constitute a *universe,* a domain, a group, etc., but it does not constitute a *world,* for a world is an organized body of objects, purposes, skills, and practices in terms of which human activities have meaning or make sense. It follows that although there is a children's world in which, among other things, there are blocks, there is no such thing as a blocks world. Or, to put this as a critique of Winograd, one cannot equate, as he does, a program which deals with "a tiny bit of the world," with a program which deals with a "mini-world."[26]

In our everyday life we are, indeed, involved in various "sub-worlds" such as the world of the theater, of business, or of mathematics, but each of these is a "mode" of our shared everyday world.[27]* That is, sub-worlds are not related like isolable physical systems to larger systems they *compose;* rather they are local elaborations of a whole which they *presuppose.* If micro-worlds *were* sub-worlds one would not have to extend and combine them to reach the everyday world, because the everyday world would have to be included already. Since, however, micro-worlds are *not* worlds, there is no way they can be combined and extended to the world of everyday life. As a result of failing to ask what a world is, five years of stagnation in AI was mistaken for progress.

Papert and Minsky's 1973 grant proposal is perhaps the last time the artificially isolated character of the micro-world is defended as a scientific virtue—at least at M.I.T.:

Artificial Intelligence, as a new technology, is in an intermediate stage of development. In the first stages of a new field, things have to be simplified so that one can *isolate* and study the *elementary* phenomena. In most successful applications, we use a strategy we call "working within a Micro-World".[28]

SHRDLU is again singled out as the most successful version of this research method. "A good example of a suitably designed Micro-world is shown in the well-known project of Winograd, which made many practical and theoretical contributions to Understanding Natural Language."[29] But while gestures are still made in the direction of generalization it is obvious that SHRDLU is running into difficulty.

Since the Winograd demonstration and thesis, several workers have been adding new elements, regulations, and features to that system. That work has not gone very far, however, because the details of implementation of the original system were quite complex.[30]

Such failures to generalize no doubt lie behind the sober evaluation in a proposal two years later:

. . . Artificial Intelligence has done well in tightly constrained domains—Winograd, for example, astonished everyone with the expertise of his blocks-world natural language system. Extending this kind of ability to larger worlds has not proved straightforward, however. . . . The time has come to treat the problems involved as central issues.[31]

But typically, it is only from the vantage point of the next phase of research, with its new hopes, that the early seventies' illusion that one can generalize work done in narrowly constrained domains is finally diagnosed and laid to rest. Winograd himself acknowledges that:

The AI programs of the late sixties and early seventies are much too literal. They deal with meaning as if it were a structure to be built up of the bricks and mortar provided by the words, rather than a design to be created based on the sketches and hints actually present in the input. This gives them a "brittle" character, able to deal well with tightly specified areas of meaning in an artificially formal conversation. They are correspondingly weak in dealing with natural utterances, full of bits and fragments, continual (unnoticed) metaphor, and reference to much less easily formalizable areas of knowledge.[32]

Another supposed breakthrough mentioned by Buchanan is Adolfo Guzman's program, SEE (1968), which analyzes two-dimensional projections of complicated scenes involving partially occluded three-dimensional polyhedra. (See Figure 1). Already as developed by Guzman this program could outdo human beings in unscrambling some classes of complicated scenes, and as generalized by David Waltz it is even more impressive. It not only demonstrates the power gained by restricting the domain analyzed, but it also shows the kind of generalization that *can* be obtained in micro-world work, as well as indirectly showing the kind of generalization that is precluded by the very nature of special-purpose heuristics.

Guzman's program analyzes scenes involving cubes and other such rectilinear solids by merging regions into bodies using evidence from the vertices. Each vertex suggests that two or more of the regions around it belong together depending on whether the vertex is shaped like an L, an arrow, a T, a K, an X, a fork, a peak, or an upside-down peak. With these eight primitives and commonsense rules for their use, Guzman's program did quite well. But it had certain weaknesses. According to Winston, "The program could not handle shadows, and it did poorly if there were holes in objects or missing lines in the drawing."[33] Waltz then generalized Guzman's work and showed that by introducing three more such primitives, a computer can be programmed to decide if a particular line in a drawing is a shadow, a crack, an obscuring edge, or an internal seam in a way analogous to the solution of sets of algebraic equations. As Winston later sums up the change:

Previously it was believed that only a program with a complicated control structure and lots of explicit reasoning power could hope to analyze scenes like that in figure [1]. Now we know that understanding the constraints the real world imposes on how boundaries, concave and convex interiors, shadows, and cracks can come together at junctions is enough to make things much simpler. A table which contains a list of the few thousand physically possible ways that line types can come together accompanied by a simple matching program are all that is required. Scene analysis is translated into a problem resembling a jigsaw puzzle or a set of linear equations. No deep problem solving effort is required; it is just a matter of executing a very simple constraint dependent, iterative process that successively throws away incompatible line arrangement combinations.[34]

This is just the kind of mathematical generalization within a domain one might expect in micro-worlds where the rule-governed relation of the primitives (in this case the set of vertices) are under some external constraint (in this case the laws of geometry and optics). What one would not expect is that the special-purpose heuristics which depend on corners for segregating rectilinear objects could in any way be generalized so as to make possible the recognition of other sorts of objects. And, indeed, none of Guzman's or Waltz's techniques, since they rely on the intersection of straight lines, have any use in analyzing a scene involving curved objects. What one gains in narrowing a domain, one loses in breadth of significance. Winston's evaluation covers up this lesson:

. . . It is wrong to think of Waltz's work as only a statement of the epistemology of line drawings of polyhedra. Instead I think it is an elegant case study of a paradigm we can expect to see again and again, and as such, it is a strong metaphoric tool for guiding our thinking, not only in vision but also in the study of other systems involving intelligence.[35]

But in a later grant proposal he acknowledges that:

To understand the real world, we must have a different set of primitives from the relatively simple line trackers suitable and sufficient for the blocks world.[36]

Waltz's work is a paradigm of the kind of generalization one can strive for *within* a micro-world all right, but for that very reason it provides

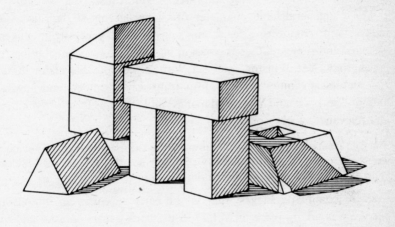

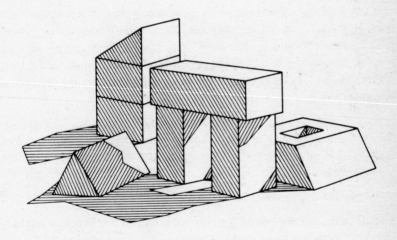

Figure 1

no way of thinking about general intelligent systems. In the light of these later evaluations my assumption that work in the early seventies did not refute my accusation of stagnation seems vindicated.

The nongeneralizable character of the programs so far discussed makes them engineering feats, not steps toward generally intelligent systems, and they are, therefore not at all promising as contributions to psychology. Yet Winston includes Waltz's work in his claim that " . . . making machines see is an important way to understand how we animals see. . . ."[37] and Winograd makes similar claims for the psychological relevance of his work:

The gain from developing AI is not primarily in the usefulness of the programs we create, but in the set of concepts we develop, and the ways in which we can apply them to understanding human intelligence.[38]

These comments suggest that in the early seventies an interesting change was taking place at M.I.T. In previous papers Minsky and his co-workers sharply distinguished themselves from workers in Cognitive Simulation, such as Simon, who presented their programs as psychological theories, insisting that the M.I.T. programs were "an attempt to build intelligent machines without any prejudice toward making the system . . . humanoid."[39] Now in their book, *Artificial Intelligence,*[40] a summary of work done at M.I.T. during the period 1967–1972, Minsky and Papert present the M.I.T. research as a contribution to psychology. They first introduce the notion of a symbolic description:

What do we mean by "description"? We do not mean to suggest that our descriptions must be made of strings of ordinary-language words (although they might be). The simplest kind of description is a structure in which some features of a situation are represented by single ("primitive") symbols, and relations between those features are represented by other symbols—or by other features of the way the description is put together.[41]

They then defend the role of symbolic descriptions in a psychological account of intelligent behavior by a constant polemic against behaviorism and gestalt theory which have opposed the use of formal models of the mind.

One can detect, underlying this change, the effect of the proliferation of micro-worlds, with their reliance on symbolic descriptions, and the disturbing failure to produce even the hint of a system with the flexibility of a six-month-old child. Instead of concluding from this frustrating situation that the special-purpose techniques which work in context-free, gamelike, micro-worlds may in no way resemble general-purpose human and animal intelligence, the AI workers seem to have taken the less embarrassing if less plausible tack of suggesting that even if they could not succeed in building intelligent systems, the *ad hoc* symbolic descriptions successful in micro-world analysis could be justified as a valuable contribution to psychology.

Such a line, however, since it involves a stronger claim than the old slogan that as long as the machine was intelligent it did not matter at all whether it performed in a humanoid way, runs the obvious risk of refutation by empirical evidence. An information-processing model must be a formal symbolic structure, however, so Minsky and Papert, making a virtue of necessity, revive the implausible intellectualist position according to which concrete perception is assimilated to the rule-governed symbolic descriptions used in abstract thought.

The Gestaltists look for simple and fundamental principles about how perception is organized, and then attempt to show how symbolic reasoning can be seen as following the same principles, while we construct a complex theory of how knowledge is applied to solve intellectual problems and then attempt to show how the symbolic description that is what one "sees" is constructed according to similar processes.[42]

Some recent work in psychology, however, points in the exactly opposite direction. Rather than showing that perception can be analyzed in terms of formal features, Erich Goldmeier's extention of early Gestalt work on the perception of similarity of simple perceptual figures—arising in part in response to "the frustrating efforts to teach pattern recognition to [computers]"[43]—has revealed sophisticated distinctions between figure and ground, matter and form, essential and accidental aspects, norms and distortions, etc., which he shows cannot be accounted for in terms of any known formal features of the phenomenal figures. They can, however, according to Goldmeier, perhaps be explained on the neurological level, where the importance of Prägnanz—i.e., singularly salient shapes and orientations—suggests underlying physical phenomena such as "regions of resonance"[44] in the brain.

Recent work in neurophysiology has suggested new mechanisms which might confirm the Gestaltist's intuition that other sorts of process than the manipulation of formal representations of the sort required by digital computers underlie perception. While still nothing definite is known about how the brain "processes information," computer models look even less likely now than in 1970, while models based on the properties of optical holograms look perhaps more promising. As John Haugeland summarizes the evidence:

First, [optical holograms] are prepared from the light bouncing off an ordinary object, and can subsequently be used to reconstruct a full three-dimensional colored image of that object. Second, the whole image can be reconstructed from any large enough portion of the hologram (i.e., there's no saying which portion of the hologram "encodes" which portion of the image). Third, a number of objects can be separately recorded on the same hologram, and there's no saying which portion records which object. Fourth, if a hologram of an arbitrary scene is suitably illuminated with the light from a reference object, bright spots will appear indicating (virtually instantaneously) the presence and location of any occurrences of the reference object in the scene (and dimmer spots indicate "similar" objects). So some neurophysiological holographic encoding might account for a number of perplexing features of visual recall and recognition, including their speed, some of their invariances, and the fact that they are only slightly impaired by large lesions in relevant areas of the brain. . . .

Another interesting property of optical holograms is that if a hologram [combining light from two separate] objects is illuminated with the light from one of them, an image of the other (absent) object appears. Thus, such a hologram can be regarded as a kind of "associator" of (not ideas, but) visual patterns. . . .[45]

Haugeland adds:

. . . Fairly detailed hypothetical models have been proposed for how holograms might be realized in neuronal structures; and there is some empirical evidence that some neurons behave in ways that would fit the models.[46]

Of course, it is still possible that the Gestaltists went too far in trying to assimilate thought to the same sort of concrete, holistic, processes they found necessary to account for perception. Thus, even though the exponents of symbolic descriptions have no account of perceptual processes, they might be right that the mechanism of everyday thinking and learning consists in constructing a formal description of the world and transforming this representation in a rule-governed way. Such a formal model of everyday learning and categorization is proposed by Winston in his 1970 thesis, "Learning Structural Descriptions from Examples."[47] Given a set of positive and negative instances, Winston's self-proclaimed "classic" program can, for example, use a descriptive repertoire to construct a formal description of the class of arches. Since, as we mentioned earlier, Winston's program (along with those of Winograd and Guzman) is often mentioned as a success of the late sixties, we must examine it in detail.

Is this program a plausible general theory of learning? Winston's commitment to a computer model dictates the conclusion that it must be:

Although this may seem like a very special kind of learning, I think the implications are far ranging, because I believe that learning by examples, learning by being told, learning by imitation, learning by reinforcement and other forms are much like one another. In the literature of learning there is frequently an unstated assumption that these various forms are fundamentally different. But I think the classical boundaries between the various kinds of learning will disappear once superficially different kinds of learning are understood in terms of processes that construct and manipulate descriptions.[48]

Yet Winston's program works only if the "student" is saved the trouble of what Charles Sanders Peirce called abduction, by being "told" a set of context-free features and relations—in this case a list of possible spacial relationships of blocks such as "left-of," "standing," "above," and "supported by"—from which to build up a description of an arch. Minsky and Papert presuppose this preselection when they say that "to eliminate objects which seem atypical . . . the program lists all relationships exhibited by more than half of the candidates in the set."[49] Lurking behind this claim is the supposition that there are only a finite number of relevant features; but without preselected features all objects share an indefinitely large number of relationships. The work of discriminating, selecting, and weighting a limited number of relevant features is the result of repeated experience and is the first stage of learning. But since in Winston's work the programmer selects and preweights the primitives, his program gives us no idea how a computer could make this selection and assign these weights. (In this respect Winston's program shows no progress beyond Newell, Shaw, and Simon's 1958 proposal; see p. 83 of this book.) Thus the Winston program, like every micro-world program, works only because it has excluded from its task domain the very ability it is supposed to explain.

If not a theory of learning, is Winston's program at least a plausible theory of categorization? Consider again the arch example. Once it has been given what Winston disarmingly calls a "good description"[50] and carefully chosen examples, the program does conclude that an arch is a structure in which a prismatic body is supported by two upright blocks that do not touch each other. But, since arches function in various ways in our everyday activity, there is no reason to suppose that these are the necessary and sufficient conditions for being an arch, or that there are any such defining features. Some prominent characteristics shared by most everyday arches are "helping to support something while leaving an important open space under it," or "being the sort of thing one can walk under and through at the same time." How does Winston propose to capture such contextual characteristics in terms of the context-free features required by his formal representation?

Winston admits that having two supports and a flat top does not begin to capture even the geometrical structure of arches. So he proposes "generalizing the machine's descriptive ability to acts and properties required by those acts"[51] by adding a functional predicate, "something to walk through."[52] But it is not at all clear how a functional predicate which refers to implicit knowledge of the bodily skill of walking through is to be formalized. Indeed, Winston himself provides a *reductio ad absurdum* of this facile appeal to formal functional predicates:

To a human, an arch may be something to walk through, as well as an appropriate alignment of bricks. And certainly, a flat rock serves as a table to a hungry person, although far removed from the image the word table usually calls to mind. But the machine does not yet know anything of walking or eating, so the programs discussed here handle only some of the physical aspects of these human notions. There is no inherent obstacle forbidding the machine to enjoy functional understanding. It is a matter of generalizing the machine's descriptive ability to acts and properties required by those acts. Then chains of pointers can link TABLE to FOOD as well as to the physical image of a table, and the machine will be perfectly happy to draw up its chair to a flat rock with the human given that there is something on that table which it wishes to eat.[53]

Progress on recognition of arches, tables, etc., must, it seems, either wait until we have captured in an abstract symbolic description much of what human beings implicitly know about walking and eating simply by having a body, or else until computers no longer have to be told what it is to walk and eat, because they have human bodies and appetites themselves!

Despite these seemingly insurmountable obstacles Winston boasts that "there will be no contentment with [concept learning] machines that only do as well as humans."[54] But it is not surprising that Winston's work is nine years old and there has been little progress in machine learning, induction, or concept formation. In their account Minsky and Papert admit that "we are still far from knowing how to design a powerful yet subtle and sensitive inductive learning program."[55] What is surprising is that they add: "but the schemata developed in Winston's work should take us a substantial part of the way."[56] The lack of progress since Winston's work was published, plus the use of predigested weighted primitives from which to produce its rigid, restricted, and largely irrelevant descriptions, makes it hard to understand in what way the program is a substantial step.

Moreover, if Winston claims to "shed some light on [the question:] How do we recognize examples of various concepts?"[57] his theory of concepts as definitions must, like any psychological theory, be subject to empirical test. It so happens that contrary to Winston's claims, recent evidence collected and analyzed by Eleanor Rosch on just this subject shows that human beings are not aware of classifying objects as instances of abstract rules but rather group objects as more or less distant from an imagined paradigm. This does not exclude the possibility of unconscious processing, but it does highlight the fact that there is no empirical evidence at all for Winston's formal model. As Rosch puts it:

Many experiments have shown that categories appear to be coded in the mind neither by means of lists of each individual member of the category, nor by means of a list of formal criteria necessary and sufficient for category membership, but, rather, in terms of a prototype of a typical category member. The most cognitively economical code for a category is, in fact, a *concrete image* of an average category member.[58]

One paradigm, it seems, is worth a thousand rules. As we shall soon see, one of the characteristics of the next phase of work in AI is to try to take account of the implications of Rosch's research.

Meanwhile, what can we conclude concerning AI's contribution to the science of psychology? No one can deny Minsky and Papert's claim that "Computer Science has brought a flood of . . . ideas, well defined and experimentally implemented, for thinking about thinking. . . ."[59] But all of these ideas can be boiled down to ways of constructing and manipulating symbolic descriptions, and, as we have seen, the notion that human cognition can be explained in terms of formal representations does not seem at all obvious in the face of actual research on perception, and everyday concept formation. Even Minsky and Papert show a commendable new modesty. They as much as admit that AI is still at the stage of astrology (not unlike alchemy), and that the much heralded breakthrough still lies in the future:

Just as astronomy succeeded astrology, following Kepler's discovery of planetary regularities, the discoveries of these many principles in empirical explorations of intellectual processes in machines should lead to a science, eventually.[60]

Happily, "should" has replaced "will" in their predictions. Indeed, this period's contribution to psychology suggests an even more modest hope: As more psychologists like Goldmeier are frustrated by the limitations of formal computer models, and others turn to investigating the function of images as opposed to symbolic representations, the strikingly limited success of AI may come to be seen as an important disconfirmation of the information processing approach.

To complete our survey of the state of AI research as it entered its second decade we need to consider briefly the state of robot research, both because work in this area received a lot of misleading publicity during this period and because, as we have just seen in discussing Winston's claims, workers in AI often take refuge in the idea that computers will finally achieve human understanding when they have humanoid bodies.

Our account will have to be brief because there is not much to report. After the usual optimistic start, the M.I.T. robot arm was stopped cold by just the problem of representing its own body space which I suspected would be its undoing (see p. 251). In the 1968–1969 AI Progress Report this problem is clearly an embarrassment:

. . . [H]ow should one represent a machine's body image? For the problem of a single, not-too-complicated arm, one can doubtless get by with cleverly coded, sparse, three-dimensional arrays, but one would like something more symbolic. And one wonders what happens in the nervous system; we have not seen anything that might be considered to be a serious theory. Consider that a normal human can place an object on a table, turn about and make a gross change in his position and posture, and then reach out and grasp within one or two inches of the object, all with his eyes closed! It seems unlikely that his cerebellum could perform the appropriate vector calculations to do this. . . .[61]

However, rather than see this as evidence that their attempt to represent the robot's arm as one more object in physical space was misguided, the authors of the report get into deeper trouble defending their faith.

. . . We would presume that this complex motor activity is made up, somehow, of a large library of *stereotypical programs,* with some heuristic interpolation scheme that fits the required action to some collection of *reasonably similar stored actions.* But we have found nowhere any serious proposal about neurological mechanisms for this, and one can hope that some plausible ideas will come out of robotics research itself.[62]

Neurophysiology offers, admittedly speculative, accounts of such similarity, but these are holographic not information processing models. As for the AI approach, it merely raises the further problem of recognizing similarity, which is discussed in connection with chess-playing programs in the next section. In the light of these problems, when the report adds: "Unfortunately, at present this area is somewhat dormant,"[63] we can only take "dormant" as a polite synonym for stagnant or even comatose.

In spite of its better press (see p. 300) the SRI robot, Shakey, was in no better shape. As Bertram Raphael frankly sums up the situation in response to exaggerated coverage by the media:

. . . Many experiments were performed with Shakey between 1968 and 1972 . . . [but] we made much less progress than various press reports might suggest toward the creation of an independent sentient robot capable of meaningful performance in a normal human environment. Responsible scientists consider this intriguing idea premature, probably by at least several decades.[64]

In effect, Shakey is another case of a micro-world success which turned into a real-world failure.

At his peak, Shakey could only function in a sterile "play-pen" environment of walls, doorways, carefully painted baseboards (so he could "see" where the walls -met the floor), and a few simply-shaped wooden blocks; he had only about a dozen pre-programmed "instinctive" abilities, such as TURN, PUSH, GO-THROUGH-DOORWAY, and CLIMB-RAMP, which could be combined in various ways by the planning programs. . . . The scientists who worked on Shakey developed a deep appreciation of how difficult it is to produce a robot even with relatively trivial abilities, let alone the true science-fiction-like independent competence.[65]

According to Raphael, Shakey and the SRI robot project have been "temporarily put aside" and there will be no interesting robot work to report until AI workers solve the basic problem of knowledge representation:

Surprisingly, the issues of how to acquire, represent, and make use of a broad store of knowledge has been the most neglected part of past robot research. The developers of the laboratory robot systems were so busy patching together existing capabilities (in vision, language, and problem solving), and filling in essential new areas (representing the physical world, providing for error recovery), that they did not attend to the fundamental issue of knowledge structures.[66]

So now we have the overall picture. In all those areas where enthusiasts saw signs of success at just the time this book appeared—language understanding, scene analysis, concept learning, and robot building—the work turned out to be based on brilliant but *nongeneralizable* exploitation of specific features of the task domain. With this realization AI finally had to face the problem of representing everyday knowledge—a difficult, decisive, and philosophically fascinating task with which it is still struggling today.

Phase IV (1972–1977) Facing the Problem of Knowledge Representation

As the restricted interest of work in restricted domains became apparent, the distinction between specific applications and research on basic principles became sharper. Feigenbaum comes to refer to his work on DENDRAL and his more recent program for inferring the rules of mass spectometry, META-DENDRAL, as "knowledge engineering"[67] while Winograd and his associates call their work "cognitive science."[68]* At M.I.T., a grant proposal from this period distinguishes between "no-holds-barred, special purpose, domain-dependent work" and "no-tricks basic study."[69] And it seems to be generally accepted that every program we discussed in Phase III, and, indeed, the whole micro-world concept, was in this straightforward sense, a trick.

We shall now see that in Phase IV the special-purpose work makes steady progress, while the basic study faces a crisis. Everyday human know-how is increasingly acknowledged to be presupposed by intelligent behavior, yet it turns out to be incredibly difficult, perhaps in principle impossible, to program.

The areas in which knowledge engineering has been successful are just those in which the first edition of *What Computers Can't Do* predicted that progress could be expected. (See Column III, of my breakdown of the field, p. 292.) As long as the domain in question can be treated as a game, i.e., as long as what is relevant is fixed, and the possibly relevant factors can be defined in terms of context-free primitives, then computers can do well in the domain. And they will do progressively better relative to people as the amount of domain-specific knowledge required is increased. In such special-purpose programs the form of knowledge representation can be limited to situation → action rules in which the situation is defined in terms of a few parameters and indicates the conditions under which a specific heuristic rule is relevant. Again, because relevance is defined beforehand, reasoning can be by inference chains with no need for reasoning by analogy.

All these features can be found in one of the most impressive practical programs to date: Shortliffe's MYCIN program (1976) for diagnosing blood infections and meningitis infections and recommending drug treatment. The rules in this case are of the form:

RULE 85

IF:

1. The site of the culture is blood, and
2. The gram stain of the organism is gramneg, and
3. The morphology of the organism is rod, and
4. The patient is a compromised host

THEN:

There is suggestive evidence (.6) that the identity of the organism is pseudomonas-aeruginosa.[70]

The program has been tested by a panel of judges:

. . . In 90% of the cases submitted to the judges, a majority of the judges said that the program's decisions were the-same-as or as-good-as the decisions they would have made.[71]*

This approach, although successful as an engineering feat, involves several assumptions which may conceal potential limitations. Feigenbaum, in his analysis of MYCIN, assumes that acquiring expert skill is acquiring rules for recognizing situations and rules for evaluating evidence.

. . . In most "crafts or branches of learning" what we call "expertise" is the essence of the art. And for the domains of knowledge that we touch with our art, it is the "rules of expertise" or the rules of "good judgment" of the expert practitioners of the domain that we seek to transfer to our programs.[72]

He conscientiously notes that the experts themselves are not aware of using rules:

. . . Experience has also taught us that much of this knowledge is private to the expert, not because he is unwilling to share publicly how he performs, but because he is unable. He knows more than he is aware of knowing. (Why else is the Ph.D. or the Internship a guild-like apprenticeship to a presumed "master of the craft"? What the masters really know is not written in the textbooks of the masters.)[73]

But Feigenbaum with his assumption that expert performance must result exclusively from following rules, is nonetheless convinced that by suitable questioning he can get the expert, as Plato would say, to "recollect" the complete set of unconscious heuristics:

. . . But we have learned also that this private knowledge can be uncovered by the careful, painstaking analysis of a second party, or sometimes by the expert himself, operating in the context of a large number of highly specific performance problems.[74]

If internship and the use of examples play an *essential* role in expert judgment, i.e., if there is a limit to what can be understood by rules, Feigenbaum would never see it—especially in domains such as medicine where there is a very large and rapidly increasing body of factual information concerning drugs and their side effects and interactions, so that the computer can make up in data-processing capacity for what it lacks in judgment. Yet, the fact remains that in each field where "knowledge engineering" has made its valuable contribution and rivaled the experts, there are still masters who do better than the machine. To determine whether this is an accident, or whether skill may involve more than rule following, it is helpful to look at developments in chess, where the domain is restricted, factual knowledge is at a minimum, and where we have some psychological evidence of what master players actually do.

Chess is an ideal micro-world in which relevance is restricted to the narrow domain of the kind of chess piece (pawn, knight, etc.), its color, and the position of the piece on the board. But while the game's circumscribed character makes a world champion chess program in principle possible, there is a great deal of evidence that human beings play chess quite differently from computers; and I was not surprised to find that up to 1971 computers played fairly low-level chess (see pp. 82–85). In July 1976, however, the Northwestern University chess program, called

CHESS 4.5, won the class B section of the Paul Masson American Chess Championship with an impressive 5 wins and no losses. It then went on in February 1977 to win the 84th Minnesota Open Tournament against experts and high-class A players.[75] Such unexpected impressive results require a reexamination of the difference between human and computer chess playing.

A chess program has the sort of situation → action rules discussed above. A situation is characterized in terms of context-free features: the position and color of each piece on the board. All possible legal moves and the positions which result are then defined in terms of these features. To evaluate and compare positions rules are provided for calculating scores on attributes such as "material balance" (where a numerical value is assigned to each piece on the board and the total score is computed for each player), or "center control" (where the number of pieces bearing on each centrally located square is counted). Finally, there must be a formula for evaluating alternative positions on the basis of these scores. Using this approach and looking at a tree of around 3 million potential positions CHESS 4.5 can beat some players at the expert level, but a chess master generally looks at the results of less than 100 possible moves (see p. 102) and yet plays a far better game. How can this be?

In Chapter 1, I note that human beings avoid the counting out of large numbers of alternatives characteristic of a computer program by "zeroing in" on the appropriate area in which to look for a move and I suggest that this ability is the result of having a sense of the developing game. While no doubt correct, this now seems to me an inadequate account, for it does not take into consideration the fact that to develop this ability to zero in, chess masters must play thousands of actual and book games. What does this apprenticeship add to their skill?

By playing over book games chess masters presumably develop the ability to recognize present positions as similar to positions which occurred in classic games. These previous positions have already been analyzed in terms of their significant aspects. Aspects of a chess position include such overall characteristics as "control of the situation" (the extent to which a player's opponent's moves can be forced by making threatening moves), "crampedness of the position" (the amount of freedom of maneuver inherent in both the player's position and the opponent's position), or "overextendedness" (the fact that while the position might be superficially quite strong, one is not in sufficient control of the situation to follow through and, with correct play by the opponent, a massive retreat will be required). The already analyzed remembered positions focus the player's attention on critical aspects of the current position, and the master can thus zero in on these critical areas before beginning to count out specific moves.

The distinction between features and aspects is central here. *Aspects* play a role in an account of human play similar to that of *features* in the computer model, but there is a crucial difference. In the computer model the *situation is* DEFINED IN TERMS OF *the features,* whereas in human play *situational understanding is* PRIOR TO *aspect specification.* For example, the numerical value of a feature such as material balance can be calculated independently of any understanding of the game, whereas an aspect like overextendedness cannot be calculated simply in terms of the position of the pieces, since the same board position can have different aspects depending on its place in the long-range strategy of a game. In a game in which white's long-range strategy is an attack on the opponent's king, the advanced position of white's pieces does not constitute overextension, whereas otherwise it would. No present or envisaged chess program attempts to include such long-range strategy, yet to recognize aspects requires some such overall interpretation of the game.

For the same reason some sort of *feature-based* matching of the present position against a stored library of previous positions won't help account for a master player's ability to use past experience to zero in. It is astronomically unlikely that two positions will ever turn out to be *identical,* so that what has to be compared are *similar* positions. But similarity cannot be defined as having a large number of pieces on identical squares. Two positions which are identical except for one pawn moved to an adjacent square can be totally different, while two positions can be similar although no pieces are on the same square in each. Thus similarity depends on the player's sense of the issues at stake, not merely on the position of the pieces. Seeing two positions as similar is exactly what requires a deep understanding of the game. And structuring the situation in terms of aspects of remembered similar situations in turn enables the human player to avoid the massive counting out required when the positions are characterized only in terms of context-free features.

Aspects also enable masters to formulate heuristic *maxims* which play a role in this account analogous to heuristic *rules* in the computer model. Polanyi calls attention to the difference between strict rules and maxims:

Maxims are rules, the correct application of which is part of the art which they govern. The true maxims of golfing or of poetry increase our insight into golfing or poetry and may even give valuable guidance to golfers and poets; but these maxims would instantly condemn themselves to absurdity if they tried to replace the golfer's skill or the poet's art. Maxims cannot be understood, still less applied by anyone not already possessing a good practical knowledge of the art.[76]

At present computers using exhaustive search, and masters using selective search guided by aspect analysis and maxims, can each look ahead about six or seven ply.[77]* Given the exponential growth of alternative moves it will not be possible without better tree-searching heuristics to significantly increase the computer's power to look ahead. Thus with present programs what is really at stake is how far computers which must use tactics based on context-free features can make up by sheer brute force for the use of long-range strategy, the recognition of similarity to other preanalyzed games, and the zeroing in on crucial aspects characteristic of advanced human play.

In general being able to see similarity to prototypical cases and to recognize shared aspects in terms of this similarity, as well as the possibility of profiting from maxims formulated in terms of these aspects, all seem to play an essential role in the acquisition and utilization of expertise. But since these abilities are not based on context-free features but depend on the overall situation they cannot be captured in the situation → action rule formalism. Thus we can expect in every area where expertise is based on experience to continue to find some experts who outperform even the most sophisticated programs.

Although chess programs and knowledge engineering in general have made remarkable progress during the past two years, discourse understanding, despite the introduction of interesting new ideas, is still in the same state of stagnation as it was in 1972. While this has led some researchers to ever more extravagant promises and claims, it has led others to sober thoughts on the difficulty of programming human understanding. In order to form a reasonable opinion about what has yet to be done to make computers intelligent, we must turn from the computer's successes in restricted domains to the stag/flation afflicting the field of discourse understanding.

The difference between programs like MYCIN and CHESS 4.5, and programs for understanding discourse, is precisely the difference between domain-specific knowledge and general intelligence; between anything-goes engineering and no-tricks basic study; or, as we can now see, the difference between areas in which relevance has been decided beforehand (Area III in my chart, p. 292), and areas in which determining what is relevant is precisely the problem (Area IV).

In the past five years, the problem of how to structure and retrieve data in situations when anything might be relevant has come to be known as the knowledge representation problem. As Patrick Winston, head of the M.I.T. AI Laboratory, puts it in a section of a 1975 research proposal entitled "The Need for Basic Studies":

... We believe that proper representation is the key to advanced vision, common sense reasoning, and expert problem solving, just as it is to many other aspects of Artificial Intelligence.[78]

Of course, the representation of knowledge was always a central problem for work in AI, but earlier periods were characterized by an attempt to repress it by seeing how much could be done with as little knowledge as possible. Now, the difficulties are being faced. As Roger Schank of Yale recently remarked:

... Researchers are starting to understand that tour-de-forces in programming are interesting but non-extendable ... the AI people recognize that how people use and represent knowledge is the key issue in the field. ...[79]

Papert and Goldstein explain the problem:

It is worthwhile to observe here that the goals of a knowledge-based approach to AI are closely akin to those which motivated Piaget to call ... himself an "epistemologist" rather than a psychologist. The common theme is the view that the process of intelligence is determined by the knowledge held by the subject. The deep and primary questions are to understand the operations and data structures involved.[80]

Another memo illustrates how ignoring the background knowledge can come back to haunt one of AI's greatest tricks in the form of nongeneralizability:

. . . Many problems arise in experiments on machine intelligence because things obvious to any person are not represented in any programs. One can pull with a string, but one cannot push with one. One cannot push with a thin wire, either. A taut inextensible cord will break under a very small lateral force. Pushing something affects first its speed; only indirectly its position! Simple facts like these caused serious problems when Charniak attempted to extend Bobrow's "Student" program to more realistic applications, and they have not been faced up to until now.[81]

The most interesting current research is directed toward the underlying problem of developing new, flexible, complex data types which will allow the representation of background knowledge in large, more structured units.

In 1972, drawing on Husserl's phenomenological analysis, I pointed out that it was a major weakness of AI that no programs made use of expectations (see pp. 241, 242, and 250). Instead of modeling intelligence as a passive receiving of context-free facts into a structure of already stored data, Husserl thinks of intelligence as a context-determined, goal-directed activity—as a *search* for anticipated facts. For him the noema, or mental representation of any type of object, provides a context or "inner horizon" of expectations or "predelineations" for structuring the incoming data: a "rule governing *possible* other consciousness of [the object] as identical—possible, as exemplifying essentially predelineated types."[82]* As I explain in Chapter 7:

. . . We perceive a house, for example, as more than a façade—as having some sort of back—some inner horizon. We respond to this whole object first and then, as we get to know the object better, fill in the details as to inside and back. [p. 241]

The noema is thus a symbolic description of all the features which can be expected with certainty in exploring a certain type of object—features which remain "inviolably the same: as long as the objectivity remains intended as *this* one and of this kind"[83] . . . plus "predelineations" of those properties which are possible but not necessary features of this type of object.

A year after my objection, Minsky proposed a new data structure remarkably similar to Husserl's for representing everyday knowledge:

A frame is a data-structure for representing a stereotyped situation, like being in a certain kind of living room, or going to a child's birthday party. . . .

We can think of a frame as a network of nodes and relations. The "top levels" of a frame are fixed, and represent things that are always true about the supposed situation. The lower levels have many *terminals*—"slots" that must be filled by specific instances or data. Each terminal can specify conditions its assignments must meet. . . .

Much of the phenomenological power of the theory hinges on the inclusion of expectations and other kinds of presumptions. A frame's terminals are normally already filled with "default" assignments.[84]

In Minsky's model of a frame, the "top level" is a developed version of what in Husserl's terminology "remains inviolably the same" in the representation, and Husserl's predelineations have been made precise as "default assignments"—additional features that can normally be expected. The result is a step forward in AI techniques from a passive model of information processing to one which tries to take account of the context of the interactions between a knower and his world. Husserl thought of his method of transcendental-phenomenological constitution, i.e., "explicating" the noema for all types of objects, as the beginning of progress toward philosophy as a rigorous science, and Patrick Winston has hailed Minsky's proposal as "the ancestor of a wave of progress in AI."[85] But Husserl's project ran into serious trouble and there are signs that Minsky's may too.

During twenty years of trying to spell out the components of the noema of everyday objects, Husserl found that he had to include more and more of what he called the "outer horizon," a subject's total knowledge of the world:

. . . To be sure, even the tasks that present themselves when we take single types of objects as restricted clues prove to be extremely complicated and always lead to extensive disciplines when we penetrate more deeply. That is the case, for example, with a transcendental theory of the constitution of a spatial object (to say nothing of a Nature) as such, of psycho-physical being and humanity as such, cultures as such.[86]

He sadly concluded at the age of seventy-five that he was "a perpetual beginner" and that phenomenology was an "infinite task"—and even that may be too optimistic. His successor, Heidegger, pointed out that since the outer horizon or background of cultural practices was the condition of the possibility of determining relevant facts and features and thus prerequisite for structuring the inner horizon, as long as the cultural context had not been clarified the proposed analysis of the inner horizon of the *noema* could not even claim progress.

There are hints in an unpublished early draft of the frame paper that Minsky has embarked on the same misguided "infinite task" that eventually overwhelmed Husserl:

Just constructing a knowledge base is a major intellectual research problem. . . . We still know far too little about the contents and structure of common-sense knowledge. A "minimal" common-sense system must "know" something about cause-effect, time, purpose, locality, process, and types of knowledge. . . . We need a serious epistemological research effort in this area.[87]

Minsky's naïveté and faith are astonishing. Philosophers from Plato to Husserl, who uncovered all these problems and more, have carried on serious epistemological research in this area for two thousand years without notable success. Moreover, the list Minsky includes in this passage deals only with natural objects, and their positions and interactions. As Husserl saw, and as I argue in Chapter 8, intelligent behavior also presupposes a background of cultural practices and institutions. Observations in the frame paper such as:

Trading normally occurs in a social context of law, trust, and convention. Unless we also represent these other facts, most trade transactions will be almost meaningless[88]

show that Minsky has understood this too. But Minsky seems oblivious to the hand-waving optimism of his proposal that programmers rush in where philosophers such as Heidegger fear to tread, and simply make explicit the totality of human practices which pervade our lives as water encompasses the life of a fish.

To make this essential point clear it helps to take an example used by

Minsky and look at what is involved in understanding a piece of everyday equipment as simple as a chair. No piece of equipment makes sense by itself. The physical object which is a chair can be defined in isolation as a collection of atoms, or of wood or metal components, but such a description will not enable us to pick out chairs. What makes an object a *chair* is its function, and what makes possible its role as equipment for sitting is its place in a total practical context. This presupposes certain facts about human beings (fatigue, the ways the body bends), and a network of other culturally determined equipment (tables, floors, lamps), and skills (eating, writing, going to conferences, giving lectures, etc.). Chairs would not be equipment for sitting if our knees bent backwards like those of flamingos, or if we had no tables as in traditional Japan or the Australian bush.

Anyone in our culture understands such things as how to sit on kitchen chairs, swivel chairs, folding chairs; and in arm chairs, rocking chairs, deck chairs, barber's chairs, sedan chairs, dentist's chairs, basket chairs, reclining chairs, wheel chairs, sling chairs, and beanbag chairs— as well as how to get out of them again. This ability presupposes a repertoire of bodily skills which may well be indefinitely large, since there seems to be an indefinitely large variety of chairs and of successful (graceful, comfortable, secure, poised, etc.) ways to sit in them. More-over, understanding chairs also includes social skills such as being able to sit appropriately (sedately, demurely, naturally, casually, sloppily, provocatively, etc.) at dinners, interviews, desk jobs, lectures, auditions, concerts (intimate enough for there to be chairs rather than seats), and in waiting rooms, living rooms, bedrooms, courts, libraries, and bars (of the sort sporting chairs, not stools).

In the light of this amazing capacity, Minsky's remarks on chairs in his frame paper seem more like a review of the difficulties than even a hint of how AI could begin to deal with our commonsense understanding in this area.

There are many forms of chairs, for example, and one should choose carefully the chair-description frames that are to be the major capitols of chair-land. These are used for rapid matching and assigning priorities to the various differences. The lower priority *features* of the *cluster* center then serve . . . as properties of the chair *types*. . . .[89]

There is no argument why we should expect to find elementary context-free *features* characterizing a chair *type,* nor any suggestion as to what these features might be. They certainly cannot be legs, back, seat, etc., since these are not context-free characteristics defined apart from chairs which then "cluster" in a chair representation, but rather legs, back, etc. come in all shapes and variety and can only be recognized as *aspects* of already recognized chairs. Minsky continues:

Difference pointers could be "functional" as well as geometric. Thus, after rejecting a first try at "chair" one might try the functional idea of "something one can sit on" to explain an unconventional form.[90]

But, as we already saw in our discussion of Winston's concept-learning program, a function so defined is not abstractable from human embodied know-how and cultural practices. A functional description such as "something one can sit on" treated merely as an additional context-free descriptor cannot even distinguish conventional chairs from saddles, thrones, and toilets. Minsky concludes:

Of course, that analysis would fail to capture toy chairs, or chairs of such ornamental delicacy that their actual use would be unthinkable. These would be better handled by the method of excuses, in which one would bypass the usual geometrical or functional explanation in favor of responding to *contexts* involving *art* or *play.*[91]

This is what is required all right, but by what elementary features are *these* contexts to be recognized? There is no reason at all to suppose that one can avoid the difficulty of formally representing our knowledge of chairs by abstractly representing even more holistic, concrete, culturally determined, and loosely organized human practices such as art and play.

Minsky in his frame article claims that: "the frame idea . . . is in the tradition of . . . the 'paradigms' of Kuhn,"[92] so it is appropriate to ask whether a theory of formal representation such as Minsky's, even if it can't account for everyday objects like chairs, can do justice to Thomas Kuhn's analysis of the role of paradigms in the practice of science. Such a comparison might seem more promising than testing the ability of frames to account for our everyday understanding, since science is a theoretical enterprise which deals with context-free data whose lawlike relations can in principle be grasped by any sufficiently powerful "pure-intellect," whether human, Martian, digital, or divine.

Paradigms, like frames, serve to set up expectations. As Kuhn notes: "In the absence of a paradigm or some candidate for paradigm, all the facts that could possibly pertain to the development of a given science are likely to seem equally relevant."[93] Minsky interprets as follows:

According to Kuhn's model of scientific evolution 'normal' science proceeds by using established *descriptive schemes*. Major changes result from new 'paradigms', new ways of describing things. Whenever our customary viewpoints do not work well, whenever we fail to find effective frame systems in memory, we must construct new ones that bring out the right *features.*[94]

But what Minsky leaves out is precisely Kuhn's claim that a paradigm or exemplar is *not* an *abstract explicit descriptive scheme* utilizing formal *features,* but rather a shared *concrete case,* which dispenses with features altogether:

The practice of normal science depends on the ability, acquired from exemplars, to group objects and situations into similarity sets which are primitive in the sense that the grouping is done without an answer to the question, "Similar with respect to what?"[95]

Thus, although it is the job of scientists to find abstractable, exact, symbolic descriptions, and *the subject matter of science* consists of such formal accounts, the *thinking* of scientists themselves does not seem to be amenable to this sort of analysis. Kuhn explicitly repudiates any formal reconstruction which claims that the scientists must be using symbolic descriptions:

I have in mind a manner of knowing which is misconstrued if reconstructed in terms of rules that are first abstracted from exemplars and thereafter function in their stead.[96]

Indeed, Kuhn sees his book as raising just those questions which Minsky refuses to face:

Why is the *concrete* scientific achievement, as a locus of professional commitment, prior to the various concepts, laws, theories, and points of view that may be *abstracted* from it? In what sense is the shared paradigm a fundamental unit for the student of scientific development, a unit that *cannot* be fully reduced to logically *atomic components* which might function in its stead?[97]

Although research based on frames cannot deal with this question and so cannot account for commonsense or scientific knowledge, the frame idea did bring the problem of how to represent our everyday knowledge into the open in AI. Moreover, it provided a model so vague and suggestive that it could be developed in several different directions. Two alternatives immediately presented themselves: either to use frames as part of a special-purpose micro-world analysis dealing with commonsense knowledge as if everyday activity took place in preanalyzed specific domains, or else to try to use frame structures in "a no-tricks basic study" of the open-ended character of everyday know-how. Of the two most influential current schools in AI, Roger Schank and his students at Yale have tried the first approach, Winograd, Bobrow, and their research group at Stanford and Xerox, the second.

Schank's version of frames are called "scripts." Scripts encode the essential steps involved in stereotypical social activities. Schank uses them to enable a computer to "understand" simple stories. Like the micro-world builders of Phase III, Schank believes he can start with isolated stereotypical situations described in terms of primitive actions and gradually work up from there to all of human life.

To carry out this project, Schank invented an event description language consisting of eleven primitive acts such as: ATRANS—the transfer of an abstract relationship such as possession, ownership, or control; PTRANS—the transfer of physical location of an object; INGEST—the taking of an object by an animal into the inner workings of that animal, etc.,[98] and from these primitives he builds gamelike scenarios which enable his program to fill in gaps and pronoun reference in stories.

Such primitive acts, of course, make sense only when the context is already interpreted in a specific piece of discourse. Their artificiality can easily be seen if one compares one of Schank's context-free primitive acts to real-life actions. Take PTRANS, the transfer of physical location of an object. At first it seems an interpretation-free fact if ever there was one. After all, either an object moves or it doesn't. But in real life things are not so simple; even what counts as physical motion depends on our purposes. If someone is standing still in a moving elevator on a moving ocean liner, is his going from A to B deck a PTRANS? What about when he is just sitting on B deck? Are we all PTRANSing around the sun? Clearly the answer depends on the situation in which the question is asked.

Such primitives can, however, be used to describe fixed situations or scripts once the relevant purposes have already been agreed upon. Schank's definition of a script emphasizes its predetermined, bounded, gamelike character:

We define a script as a *predetermined* causal chain of conceptualizations that describe the *normal sequence of things* in a familiar situation. Thus there is a restaurant script, a birthday-party script, a football game script, a classroom script, and so on. Each script has in it a *minimum number of players* and objects that assume certain roles within the script . . . [E]ach *primitive* action given stands for the most important *element* in a *standard set* of actions.[99]

His illustration of the restaurant script spells out in terms of primitive actions the rules of the restaurant game:

Script: restaurant
Roles: customer; waitress; chef; cashier
Reason: to get food so as to go down in hunger and up in pleasure

Scene 1 entering

PTRANS—go into restaurant
MBUILD—find table
PTRANS—go to table
MOVE—sit down

Scene 2 ordering

ATRANS—receive menu
ATTEND—look at it
MBUILD—decide on order
MTRANS—tell order to waitress

Scene 3 eating

ATRANS—receive food
INGEST—eat food

Scene 4 exiting

MTRANS—ask for check
ATRANS—give tip to waitress
PTRANS—go to cashier
ATRANS—give money to cashier
PTRANS—go out of restaurant[100]

No doubt many of our social activities are stereotyped and there is nothing in principle misguided in trying to work out primitives and rules for a restaurant game, the way the rules of Monopoly are meant to capture a simplified version of the typical moves in the real estate business. But Schank claims that he can use this approach to understand stories about *actual* restaurant-going—that in effect he can treat the sub-world of restaurant going as if it were an isolated micro-world. To do this, however, he must artificially limit the possibilities; for, as one might suspect, no matter how stereotyped, going to the restaurant is not a self-contained game but a highly variable set of behaviors which open out into the rest of human activity. What "normally" happens when one goes to a restaurant can be preselected and formalized by the programmer as default assignments, but the background has been left out so that a program using such a script cannot be said to understand going to a restaurant at all. This can easily be seen by imagining a situation that deviates from the norm. What if when one tries to order he finds that the item in question is not available, or before paying he finds that the bill is added up wrongly? Of course, Schank would answer that he could build these normal ways restaurant-going breaks down into his script. But there are always *abnormal* ways everyday activities can break down: the juke box might be too noisy, there might be too many flies on the counter, or as in the film *Annie Hall,* in a New York delicatessen one's girl friend might order a pastrami sandwich on white bread with mayonnaise. When we understand going to a restaurant we understand how to cope with even these abnormal possibilities because going to a restaurant is part of our everyday activities of going into buildings, getting things we want, interacting with people, etc.

To deal with this sort of objection Schank has added some general rules for coping with unexpected disruptions. The general idea is that in a story "it is usual for non-standard occurrences to be explicitly mentioned"[101] so the program can spot the abnormal events and understand the subsequent events as ways of coping with them. But here we can see that dealing with stories allows Schank to bypass the basic problem, since it is the *author's* understanding of the situation which enables him to decide which events are disruptive enough to mention.

This *ad hoc* way of dealing with the abnormal can always be revealed by asking further questions, for the program has not understood a restaurant story the way people in our culture do, until it can answer such simple questions as: When the waitress came to the table did she wear clothes? Did she walk forward or backward? Did the customer eat his food with his mouth or his ear? If the program answers, "I don't know," we feel that all of its right answers were tricks or lucky guesses and that it has not understood anything of our everyday restaurant behavior.[102]* The point here, and throughout, is not that there are subtle things human beings can do and recognize which are beyond the low-level understanding of present programs, but that in any area there are simple taken-for-granted responses central to human understanding, lacking which a computer program cannot be said to have any understanding at all.

Schank's claim, then, that "the paths of a script are the possibilities that are extant in a situation"[103] is insidiously misleading. Either it means that the script accounts for the possibilities in the restaurant game defined by Schank, in which case it is true but uninteresting; or he is claiming that he can account for the possibilities in an everyday restaurant situation which is impressive but, by Schank's own admission, false.

Real short stories pose a further problem for Schank's approach. In a script what the primitive actions and facts are is determined beforehand, but in a short story *what counts as the relevant facts depends on the story itself.* For example, a story which describes a bus trip contains in its script that the passenger thanks the driver (a Schank example). But the fact that the passenger thanked the driver would not be important in a story in which the passenger simply took the bus as a part of a longer journey, while it might be crucially important if the story concerned a misanthrope who had never thanked anyone before, or a very law-abiding young man who had courageously broken the prohibition against speaking to drivers in order to speak to the attractive woman driving the bus. Overlooking this point, Schank claimed at a recent meeting that his program which can extract death statistics from newspaper accident reports had answered my challenge that a computer would count as intelligent only if it could summarize a short story.[104] But Schank's newspaper program cannot provide a clue concerning judgments of what to include in a story summary because it works only where relevance and significance have been predetermined, and thereby avoids dealing with the world built up in a story in terms of which judgments of relevance and importance are made.

Another way to see that script analysis of story understanding leaves out something essential is to consider the question: In reading a story how do we call up the appropriate script? In discussing this question Schank points out:

... While the restaurant script can be a subpart of a larger script (such as $TRIP) [In Schank's notation the dollar sign indicates a script.] it must be marked as not being capable of being subsumed by $DELIVERY.[105]

But this "solution" raises the problem of negative information which dogs a proposal like Schank's. It seems implausible to suppose that one could mark the restaurant script as *not* subsumed under such other scripts as making a phone call, answering a call for help, retrieving a lost object, looking for a job, getting signatures for a petition, repairing equipment, coming to work, doing an inspection, leaving a bomb, arranging a banquet, collecting for the Mafia, looking for change for the meter, buying cigarettes, hiding from the police, etc., etc., which might lead one to enter a restaurant *without* intending to eat. It would be more manageable to write a program which, *whenever* someone in a story enters a restaurant, follows the restaurant script until the understander's expectations fail to be fulfilled. Presumably because he thinks of his programs as having psychological reality, Schank neglects this alternative, and on this point he is right. Normally in reading a story we do not suppose that a person who enters a restaurant for a purpose that does not involve eating is preparing to eat; so we do not have to be jolted out of this hypothesis by the fact that the waitress does not bring him a menu. But

Schank's proposal leaves completely unanswered the problem of how we *do* choose the right script.

Schank's latest book does have some interesting ideas about how to go beyond scripts, since he readily admits that much of our everyday activities is not scripted. He introduces "plans" as our way of dealing with stories about situations which don't have fixed scripts. And he points out that plans are made up of subplans or planboxes, which are useful in many situations. For example,

one kind of instrumental goal is a general building block in many planning processes. In a plan for satisfying hunger, one of the crucial steps is to go to where food is. Going to an intended location is a very general process, useful in all sorts of specific plans.[106]

Thus a planbox is used whenever no script is available. If a planbox is used often enough, it will generate a script that eliminates the need for the planbox *as long as the surrounding context stays the same.*[107]

But here the persistent problem of recognizing similarity again arises. How can we tell whether the surrounding context is the same? It won't be identical, and Schank gives us no theory of how to recognize contexts as similar.

Finally, Schank has to deal with the short-term goals which motivate everyday plans, the long range goals which generate the short term ones, and the life themes, in terms of which people organize their goal-oriented activities.

. . . The expectations that we generate from themes are an important part of understanding stories because they generate the goals that generate the plans that we expect to be carried out.[108]

Here Schank has to face the important way desires, emotions, and a person's interpretation of what it means to be a human being open up endless possibilities for human life. If the themes which organize our lives turn out to be unprogrammable Schank is in trouble and so is all of AI. But Schank again imperturbably uses his engineering approach and starts making lists of life themes. This leads to what would seem to be an in-principle problem:

Because life themes are continuous goal generators, it is not really possible to delimit a set of possible life themes. There are as many life themes as there are possible long term goals.[109]

But Schank passes over this difficulty, as he does all others, by stipulating a few more *ad hoc* primitives.

. . . As understanders we attempt to type people we hear about in terms of one of our standard life themes. As we hear of differences from the normal type we create a private life theme for the individual we are hearing about. The infinity of possible life themes comes from this possibility of the unique combination of goals for any individual. What makes life themes manageable is that the number of life theme types is small (six) and the number of standard life themes within those typings is a tractable size (say 10 to 50 for each type).[110]

If these primitives don't account for our understanding of the variety of possible human lives, Schank is ready, as always, to add a few more.

Nothing could ever call into question Schank's basic assumption that all human practice and know-how is represented in the mind as a system of beliefs constructed from context-free primitive actions and facts, but there are signs of trouble. Schank does admit that an individual's "belief system" cannot be fully elicited from him; although he never doubts that it exists and that it could in principle be represented in his formalism. He is therefore led to the desperate idea of a program which could learn about everything from restaurants to life themes the way people do. In a recent paper he concludes:

We hope to be able to build a program that can learn, as a child does, how to do what we have described in this paper instead of being spoon-fed the tremendous information necessary. In order to do this it might be necessary to await an effective automatic hand-eye system and an image processor.[111]

For Schank's *ad hoc* approach there is no way of ever facing an interesting failure, but the fact that robot makers such as Raphael report that progress in their area must await an adequate scheme for knowledge representation, and that those like Schank who hope to provide such representation systems finally fall back on robots as a means for acquiring them, suggests that the field is in a loop—the computer world's conception of a crisis.

In any case, Schank's appeal to learning is at best another evasion. Developmental psychology has shown that children's learning does not consist merely in acquiring more and more information about specific routine situations by adding new primitives and combining old ones as Schank's view would lead one to expect. Rather learning of specific details takes place on a background of shared practices which seem to be picked up in everyday interactions not as facts and beliefs but as bodily skills for coping with the world. Any learning presupposes this background of implicit know-how which gives significance to details. Since Schank admits that he cannot see how this background can be made explicit so as to be given to a computer, and since the background is presupposed for the kind of script learning Schank has in mind, it seems that his project of using preanalyzed primitives to capture commonsense understanding is doomed.

A more plausible, even if in the last analysis perhaps no more promising, approach would be to use the new theoretical power of frames or stereotypes to dispense with the need to preanalyze everyday situations in terms of a set of primitive features whose *relevance is independent of context.* This approach starts with the recognition that in everyday communication " 'Meaning' is multi-dimensional, formalizable only in terms of the entire complex of goals and knowledge [of the world] being applied by both the producer and understander."[112] This knowledge, of course, is assumed to be "A body of specific beliefs (expressed as symbol structures . . .) making up the person's 'model of the world'."[113] Given these assumptions Terry Winograd and his co-workers are developing a new knowledge representation language (KRL), which they hope will enable programmers to capture these beliefs in symbolic descriptions of multidimensional prototypical objects whose *relevant aspects are a function of their context.*

Prototypes would be structured so that any sort of description from proper names to procedures for recognizing an example could be used to fill in any one of the nodes or slots that are attached to a prototype. This allows representations to be defined in terms of each other, and results in what the author calls "a *wholistic* as opposed to *reductionistic* view of representation."[114] For example, since any description could be part of any other, chairs could be described as having aspects such as seats and backs, and seats and backs in turn could be described in terms of their function in chairs. Furthermore, each prototypical object or situation could be described from many different perspectives. Thus nothing need be defined in terms of its necessary and sufficient features in the way Winston and traditional philosophers have proposed, but rather, following Rosch's research on prototypes, objects would be classified as more or less resembling certain prototypical descriptions.

Winograd illustrates this idea using the traditional philosophers' favorite example:

The word "bachelor" has been used in many discussions of semantics, since (save for obscure meanings involving aquatic mammals and medieval chivalry) it seems to have a formally tractable meaning which can be paraphrased "an adult human male who has never been married". . . . In the realistic use of the word, there are many problems which are not as simply stated and formalized. Consider the following exchange:

Host: I'm having a big party next weekend. Do you know any nice bachelors I could invite?
Friend: Yes, I know this fellow X. . . .

The problem is to decide, given the facts below, for which values of X the response would be a reasonable answer in light of the normal meaning of the word "bachelor". A simple test is to ask for which ones the host might fairly complain "You lied. You said X was a bachelor.":

A: Arthur has been living happily with Alice for the last five years. They have a two year old daughter and have never officially married.

B: Bruce was going to be drafted, so he arranged with his friend Barbara to have a justice of the peace marry them so he would be exempt. They have never lived together. He dates a number of women, and plans to have the marriage annulled as soon as he finds someone he wants to marry.

C: Charlie is 17 years old. He lives at home with his parents and is in high school.

D: David is 17 years old. He left home at 13, started a small business, and is now a successful young entrepreneur leading a playboy's life style in his penthouse apartment.

E: Eli and Edgar are homosexual lovers who have been living together for many years.

F: Faisal is allowed by the law of his native Abu Dhabi to have three wives. He currently has two and is interested in meeting another potential fiancee.

G: Father Gregory is the bishop of the Catholic cathedral at Groton upon Thames.

[This] cast of characters could be extended indefinitely, and in each case there are problems in deciding whether the word "bachelor" could appropriately be applied. In normal use, a word does not convey a clearly definable combination of primitive propositions, but evokes an *exemplar* which possesses a number of properties. This exemplar is not a specific individual in the experience of the language user, but is more abstract, representing a conflation of typical properties. A prototypical bachelor can be described as:

1. a person
2. a male
3. an adult
4. not currently officially married
5. not in a marriage-like living situation
6. potentially marriageable
7. leading a bachelor-like life style
8. not having been married previously
9. having an intention, at least temporarily, not to marry
10. . . .

Each of the men described above fits some but not all of these characterizations. Except for narrow legalistic contexts, there is no significant sense in which a subset of the characteristics can be singled out as the "central meaning" of the word. In fact, among native English speakers there is little agreement about whether someone who has been previously married can properly be called a "bachelor" and fairly good agreement that it should not apply to someone who is not potentially marriageable (e.g. has taken a vow of celibacy).

Not only is this list [of properties] open-ended, but the individual terms are themselves not definable in terms of primitive notions. In reducing the meaning of 'bachelor' to a formula involving 'adult' or 'potentially marriageable', one is led into describing these in terms of exemplars as well. 'Adult' cannot be defined in terms of years of age for any but technical legal purposes and in fact even in this restricted sense, it is defined differently for different aspects of the law. Phrases such as 'marriage-like living situation' and 'bachelor-like life style' reflect directly in their syntactic form the intention to convey stereotyped exemplars rather than formal definitions.[115]

Obviously if KRL succeeds in enabling AI researchers to use such prototypes to write flexible programs, such a language will be a major breakthrough and will avoid the *ad hoc* character of the "solutions" typical of micro-world programs. Indeed, the future of AI depends on some such work as that begun with the development of KRL. But there are problems with this approach. Winograd's analysis has the important consequence that in comparing two prototypes, what counts as a match and thus what counts as the relevant aspects which justify the match will be a result of the program's understanding of the current context.

The result of a matching process is not a simple true/false answer. It can be stated in its most general form as: "Given the set of alternatives which I am currently considering . . . and looking in order at those stored structures which are most accessible in the *current context,* here is the best match, here is the degree to which it seems to hold, and here are the specific detailed places where match was not found. . . ."

The selection of the order in which sub-structures of the description will be compared is a function of their current accessibility, which depends both on the form in which they are stored and the *current context.* [116]

This raises four increasingly grave difficulties. First, for there to be "a class of cognitive 'matching' processes which operate on the descriptions (symbol structures) available for two entities, looking for correspondences and differences" [117] there must be a finite set of prototypes to be matched. To take Winograd's example:

A single object or event can be described with respect to several prototypes, with further specifications from the perspective of each. The fact that last week *Rusty flew to San Francisco* would be expressed by describing the event as a typical instance of *Travel* with the mode specified as *Airplane,* destination *San Francisco,* etc. It might also be described as a *Visit* with the actor being *Rusty,* the friends a particular group of people, the interaction warm, etc. [118]

But *etc.* covers what might, without predigestion for a specific purpose, be a hopeless proliferation. The same flight might also be a test flight, a check of crew performance, a stopover, a mistake, a golden opportunity, not to mention a visit to brother, sister, thesis adviser, guru, etc., etc., etc. Before the program can function at all the total set of possible alternatives must be pre-selected by the programmer.

Second, the matching makes sense only *after* the current candidates for comparison have been found. In chess, for example, positions can be compared only after the chess master calls to mind past positions the current board positions might plausibly resemble. And, as we saw in the chess case, the discovery of the relevant candidates which makes the matching of aspects possible requires experience and intuitive association.

We saw also, in both the chess and the robot cases, that the discovery of this prior similarity seems to point to some entirely different sort of processing than symbolic description—perhaps the sort of processing provided by some brain equivalent of holograms in which similarity is basic. The only way a KRL-based program (which must use symbolic descriptions) could proceed would be to guess some frame on the basis of what was already "understood" by the program, and then see if that frame's features could be matched to some current description. If not, the program would have to backtrack and try another prototype until it found one into whose slots or default terminals the incoming data could be fitted. This seems an altogether implausible and inefficient model of how we perform, and only rarely occurs in our conscious life (see p. 248 of this book for a Husserlian discussion of this problem). Of course, cognitive scientists could answer the above objection by maintaining, in spite of the implausibility, that we try out the various prototypes very quickly and are simply not aware of the frantic shuffling of hypotheses going on in our unconscious. But, in fact, most would agree with Winograd that at present the frame selection problem is unsolved.

The problem of choosing the frames to try is another very open area. There is a selection problem, since we cannot take all of our possible frames for different kinds of events and match them against what is going on.[119]

There is, moreover, a third and more basic question which may pose an in-principle problem for any formal holistic account in which the significance of any fact, indeed what counts as a fact, always depends on context. Winograd stresses the critical importance of context:

The results of human reasoning are *context dependent,* the structure of memory includes not only the long-term storage organization (what do I know?) but also a current context (what is in focus at the moment?). We believe that this is an important feature of human thought, not an inconvenient limitation.[120]

He further notes that "the problem is to find a formal way of talking about . . . current attention focus and goals. . . ."[121] Yet he gives no formal account of how a computer program written in KRL could determine the current context.

Winograd's work does contain suggestive claims such as his remark that "the procedural approach formalizes notions such as 'current context' . . . and 'attention focus' in terms of the processes by which cognitive state changes as a person comprehends or produces utterances."[122] There are also occasional parenthetical references to "current goals, focus of attention, set of words recently heard, etc."[123] But reference to recent words has proven useless as a way of determining what the current context is, and reference to current goals and focus of attention is vague and perhaps even question-begging. If a human being's current goal is, say, to find a chair to sit on, his current focus might be on recognizing whether he is in a living room or a warehouse. He will also have short-range goals like finding the walls, longer-range goals like finding the light switch, middle-range goals like wanting to write or rest; and what counts as satisfying these goals will in turn depend on his ultimate goals and interpretation of himself as, say, a writer, or merely as easily exhausted and deserving comfort. So Winograd's appeal to "current goals and focus" covers too much to be useful in determining what specific situation the program is in.

To be consistent, Winograd would have to treat each type of situation the computer could be in as an object with *its* prototypical description; then in recognizing a specific situation, the situation or context in which *that* situation was encountered would determine which foci, goals, etc. were relevant. But where would such a regress stop? Human beings, of course, don't have this problem. They are, as Heidegger puts it, already in a situation, which they constantly revise. If we look at it genetically, this is no mystery. We can see that human beings are gradually trained into their cultural situation on the basis of their embodied precultural situation, in a way no programmer using KRL is trying to capture. But for this very reason a program in KRL is not always-already-in-a-situation. Even if it represents all human knowledge in its stereotypes, including all possible types of human situations, it represents them from the outside like a Martian or a god. It isn't situated in any one of them, and it may be impossible to program it to behave as if it were.

This leads to my fourth and final question: Is the know-how which enables human beings constantly to sense what specific situation they are in, the sort of know-how which can be represented as a kind of knowledge in *any* knowledge representation language no matter how ingenious and complex? It seems that our sense of our situation is determined by our changing moods, by our current concerns and projects, by our long-range self-interpretation and probably also by our sensory-motor skills for coping with objects and people—skills we develop by practice without ever having to represent to ourselves our body as an object, our culture as a set of beliefs, and our propensities as situation → rules. All these uniquely human capacities provide a "richness" or a "thickness" to our way of being-in-the-world and thus seem to play an essential role in situatedness, which in turn underlies all intelligent behavior.

There is no reason to suppose that moods, mattering, and embodied skills can be captured in any formal web of belief, and except for Kenneth Colby, whose view is not accepted by the rest of the AI community, no current work assumes that they can. Rather, all AI workers and cognitive psychologists are committed, more or less lucidly, to the view that such noncognitive aspects of the mind can simply be ignored. This belief that a significant part of what counts as intelligent behavior can be captured in purely cognitive structures defines cognitive science and is a version of what, in Chapter 4, I call the psychological assumption. Winograd makes it explicit:

AI is the general study of those aspects of cognition which are common to all physical symbol systems, including humans and computers.[124]*

But this definition merely delimits the field; it in no way shows there is anything to study, let alone guarantees the project's success.

Seen in this light, Winograd's grounds for optimism contradict his own basic assumptions. On the one hand, he sees that a lot of what goes on in human minds cannot be programmed, so he only hopes to program a significant part:

[C]ognitive science . . . does not rest on an assumption that the analysis of mind as a physical symbol system provides a *complete* understanding of human thought. . . . For the paradigm to be of value, it is only necessary that there be *some significant aspects* of thought and language which can be profitably understood through analogy with other symbol systems we know how to construct.[125]

On the other hand, he sees that human intelligence is "wholistic" and that meaning depends on "the entire complex of goals and knowledge." What our discussion suggests is that all aspects of human thought, including nonformal aspects like moods, sensory-motor skills, and long-range self-interpretations, are so interrelated that one cannot substitute an abstractible web of explicit beliefs for the whole cloth of our concrete everyday practices.

What lends plausibility to the cognitivist position is the conviction that such a web of beliefs must finally fold back on itself and be complete, since we can know only a finite number of facts and procedures describable in a finite number of sentences. But since facts are descriminated and language is used only in a context, the argument that the web of belief must in principle be completely formalizable does not show that such a belief system can account for intelligent behavior. This would be true only if the context could also be captured in the web of facts and procedures. But if the context is determined by moods, concerns, and skills, then the fact that our beliefs can in principle be completely represented does not show that representations are sufficient to account for cognition. Indeed, if nonrepresentable capacities play an essential role in situatedness, and the situation is presupposed by all intelligent behavior, then the "aspects of cognition which are common to all physical symbol systems" will not be able to account for any cognitive *performance* at all.

In the end the very idea of a holistic information processing model in which the relevance of the facts depends on the context may involve a contradiction. To recognize any context one must have already selected from the indefinite number of possibly descriminable features the possibly relevant ones, but such a selection can be made only after the context has already been recognized as similar to an already analyzed one. The holist thus faces a vicious circle: relevance presupposes similarity and similarity presupposes relevance. The only way to avoid this loop is to be always-already-in-a-situation without representing it so that the problem of the priority of context and features does not arise, or else to return to the reductionist project of preanalyzing all situations in terms of a fixed set of possibly relevant primitives—a project which has its own practical problems, as our analysis of Schank's work has shown, and, as we shall see in the conclusion, may have its own internal contradiction as well.

Whether this is, indeed, an in-principle obstacle to Winograd's approach only further research will tell. Winograd himself is admirably cautious in his claims:

If the procedural approach is successful, it will eventually be possible to describe the mechanisms at such a level of detail that there will be a verifiable fit with many aspects of detailed human performance . . . but we are nowhere near having explanations which cover language processing as a whole, including meaning.[126]

If problems do arise because of the necessity in any formalism of isolating beliefs from the rest of human activity, Winograd will no doubt have the courage to analyze and profit from the discovery. In the meantime everyone interested in the philosophical project of cognitive science will be watching to see if Winograd and company can produce a moodless, disembodied, concernless, already adult surrogate for our slowly acquired situated understanding.

Conclusion

Given the fundamental supposition of the information processing approach that all that is relevant to intelligent behavior can be formalized in a structured description, all problems must appear to be merely problems of complexity. Bobrow and Winograd put this final faith very clearly at the end of their description of KRL:

The system is complex, and will continue to get more so in the near future. . . . [W]e do not expect that it will ever be reduced to a very small set of mechanisms. Human thought, we believe, is the product of the interaction of a fairly large set of interdependent processes. Any representation language which is to be used in modeling thought or achieving "intelligent" performance will have to have an extensive and varied repertoire of mechanisms.[127]

Underlying this mechanistic assumption is an even deeper assumption which has gradually become clear during the past ten years of research. During this period AI researchers have consistently run up against the problem of representing everyday context, just as I predicted they would in the first edition of this book. Work during the first five years (1967–1972) demonstrated the futility of trying to evade the importance of everyday context by creating artificial gamelike contexts preanalyzed in terms of a list of fixed-relevance features. More recent work has thus been forced to deal directly with the background of commonsense know-how which guides our changing sense of what counts as the relevant facts. Faced with this necessity researchers have implicitly tried to treat the broadest context or background as an object with its own set of prese-lected descriptive features. This assumption, that the background can be treated as just another object to be represented in the same sort of structured description in which everyday objects are represented, is es-sential to our whole philosophical tradition. Following Heidegger, who is the first to have identified and criticized this assumption, I will call it the metaphysical assumption.

The obvious question to ask in conclusion is: Is there any evidence besides the persistent difficulties and history of unfulfilled promises in AI for believing that the metaphysical assumption is unjustified? It may be that no argument can be given against it, since facts put forth to show that the background of practices is unrepresentable are in that very act shown to be the sort of facts which *can* be represented. Still, since the value of this whole dialogue is to help each side to become as clear as possible concerning its presuppositions and their possible justification, I will attempt to lay out the argument which underlies my antiformalist, and, therefore, antimechanist convictions.

My thesis, which owes a lot to Wittgenstein,[128]* is that whenever human behavior is analyzed in terms of rules, these rules must always contain a *ceteris paribus* condition, i.e., they apply "everything else being equal," and what "everything else" and "equal" means in any specific situation can never be fully spelled out without a regress. Moreover, this *ceteris paribus* condition is not merely an annoyance which shows that the analysis is not yet complete and might be what Husserl called an "infinite task." Rather the *ceteris paribus* condition points to a background of practices which are the condition of the possibility of all rulelike activity. In explaining our actions we must always sooner or later fall back on our everyday practices and simply say "this is what we do" or "that's what it is to be a human being." Thus in the last analysis all intelligibility and all intelligent behavior must be traced back to our sense of what we *are,* which is, according to this argument, necessarily, on pain of regress, something we can never explicitly *know.*

This argument can be best worked out in terms of an example. Back in 1972 when Minsky was working on the frame concept, one of his students, Eugene Charniak, was developing a scriptlike approach for dealing with children's stories. Papert and Goldstein provide a revealing analysis of this approach:

. . . [C]onsider the following story fragment from Charniak,

> Today was Jack's birthday. Penny and Janet went to the store. They were going to get presents. Janet decided to get a kite. "Don't do that," said Penny. "Jack has a kite. He will make you take *it* back."

The goal is to construct a theory that explains how the reader understands that *"it"* refers to the new kite, not the one Jack already owns. Purely syntactic criteria (such as assigning the referent of *"it"* to the last mentioned noun) are clearly inadequate, as the result would be to mistakenly understand the last sentence of the story as meaning that Jack will make Janet take back the kite *he already owns.* . . . [I]t is clear that one cannot know that *"it"* refers to the new kite without knowledge about the trading habits of our society. One could imagine a different world in which newly bought objects are never returned to the store, but old ones are. The question we raise here is how this knowledge might be represented, stored and made available to the process of understanding Charniak's story.[129]

Their answer to this question is, of course, dictated by the metaphysical assumption. They try to make the background of practices involved explicit as a set of beliefs:

Charniak's formal realization of a *frame* was in the form of *base-knowledge* about a large variety of situations that arise in the context of these stories. The mechanism of his program was for the content of sentences to evoke this base knowledge with the following effect: demons ("frame-keepers" in our terminology) were created to monitor the possible occurrence in later sentences of likely (but not inevitable) consequences of the given situation. Thus, for our story fragment the birthday knowledge creates expectations about the need for participants of the party to buy presents and the possible consequence of having to return these gifts. Hence, these demons expect the possibility of Jack already possessing the present and the resulting need for Janet to return *it,* where *it* is known to be the present.[130]

But once games and micro-worlds are left behind, a yawning abyss threatens to swallow up those who try to carry out such a program. Papert and Goldstein march bravely in:

. . . But the story does not include explicitly all important facts. Look back at the story. Some readers will be surprised to note that the text itself does not state (a) that the presents bought by Penny and Janet were for *Jack,* (b) that the [kite] bought by Janet was intended as a present, and (c) that having an object implies that one does not want another. All of the above facts are inserted into the database by other demons made activated by the birthday frame.[131]

Our example turns on the question: How does one store the "facts" mentioned in (c) above about returning presents? To begin with there are perhaps indefinitely many reasons for taking a present back. It may be the wrong size, run on the wrong voltage, be carcinogenic, make too much noise, be considered too childish, too feminine, too masculine, too American, etc., etc. And each of these facts requires further facts to be understood. But we will concentrate on the reason mentioned in (c): that normally, i.e., *everything else being equal,* if one has an object, one does not want another just like it. Of course, this cannot simply be entered as a true proposition. It does not hold for dollar bills, cookies, or marbles. (It is not clear it even holds for kites.) Papert and Goldstein would answer that, of course, once we talk of the norm we must be prepared to deal with exceptions:

[T]he typical situation in comprehension is to be faced with a set of clues that evoke a rich and detailed knowledge structure, the frame, that supplies the unstated details. Naturally, these defaults may be inappropriate for some situations and, in those cases, the text must supply the exceptions.[132]

But here the desperate hand waving begins, for the text need not explicitly mention the exceptions at all. If the gift was marbles or cookies the text surely would not mention that these were exceptions to the general rule that one of a kind is enough. So the data base would have to contain *an account of all possible exceptions* to augment the text—if it even makes sense to think of this as a definite list. Worse, even if one listed all the exceptional cases where one would be glad to possess more than one specimen of a certain type of object, there are situations which allow an exception to this exception: already having one cookie is more than enough if the cookie in question is three feet in diameter; one thousand marbles is more than a normal child can handle, etc. Must we then list the situations which lead one to expect exceptions to the exceptions? But these exceptions too can be overriden in the case of, say, a cookie monster or a marble freak, and so it goes. . . . The computer programmer writing a story understander must try to list all possibly relevant information, and once that information contains appeals to the *normal* or *typical* there is no way to avoid an infinite regress of qualifications for applying that knowledge to a specific situation.

The only "answer" the M.I.T. group offers is the metaphysical assumption that the background of everyday life is a set of rigidly defined situations in which the relevant facts are as clear as in a game:

The fundamental frame assumption is the thesis that . . . [m]ost situations in which people find themselves *have sufficient in common* with previously encountered situations for the salient features to be *pre-analyzed* and stored in a *situation-specific* form.[133]

But this "solution" is untenable for two reasons:[134]*

1. Even if the current situation is, indeed, *similar* to a preanalyzed one, we still have the problem of deciding which situation it is similar to. We have already seen that even in games such as chess no two positions are likely to be identical so a deep understanding of what is going on is required to decide what counts as a similar position in any two games. This should be even more obvious in cases where the problem is to decide

which preanalyzed situation a given real-world situation most resembles, for example whether a situation where there are well-dressed babies and new toys being presented has more in common with a birthday party or a beauty contest.

2. Even if all our lives *were* lived in identical stereotypical situations, we have just seen that any real-world frame must be described in terms of the normal, and that appeal to the normal necessarily leads to a regress when we try to characterize the conditions which determine the applicability of the norm to a specific case. Only our *general* sense of what is typical can decide here, and *that* background understanding by definition cannot be "situation-specific."

This is the other horn of the dilemma facing the information-processing model. We have seen in discussing KRL that the holistic approach leads to a circle as to which comes first, similarity or relevant aspects, now it turns out that the reductionist alternative leads to a regress.

Still, to this dilemma the AI researchers might plausibly respond: "Whatever the background of shared interests, feelings, and practices necessary for understanding specific situations, that knowledge *must* somehow be represented in the human beings who have that understanding. And how else could such knowledge be represented but in some explicit data structure?" Indeed, the kind of computer programming accepted by all workers in AI would require such a data structure, and so would philosophers who hold that all knowledge must be explicitly represented in our minds, but there are two alternatives which would avoid the contradictions inherent in the information-processing model by avoiding the idea that everything we know must be in the form of some explicit symbolic representation.

One response, shared by existential phenomenologists such as Merleau-Ponty and ordinary language philosophers such as Wittgenstein, is to say that such "knowledge" of human interests and practices need not be represented at all. Just as it seems plausible that I can learn to swim by practicing until I develop the necessary patterns of responses, without representing my body and muscular movements in some data structure, so too what I "know" about the cultural practices which enables me to recognize and act in specific situations has been gradually acquired through training in which no one ever did or could, again on pain of regress, make explicit what was being learned.

Another possible account would allow a place for representations, at least in special cases where I have to stop and reflect, but such a position would stress that these are usually nonformal representations, more like images, by means of which I explore what I *am,* not what I *know.* On this view I don't normally represent to myself that I have desires, or that standing up requires balance, or, to take an example from Schank's attempt to make explicit our interpersonal knowledge, that:

[I]f two people are positively emotionally related, then a negative change in one person's state will cause the other person to develop the goal of causing a positive change in the other's state.[135]

Still, when it is helpful, I can picture myself in a specific situation and ask myself what would I do or how would I feel—if I were in Jack's place how would I react to being given a second kite—without having to make explicit all that a computer would have to be told to come to a similar conclusion. We thus appeal to *concrete* representations (images or memories) based on our own experience without having to make explicit the strict rules and their spelled out *ceteris paribus* conditions required by *abstract* symbolic representations.

Indeed, it is hard to see how the subtle variety of ways things can matter to us could be exhaustively spelled out. We can anticipate and understand Jack's reaction because we remember what it feels like to be amused, amazed, incredulous, disappointed, disgruntled, saddened, annoyed, disgusted, upset, angry, furious, outraged, etc., and we recognize the impulses to action associated with these various degrees and kinds of concerns. A computer model would have to be given a description of each shade of feeling as well as each feeling's normal occasion and likely result.

The idea that feelings, memories, and images *must* be the conscious tip of an unconscious framelike data structure runs up against both *prima facie* evidence and the problem of explicating the *ceteris paribus* conditions. Moreover, the formalist assumption is not supported by one shred of scientific evidence from neurophysiology or psychology, or from the past successes of AI, whose repeated failures required appeal to the metaphysical assumption in the first place.

AI's current difficulties, moreover, become intelligible in the light of this alternative view. The proposed formal representation of the background of practices in symbolic descriptions, whether in terms of situation-free primitives or more sophisticated data structures whose building blocks can be descriptions of situations, would, indeed, look more and more complex and intractable if minds were not physical symbol systems. If belief structures are the result of abstraction from the concrete practical context rather than the true building blocks of our world, it is no wonder the formalist finds himself stuck with the view that they are endlessly explicatable. On my view "the organization of world knowledge provides the largest stumbling block"[136] to AI precisely because the programmer is forced to treat the world as an object, and our know-how as knowledge.

But this metaphysical assumption definitive of cognitive science is never questioned by its practitioners. John McCarthy notes that "it is quite difficult to formalize the facts of common knowledge,"[137] but he never doubts that common knowledge can be accounted for in terms of facts.

The epistemological part of AI studies what kinds of *facts* about the world are available to an observer with given opportunities to observe, how these facts can be represented in the memory of a computer, and what *rules* permit legitimate conclusions to be drawn from these facts.[138]

When AI workers finally face and analyze their failures it might well be this metaphysical assumption that they will find they have to reject.

Looking back over the past ten years of AI research we might say that the basic point which has emerged is that *since intelligence must be situated it cannot be separated from the rest of human life.* The persistent denial of this seemingly obvious point cannot, however, be laid at the door of AI. It starts with Plato's separation of the intellect or rational soul from the body with its skills, emotions, and appetites. Aristotle continued this unlikely dichotomy when he separated the theoretical from the practical, and defined man as a rational animal—as if one could separate man's rationality from his animal needs and desires. If one thinks of the importance of the sensory-motor skills in the development of our ability to recognize and cope with objects, or of the role of needs and desires in structuring all social situations, or finally of the whole cultural background of human self-interpretation involved in our simply knowing how to pick out and use chairs, the idea that we can simply ignore this know-how while formalizing our intellectual understanding as a complex system of facts and rules is highly implausible.

However incredible, this dubious dichotomy now pervades our thinking about everything including computers. In the *Star Trek* TV series, the episode entitled "The Return of the Archons" tells of a wise states-man named Landru who programmed a computer to run a society. Unfortunately, he could give the computer only his abstract intelligence, not his concrete wisdom, so it turned the society into a rational plannified hell. No one stops to wonder how, without Landru's embodied skills, feelings, and concerns, the computer could understand everyday situations and so run a society at all.

In *Computer Power and Human Reason,*[139] Joseph Weizenbaum, a well-known contributor to work in AI (see pp. 218 ff.) makes this same mistake. Indeed, the radical separation of intelligence and wisdom is the basic assumption which seems to support but actually undermines the thesis of his otherwise eloquent book. Weizenbaum warns that we de-mean ourselves if we come to think of human beings on the AI model as devices for solving technical problems. But to make the argument that we are not such devices he embraces the very dichotomy which gives plausibility to AI. Weizenbaum argues, for example, that since a com-puter cannot understand loneliness it cannot *fully* understand the sen-tence " 'Will you come to dinner with me this evening' . . . to mean a shy young man's desperate longing for love"[140]* (a point which workers in AI would readily admit), while at the same time Weizenbaum grants the dubious AI assumption that "it may be possible, following Schank's procedures, to construct a conceptual structure that corresponds to the meaning of the sentence."[141] Stressing these extremes of emphathetic wisdom and formalized meaning leads Weizenbaum to overlook the essential point that all meaningful discourse must take place in a shared context of concerns.

Ironically, Weizenbaum was the first major contributor to AI to recognize the essential relation of meaning and pragmatic context. As he put it in 1968: "[I]n real conversation global context assigns meaning to what is being said. . . ."[142] But once he overlooks this essential connection there is no way he can resist the conclusions of his AI colleagues. Thus, in spite of his well-documented claim that each culture has what Justice Oliver W. Holmes called its "tacit assumptions" and "unwritten practices,"[143] and his commitment to the strong thesis argued for in this book that these practices "cannot be explicated in any form but life itself,"[144]* Weizenbaum, like Minsky, concludes: "I see no way to put a bound on the degree of intelligence such an organism [i.e., a computer] could, at least in principle attain."[145]

This surprising admission can be explained only if Weizenbaum holds the AI view that the unexplicatable assumptions and unwritten practices of a culture play no essential role in the intelligent behavior of its members. Indeed, at times Weizenbaum seems to embrace the most implausible implications of this implausible view, viz., that these tacit assumptions and practices play no role in everyday linguistic communication, for he concedes that:

It is technically feasible to build a computer system that will interview patients applying for help at a psychiatric out-patient clinic and will produce their psychiatric profiles complete with charts, graphs, and natural-language commentary.[146]

Consistent with this view that intelligence and natural language communication—as distinct from intuition and wisdom—are in-principle completely formalizable, Weizenbaum further allows that:

. . . the view of man as a species of the more general genus "information-processing system" does concentrate our attention on one aspect of man. . . .[147]*

He calls to aid in justifying this claim the latest "scientific" version of the Platonic dichotomy—the split brain. This is a natural association, since pop literature on the split brain seems to support the science-fiction illusion of the separation of intuition and pure intelligence. As Weizenbaum explains it:

The LH [Left Hemisphere] thinks, so to speak, in an orderly, sequential, and, we might call it, *logical fashion*. The RH [Right Hemisphere], on the other hand, appears to think in terms of *holistic* images. *Language processing* appears to be almost exclusively centered in the LH. . . .[148]

Here again linguistic capacity is isolated and equated with context-free logicality, forgetting, what Weizenbaum was the first AI worker to see, that when language is used in communication (and the Left Hemisphere alone is perfectly able to use language to communicate), "a global [holistic] context assigns meaning to what is being said. . . ."[149]

After these damaging admissions Weizenbaum is left with only the moralistic position that "however intelligent machines may be made to be, there are some acts of thought that ought to be attempted only by humans."[150]* This stricture presumably follows from the notion that although the background of cultural practices plays no essential role in intelligent behavior, including everyday conversation, it does play a role in the wisdom required in making sound legal decisions and psychiatric evaluations—although even here Weizenbaum is wary of making any in-principle claim. And he has good reason for caution, since once everyday activity has been admitted to be a technical problem amenable to the powers of pure formal intelligence it is impossible to draw a line limiting what computers may ultimately be able to do. All Weizenbaum has left is the high-minded platitude that "since we do not now have any ways of making computers wise, we ought not now to give computers tasks which demand wisdom."[151]*

From the perspective we have been laying out here the real problem is that Weizenbaum accepts the metaphysical assumption that whatever is required for everyday intelligence can be objectified and represented in a belief system. Whether this assumption takes the form of the deep philosophical claim that goes back to Leibniz and is still made by Husserl that the perceptions and practices required for situated intelligence can all be represented in a symbolic description, or the shallow technological view, shared by Weizenbaum and the "artificial intelligentsia" he opposes, that everyday understanding and natural language communication does not essentially involve our embodied, socialized skills, this assumption distorts our perception of our humanity.

Great artists have always sensed the truth, stubbornly denied by both philosophers and technologists, that the basis of human intelligence cannot be isolated and explicitly understood. In *Moby Dick* Melville writes of the tattooed savage, Queequeg, that he had "written out on his body a complete theory of the heavens and the earth, and a mystical treatise on the art of attaining truth; so that Queequeg in his own proper person was a riddle to unfold; a wondrous work in one volume; but whose mysteries not even himself could read. . . ."[152] Yeats puts it even more succinctly: "I have found what I wanted—to put it in a phrase, I say, 'Man can embody the truth, but he cannot know it'."

Hubert L. Dreyfus
1979

Introduction

I

Since the Greeks invented logic and geometry, the idea that all reasoning might be reduced to some kind of calculation—so that all arguments could be settled once and for all—has fascinated most of the Western tradition's rigorous thinkers. Socrates was the first to give voice to this vision. The story of artificial intelligence might well begin around 450 B.C. when (according to Plato) Socrates demands of Euthyphro, a fellow Athenian who, in the name of piety, is about to turn in his own father for murder: "I want to know what is characteristic of piety which makes all actions pious . . . that I may have it to turn to, and to use as a standard whereby to judge your actions and those of other men."[1]§ Socrates is asking Euthyphro for what modern computer theorists would call an "effective procedure," "a set of rules which tells us, from moment to moment, precisely how to behave."[2]

Plato generalized this demand for moral certainty into an epistemological demand. According to Plato, all knowledge must be stateable in explicit definitions which anyone could apply. If one could not state his know-how in terms of such explicit instructions—if his knowing *how*

§Notes begin on p. 307. [Citations are indicated by a superior figure. Substantive notes are indicated by a superior figure and an astersik.]

could not be converted into knowing *that*—it was not knowledge but mere belief. According to Plato, cooks, for example, who proceed by taste and intuition, and poets who work from inspiration, have no knowledge: what they do does not involve understanding and cannot be understood. More generally, what cannot be stated explicitly in precise instructions—all areas of human thought which require skill, intuition, or a sense of tradition—are relegated to some kind of arbitrary fumbling.

But Plato was not yet fully a cyberneticist (although according to Norbert Wiener he was the first to use the term), for Plato was looking for *semantic* rather than *syntactic* criteria. His rules presupposed that the person understood the meanings of the constitutive terms. In the *Republic* Plato says that Understanding (the rulelike level of his divided line representing all knowledge) depends on Reason, which involves a dialectical analysis and ultimately an intuition of the meaning of the fundamental concepts used in understanding. Thus Plato admits his instructions cannot be completely formalized. Similarly, a modern computer expert, Marvin Minsky, notes, after tentatively presenting a Platonic notion of effective procedure: "This attempt at definition is subject to the criticism that the *interpretation* of the rules is left to depend on some person or agent."[3]

Aristotle, who differed with Plato in this as in most questions concerning the application of theory to practice, noted with satisfaction that intuition was necessary to apply the Platonic rules:

Yet it is not easy to find a formula by which we may determine how far and up to what point a man may go wrong before he incurs blame. But this difficulty of definition is inherent in every object of perception; such questions of degree are bound up with the circumstances of the individual case, where our only criterion *is* the perception.[4]

For the Platonic project to reach fulfillment one breakthrough is required: all appeal to intuition and judgment must be eliminated. As Galileo discovered that one could find a pure formalism for describing physical motion by ignoring secondary qualities and teleological considerations, so, one might suppose, a Galileo of human behavior might succeed in reducing all semantic considerations (appeal to meanings) to the techniques of syntactic (formal) manipulation.

The belief that such a total formalization of knowledge must be possible soon came to dominate Western thought. It already expressed a basic moral and intellectual demand, and the success of physical science seemed to imply to sixteenth-century philosophers, as it still seems to suggest to thinkers such as Minsky, that the demand could be satisfied. Hobbes was the first to make explicit the syntactic conception of thought as calculation: "When a man *reasons,* he does nothing else but conceive a sum total from addition of parcels," he wrote, "for REASON . . . is nothing but reckoning. . . ."[5]

It only remained to work out the univocal parcels or "bits" with which this purely syntactic calculator could operate; Leibniz, the inventor of the binary system, dedicated himself to working out the necessary unambiguous formal language.

Leibniz thought he had found a universal and exact system of notation, an algebra, a symbolic language, a "universal characteristic" by means of which "we can assign to every object its determined characteristic number."[6] In this way all concepts could be analyzed into a small number of original and undefined ideas; all knowledge could be expressed and brought together in one deductive system. On the basis of these numbers and the rules for their combination all problems could be solved and all controversies ended: "if someone would doubt my results," Leibniz said, "I would say to him: 'Let us calculate, Sir,' and thus by taking pen and ink, we should settle the question."[7]

Like a modern computer theorist announcing a program about to be written, Leibniz claims:

Since, however, the wonderful interrelatedness of all things makes it extremely difficult to formulate explicitly the characteristic numbers of individual things, I have invented an elegant artifice by virtue of which certain relations may be represented and fixed numerically and which may thus then be further determined in numerical calculation.[8]

Nor was Leibniz reticent about the importance of his almost completed program.

Once the characteristic numbers are established for most concepts, mankind will then possess a new instrument which will enhance the capabilities of the mind to far greater extent than optical instruments strengthen the eyes, and will supersede the microscope and telescope to the same extent that reason is superior to eyesight.[9]

With this powerful new tool, the skills which Plato could not formalize, and so treated as confused thrashing around, could be recuperated as theory. In one of his "grant proposals"—his explanations of how he could reduce all thought to the manipulation of numbers if he had money enough and time—Leibniz remarks:

the most important observations and turns of skill in all sorts of trades and professions are as yet unwritten. This fact is proved by experience when passing from theory to practice we desire to accomplish something. *Of course, we can also write up this practice, since it is at bottom just another theory more complex and particular. . . .*[10]

Leibniz had only promises, but in the work of George Boole, a mathematician and logician working in the early nineteenth century, his program came one step nearer to reality. Like Hobbes, Boole supposed that reasoning was calculating, and he set out to "investigate the fundamental laws of those operations of the mind by which reasoning is performed, to give expression to them in the symbolic language of a Calculus. . . ."[11]

Boolean algebra is a binary algebra for representing elementary logical functions. If "a" and "b" represent variables, "." represents "and," " + " represents "or," and "1" and "0" represent "true" and "false" respectively, then the rules governing logical manipulation can be written in algebraic form as follows:

$$a + a = a \quad a + 0 = a \quad a + 1 = 1$$
$$a \cdot a = a \quad\quad a \cdot 0 = 0 \quad\quad a \cdot 1 = a$$

Western man was now ready to begin the calculation.

Almost immediately, in the designs of Charles Babbage (1835), practice began to catch up to theory. Babbage designed what he called an "Analytic Engine" which, though never built, was to function exactly like a modern digital computer, using punched cards, combining logical and arithmetic operations, and making logical decisions along the way based upon the results of its previous computations.

An important feature of Babbage's machine was that it was digital. There are two fundamental types of computing machines: analogue and digital. Analogue computers do not compute in the strict sense of the word. They operate by measuring the magnitude of physical quantities. Using physical quantities, such as voltage, duration, angle of rotation of a disk, and so forth, proportional to the quantity to be manipulated, they combine these quantities in a physical way and *measure* the result. A slide rule is a typical analogue computer. A digital computer—as the word *digit,* Latin for "finger," implies—represents all quantities by discrete states, for example, relays which are open or closed, a dial which can assume any one of ten positions, and so on, and then literally *counts* in order to get its result.

Thus, whereas analogue computers operate with continuous quantities, all digital computers are discrete state machines. As A. M. Turing, famous for defining the essence of a digital computer, puts it:

[Discrete state machines] move by sudden jumps or clicks from one quite definite state to another. These states are sufficiently different for the possibility of confusion between them to be ignored. Strictly speaking there are no such machines. Everything really moves continuously. But there are many kinds of machines which can profitably be *thought of* as being discrete state machines. For instance in considering the switches for a lighting system it is a convenient fiction that each switch must be definitely on or definitely off. There must be intermediate positions, but for most purposes we can forget about them.[12]

Babbage's ideas were too advanced for the technology of his time, for there was no quick efficient way to represent and manipulate the digits. He had to use awkward mechanical means, such as the position of cogwheels, to represent the discrete states. Electric switches, however, provided the necessary technological breakthrough. When, in 1944, H. H. Aiken actually built the first practical digital computer, it was electromechanical, using about 3000 telephone relays. These were still slow, however, and it was only with the next generation of computers using vacuum tubes that the modern electronic computer was ready.

Ready for anything. For, since a digital computer operates with abstract symbols which can stand for anything, and logical operations which can relate anything to anything, any digital computer (unlike an analogue computer) is a universal machine. First, as Turing puts it, it can simulate any other digital computer.

This special property of digital computers, that they can mimic any discrete state machine, is described by saying that they are *universal* machines. The existence of machines with this property has the important consequence that, considerations of speed apart, it is unnecessary to design various new machines to do various computing processes. They can all be done with one digital computer, suitably programmed for each case. It will be seen that as a consequence of this all digital computers are in a sense equivalent.[13]

Second, and philosophically more significant, *any* process which can be formalized so that it can be represented as series of instructions for the manipulation of discrete elements, can, at least in principle, be reproduced by such a machine. Thus even an analogue computer, provided that the relation of its input to its output can be described by a precise mathematical function, can be simulated on a digital machine.[14]*

But such machines might have remained overgrown adding machines, had not Plato's vision, refined by two thousand years of metaphysics, found in them its fulfillment. At last here was a machine which operated according to syntactic rules, on bits of data. Moreover, the rules were built into the circuits of the machine. Once the machine was programmed there was no need for interpretation; no appeal to human intuition and judgment. This was just what Hobbes and Leibniz had ordered, and Martin Heidegger appropriately saw in cybernetics the culmination of the philosophical tradition.[15]*

Thus while practical men like Eckert and Mauchly, at the University of Pennsylvania, were designing the first electronic digital machine, theorists, such as Turing, trying to understand the essence and capacity of such machines, became interested in an area which had thus far been the province of philosophers: the nature of reason itself.

In 1950, Turing wrote an influential article, "Computing Machinery and Intelligence," in which he points out that "the present interest in 'thinking machines' has been aroused by a particular kind of machine, usually called an 'electronic computer' or a 'digital computer.' "[16] He then takes up the question "Can [such] machines think?"

To decide this question Turing proposes a test which he calls the imitation game:

The new form of the problem can be described in terms of a game which we call the "imitation game." It is played with three people, a man (A), a woman (B), and an interrogator (C) who may be of either sex. The interrogator stays in a room apart from the other two. The object of the game for the interrogator is to determine which of the other two is the man and which is the woman. He knows them by labels X and Y, and at the end of the game he says either "X is A and Y is B" or "X is B and Y is A." The interrogator is allowed to put questions to A and B thus:

C: Will X please tell me the length of his or her hair? Now suppose X is actually A, then A must answer. It is A's object in the game to try to cause C to make the wrong identification. His answer might therefore be

"My hair is shingled, and the longest strands are about nine inches long."

In order that tones of voice may not help the interrogator the answers should be written, or better still, typewritten. The ideal arrangement is to have a tele-printer communicating between the two rooms. Alternatively, the question and answers can be repeated by an intermediary. The object of the game for the third player (B) is to help the interrogator. The best strategy for her is probably to give truthful answers. She can add such things as "I am the woman, don't listen to him!" to her answers, but it will avail nothing as the man can make similar remarks.

We now ask the question, "What will happen when a machine takes the part of A in this game?" Will the interrogator decide wrongly as often when the game is played like this as he does when the game is played between a man and a woman? These questions replace our original, "Can machines think?"[17]

This test has become known as the Turing Test. Philosophers may doubt whether merely behavioral similarity could ever give adequate ground for the attribution of intelligence,[18] but as a goal for those actually trying to construct thinking machines, and as a criterion for critics to use in evaluating their work, Turing's test was just what was needed.

Of course, no digital computer immediately volunteered or was drafted for Turing's game. In spite of its speed, accuracy, and universality, the digital computer was still nothing more than a general-symbol manipulating device. The chips, however, were now down on the old Leibnizian bet. The time was ripe to produce the appropriate symbolism and the detailed instructions by means of which the rules of reason could be incorporated in a computer program. Turing had grasped the possibility and provided the criterion for success, but his article ended with only the sketchiest suggestions about what to do next:

We may hope that machines will eventually compete with men in all purely intellectual fields. But which are the best ones to start with? Even this is a difficult decision. Many people think that a very abstract activity, like the playing of chess, would be best. It can also be maintained that it is best to provide the machine with the best sense organs that money can buy, and then teach it to understand and speak English. This process could follow the normal teaching of a child. Things would be pointed out and named, etc. Again I do not know what the right answer is, but I think both approaches should be tried.[19]

A technique was still needed for finding the rules which thinkers from Plato to Turing assumed must exist—a technique for converting any practical activity such as playing chess or learning a language into the set of instructions Leibniz called a theory. Immediately, as if following Turing's hints, work got under way on chess and language. The same year Turing wrote his article, Claude E. Shannon, the inventor of information theory, wrote an article on chess-playing machines in which he discussed the options facing someone trying to program a digital computer to play chess.

Investigating one particular line of play for 40 moves would be as bad as investigating all lines for just two moves. A suitable compromise would be to examine only the important possible variations—that is, forcing moves, captures and main threats—and carry out the investigation of the possible moves far enough to make the consequences of each fairly clear. It is possible to set up some rough criteria for selecting important variations, not as efficiently as a chess master, but sufficiently well to reduce the number of variations appreciably and thereby permit a deeper investigation of the moves actually considered.[20]

Shannon did not write a chess program, but he believed that "an electronic computer programmed in this manner would play a fairly strong game at speeds comparable to human speeds."[21]

In 1955 Allen Newell wrote a sober survey of the problems posed by the game of chess and suggestions as to how they might be met. Newell notes that "These [suggested] mechanisms are so complicated that it is impossible to predict whether they will work."[22] The next year, however, brought startling success. A group at Los Alamos produced a program which played poor but legal chess on a reduced board. In a review of this work, Allen Newell, J. C. Shaw, and H. A. Simon concluded: "With very little in the way of complexity, we have at least entered the arena of human play—we can beat a beginner."[23] And by 1957, Alex Bernstein had a program for the IBM 704 which played two "passable amateur games."[24]

Meanwhile, Anthony Oettinger was working on the other Turing line. Having already in 1952 programmed a machine which simulated simple conditioning, increasing or decreasing a set response on the basis of positive or negative reinforcement, Oettinger turned to the problem of language translation and programmed a Russian-English mechanical dictionary. Further research in these directions, it seemed, might lead to a computer which could be taught to associate words and objects.

But neither of these approaches offered anything like a general theory of intelligent behavior. What was needed were rules for converting any sort of intelligent activity into a set of instructions. At this point Herbert Simon and Allen Newell, analyzing the way a student proceeded to solve logic problems, noted that their subjects tended to use rules or shortcuts which were not universally correct, but which often helped, even if they sometimes failed. Such a rule of thumb might be, for example: always try to substitute a shorter expression for a longer one. Simon and Newell decided to try to simulate this practical intelligence. The term "heuristic program" was used to distinguish the resulting programs from programs which are guaranteed to work, so-called algorithmic programs which follow an exhaustive method to arrive at a solution, but which rapidly become unwieldy when dealing with practical problems.

This notion of a rule of practice provided a breakthrough for those looking for a way to program computers to exhibit general problem-solving behavior. Something of the excitement of this new idea vibrates in the first paragraph of Newell, Shaw, and Simon's classic article "Empirical Explorations with the Logic Theory Machine: A Case Study in Heuristics."

This is a case study in problem-solving, representing part of a program of research on complex information-processing systems. We have specified a system for finding proofs of theorems in elementary symbolic logic, and by programming a computer to these specifications, have obtained empirical data on the problem-solving process in elementary logic. The program is called the Logic Theory Machine (LT); it was devised to learn how it is possible to solve difficult problems such as proving mathematical theorems, discovering scientific laws from data, playing chess, or understanding the meaning of English prose.

The research reported here is aimed at understanding the complex processes (heuristics) that are effective in problem-solving. Hence, we are not interested in methods that guarantee solutions, but which require vast amounts of computation. Rather, we wish to understand how a mathematician, for example, is able to prove a theorem even though he does not know when he starts how, or if, he is going to succeed.[25]

But Newell and Simon soon realized that even this approach was not general enough. The following year (1957) they sought to abstract the heuristics used in the logic machine, and apply them to a range of similar problems. This gave rise to a program called the *General Problem Solver* or GPS. The motivation and orientation of the work on the General Problem Solver are explained in Newell, Shaw, and Simon's first major report on the enterprise.

This paper . . . is part of an investigation into the extremely complex processes that are involved in intelligent, adaptive, and creative behavior. . . .

Many kinds of information can aid in solving problems: information may suggest the order in which possible solutions should be examined; it may rule out a whole class of solutions previously thought possible; it may provide a cheap test to distinguish likely from unlikely possibilities; and so on. All these kinds of information are *heuristics*—things that aid discovery. Heuristics seldom provide infallible guidance. . . . Often they "work," but the results are variable and success is seldom guaranteed.[26]

To convey a sense of the general heuristics their program employed, Newell and Simon introduced an example of everyday intelligent behavior:

I want to take my son to nursery school. What's the difference between what I have and what I want? One of distance. What changes distance? My automobile. My automobile won't work. What's needed to make it work? A new battery. What has new batteries? An auto repair shop. I want the repair shop to put in a new battery; but the shop doesn't know I need one. What is the difficulty? One of communication. What allows communication? A telephone. . . . And so on.

This kind of analysis—classifying things in terms of the functions they serve, and oscillating among ends, functions required, and means that perform them —forms the basic system of heuristic of GPS. More precisely, this means-end system of heuristic assumes the following:

1. If an object is given that is not the desired one, differences will be detectable between the available object and the desired object.

2. Operators affect some features of their operands and leave others unchanged. Hence operators can be characterized by the changes they produce and can be used to try to eliminate differences between the objects to which they are applied and desired objects.

3. Some differences will prove more difficult to affect than others. It is profitable, therefore, to try to eliminate "difficult" differences, even at the cost of introducing new differences of lesser difficulty. This process can be repeated as long as progress is being made toward eliminating the more difficult differences.[27]

With digital computers solving such problems as how to get three cannibals and three missionaries across a river without the cannibals eating the missionaries, it seemed that finally philosophical ambition had found the necessary technology: that the universal, high-speed computer had been given the rules for converting reasoning into reckoning. Simon and Newell sensed the importance of the moment and jubilantly announced that the era of intelligent machines was at hand.

We have begun to learn how to use computers to solve problems, where we do not have systematic and efficient computational algorithms. And we now know, at least in a limited area, not only how to program computers to perform such problem-solving activities successfully; we know also how to program computers to *learn* to do these things.

In short, we now have the elements of a theory of heuristic (as contrasted with algorithmic) problem solving; and we can use this theory both to understand human heuristic processes and to simulate such processes with digital computers. Intuition, insight, and learning are no longer exclusive possessions of humans: any large high-speed computer can be programmed to exhibit them also.[28]

This field of research, dedicated to using digital computers to simulate intelligent behavior, soon came to be known as "artificial intelligence." One should not be misled by the name. No doubt an artificial nervous system sufficiently like the human one, with other features such as sense organs and a body, would be intelligent. But the term "artificial" does not mean that workers in artificial intelligence are trying to build an artificial man. Given the present state of physics, chemistry, and neurophysiology, such an undertaking is not feasible. Simon and the pioneers of artificial intelligence propose to produce something more limited: a heuristic program which will enable a digital information-processing machine to exhibit intelligence.

Likewise, the term "intelligence" can be misleading. No one expects the resulting robot to reproduce everything that counts as intelligent behavior in human beings. It need not, for example, be able to pick a good wife, or get across a busy street. It must only compete in the more objective and disembodied areas of human behavior, so as to be able to win at Turing's game.

This limited objective of workers in artificial intelligence is just what gives such work its overwhelming significance. These last metaphysicians are staking everything on man's ability to formalize his behavior; to bypass brain and body, and arrive, all the more surely, at the essence of rationality.

Computers have already brought about a technological revolution comparable to the Industrial Revolution. If Simon is right about the imminence of artificial intelligence, they are on the verge of creating an even greater conceptual revolution—a change in our understanding of man. Everyone senses the importance of this revolution, but we are so near the events that it is difficult to discern their significance. This much, however, is clear. Aristotle defined man as a rational animal, and since then reason has been held to be of the essence of man. If we are on the threshold of creating artificial intelligence we are about to see the triumph of a very special conception of reason. Indeed, if reason can be programmed into a computer, this will confirm an understanding of man as an object, which Western thinkers have been groping toward for two thousand years but which they only now have the tools to express and implement. The incarnation of this intuition will drastically change our understanding of ourselves. If, on the other hand, artificial intelligence should turn out to be impossible, then we will have to distinguish human from artificial reason, and this too will radically change our view of ourselves. Thus the moment has come either to face the truth of the tradition's deepest intuition or to abandon the mechanical account of man's nature which has been gradually developing over the past two thousand years.

Although it is perhaps too early for a full answer, we must make an attempt to determine the scope and limits of the sort of reason which has come fully into force since the perfection of the "analytical engine." We must try to understand to what extent artificial intelligence is possible, and if there are limits to the possibility of computer simulation of intelligent behavior, we must determine those limits and their significance. What we learn about the limits of intelligence in computers will tell us something about the character and extent of human intelligence. What is required is nothing less than a critique of artificial reason.

II

The need for a critique of artificial reason is a special case of a general need for critical caution in the behavioral sciences. Chomsky remarks that in these sciences "there has been a natural but unfortunate tendency to 'extrapolate,' from the thimbleful of knowledge that has been attained in careful experimental work and rigorous data-processing, to issues of much wider significance and of great social concern." He concludes that

the experts have the responsibility of making clear the actual limits of their understanding and of the results they have so far achieved. A careful analysis of these limits will demonstrate that in virtually every domain of the social and behavioral sciences the results achieved to date will not support such "extrapolation."[29]

Artificial intelligence, at first glance, seems to be a happy exception to this pessimistic principle. Every day we read that digital computers play chess, translate languages, recognize patterns, and will soon be able to take over our jobs. In fact this now seems like child's play. Literally! In a North American Newspaper Alliance release, dated December 1968, entitled "A Computer for Kids" we are told that

Cosmos, the West German publishing house . . . has come up with a new idea in gifts. . . . It's a genuine (if small) computer, and it costs around $20. Battery operated, it looks like a portable typewriter. But it can be programmed like any big computer to translate foreign languages, diagnose illnesses, even provide a weather forecast.

And in a *Life* magazine article (Nov. 20, 1970) entitled "Meet Shakey, The First Electronic Person," the wide-eyed reader is told of a computer "made up of five major systems of circuitry that correspond quite closely to basic human faculties—sensation, reason, language, memory [and] ego." According to the article, this computer "sees," "understands," "learns," and, in general, has "demonstrated that machines can think." Several distinguished computer scientists are quoted as predicting that in from three to fifteen years "we will have a machine with the general intelligence of an average human being . . . and in a few months [thereafter] it will be at genius level. . . ."

The complete robot may be a few years off, of course, but anyone interested in the prospective situation at the turn of the century can see in the film *2001: A Space Odyssey* a robot named HAL who is cool, conversational, and very nearly omniscient and omnipotent. And this film is not simply science-fiction fantasy. *A Space Odyssey* was made with scrupulous documentation. The director, Stanley Kubrick, consulted the foremost computer specialists so as not to be misled as to what was at least remotely possible. Turing himself had in 1950 affirmed his belief that "at the end of the century the use of words and general educated opinion will have altered so much that one will be able to speak of machines thinking without expecting to be contradicted."[30] And the technical consultant for the film, Professor Marvin Minsky, working on an early prototype of HAL in his laboratory at M.I.T., assured Kubrick that Turing was, if anything, too pessimistic.

That Minsky was not misunderstood by Kubrick is clear from Minsky's editorial for *Science Journal,* which reads like the scenario for *2001:*

At first machines had simple claws. Soon they will have fantastically graceful articulations. Computers' eyes once could sense only a hole in a card. Now they recognize shapes on simple backgrounds. Soon they will rival man's analysis of his environment. Computer programs once merely added columns of figures. Now they play games well, understand simple conversations, weigh many factors in decisions. What next?

Today, machines solve problems mainly according to the principles we build into them. Before long, we may learn how to set them to work upon the very special problem of improving their own capacity to solve problems. Once a certain threshold is passed, this could lead to a spiral of acceleration and it may be hard to perfect a reliable 'governor' to restrain it.[31]

It seems that there may be no limit to the range and brilliance of the properly programmed computer. It is no wonder that among philosophers of science one finds an assumption that machines can do everything people can do, followed by an attempt to interpret what this bodes for the philosophy of mind; while among moralists and theologians one finds a last-ditch retrenchment to such highly sophisticated behavior as moral choice, love, and creative discovery, claimed to be beyond the scope of any machine. Thinkers in both camps have failed to ask the preliminary question whether machines can in fact exhibit even elementary skills like playing games, solving simple problems, reading simple sentences and recognizing patterns, presumably because they are under the impression, fostered by the press and artificial-intelligence researchers such as Minsky, that the simple tasks and even some of the most difficult ones have already been or are about to be accomplished. To begin with, then, these claims must be examined.

It is fitting to begin with a prediction made by Herbert Simon in 1957 as his General Problem Solver seemed to be opening up the era of artificial intelligence:

It is not my aim to surprise or shock you. . . . But the simplest way I can summarize is to say that there are now in the world machines that think, that learn and that create. Moreover, their ability to do these things is going to increase rapidly until—in a visible future—the range of problems they can handle will be coextensive with the range to which the human mind has been applied.

Simon then predicts, among other things,

1. That within ten years a digital computer will be the world's chess champion, unless the rules bar it from competition.

2. That within ten years a digital computer will discover and prove an important new mathematical theorem.
3. That within ten years most theories in psychology will take the form of
computer programs, or of qualitative statements about the characteristics of
computer programs.[32]

Unfortunately, the tenth anniversary of this historic talk went unnoticed, and workers in artificial intelligence did not, at any of their many
national and international meetings, take time out from their progress
reports to confront these predictions with the actual achievements. Now
fourteen years have passed, and we are being warned that it may soon
be difficult to control our robots. It is certainly high time to measure this
original prophecy against reality.

Already in the five years following Simon's predictions, publications
suggested that the first of Simon's forecasts had been half-realized, and
that considerable progress had been made in fulfilling his second prediction. This latter, the theorem-discovery prediction, was "fulfilled" by W.
R. Ashby (one of the leading authorities in the field) when, in a review
of Feigenbaum and Feldman's anthology *Computers and Thought,* he
hailed the mathematical power of the properly programmed computer:
"Gelernter's theorem-proving program has discovered a new proof of the
pons asinorum that demands no construction." This proof, Dr. Ashby
goes on to say, is one which "the greatest mathematicians of 2000 years
have failed to notice . . . which would have evoked the highest praise had
it occurred."[33]

The theorem sounds important, and the naive reader cannot help
sharing Ashby's enthusiasm. A little research, however, reveals that the
pons asinorum, or ass's bridge, is the elementary theorem proved in
Euclidian geometry—namely that the opposite angles of an isosceles
triangle are equal. Moreover, the first announcement of the "new" proof
"discovered" by the machine is attributed to Pappus (A.D. 300).[34] There
is a striking disparity between Ashby's excitement and the antiquity and
simplicity of this proof. We are still a long way from "the important
mathematical theorem" to be found by 1967.

The chess-playing story is more involved and might serve as a model
for a study of the production of intellectual smog in this area. In 1958,

the year after Simon's prediction, Newell, Shaw, and Simon presented an elaborate chess-playing program. As described in their classic paper, "Chess-Playing Programs and the Problem of Complexity," their program was "not yet fully debugged," so that one "cannot say very much about the behavior of the program."[35] Still, it is clearly "good in [the] . . . opening."[36] This is the last detailed published report on the program. In the same year, however, Newell, Shaw, and Simon announced: "We have written a program that plays chess,"[37] and Simon, on the basis of this success, revised his earlier prediction:

In another place, we have predicted that within ten years a computer will discover and prove an important mathematical theorem. On the basis of our experience with the heuristics of logic and chess, we are willing to add the further prediction that only moderate extrapolation is required from the capacities of programs already in existence to achieve the additional problem-solving power needed for such simulation.[38]

Public gullibility and Simon's enthusiasm was such that Newell, Shaw, and Simon's claims concerning their still bugged program were sufficient to launch the chess machine into the realm of scientific mythology. In 1959, Norbert Wiener, escalating the claim that the program was "good in the opening," informed the NYU Institute of Philosophy that "chess-playing machines as of now will counter the moves of a master game with the moves recognized as right in the text books, up to some point in the middle game."[39] In the same symposium, Michael Scriven moved from the ambiguous claim that "machines now play chess" to the positive assertion that "machines are already capable of a good game."[40]

In fact, in its few recorded games, the Newell, Shaw, Simon program played poor but legal chess, and in its last official bout (October 1960) was beaten in 35 moves by a ten-year-old novice. Fact, however, had ceased to be relevant.

While their program was losing its five or six poor games—and the myth they had created was holding its own against masters in the middle game—Newell, Shaw, and Simon kept silent. When they speak again, three years later, they do not report their difficulties and disappointment. Rather, as if to take up where the myth left off, Simon published an article in *Behavioral Science* announcing a program which played "highly creative" chess end games involving "combinations as difficult as any that have been recorded in chess history."[41] That the program restricts these end games to dependence on continuing checks, so that the number of relevant moves is greatly reduced, is mentioned but not emphasized. On the contrary, it is misleadingly implied that similar simple heuristics would account for master play even in the middle game.[42]* Thus, the article gives the impression that the chess prediction is almost realized. With such progress, the chess championship may be *claimed* at any moment. Indeed, a Russian cyberneticist, upon hearing of Simon's ten-year estimate, called it "conservative."[43] And Fred Gruenberger at RAND suggested that a world champion is not enough —that we should aim for "a program which plays better than any man could."[44] This regenerating confusion makes one think of the mythical French beast which is supposed to secrete the fog necessary for its own respiration.

Reality comes limping along behind these impressive pronouncements. Embarrassed by my exposé of the disparity between their enthusiasm and their results, AI workers finally produced a reasonably competent program. R. Greenblatt's program called MacHack did in fact beat the author,[45]* a rank amateur, and has been entered in several tournaments in which it won a few games. This limited success revived hopes and claims. Seymour Papert, the second in command at the M.I.T. robot project, leaped in to defend Simon's prediction, asserting that "as a statement of what researchers in the field consider to be a possible goal for the near future, this is a reasonable statement."[46] And on page 1 of the October 1968 issue of *Science Journal,* Donald Michie, the leader of England's artificial intelligentsia, writes that "today machines can play chess at championship level."[47] However, chess master de Groot, discussing the earlier chess programs, once said: "programs are still very poor chess players and I do not have much hope for substantial improvement in the future." And another chess master, Eliot Hearst, discussing the M.I.T. program in *Psychology Today,* adds: "De Groot's comment was made in 1964 and MacHack's recent tournament showing would not require him to revise his opinion."[48] Nor would most recent events. Greenblatt's program has been gradually improved, but it seems to have reached a point of saturation. During the past two years, it lost all games in the tournaments in which it had been entered, and received no further publicity. We shall soon see that given the limitations of digital computers this is just what one would expect.

It is to Greenblatt's credit that even in the heyday of MacHack he made no prediction; as for Simon and the world championship, the ten years are well up, and the computer is at best a class C amateur.[49]*

This rapid rundown of the state of the art vis-à-vis two of Simon's predictions has, I hope, cleared the air. It is essential to be aware at the outset that despite predictions, press releases, films, and warnings, artificial intelligence is a promise and not an accomplished fact. Only then can we begin our examination of the actual state and future hopes of artificial intelligence at a sufficiently rudimentary level.

The field of artificial intelligence has many divisions and subdivisions, but the most important work can be classified into four areas: game playing, language translating, problem solving, and pattern recognition. We have already discussed the state of game-playing research. We shall now look at the work in the remaining three fields in detail. In Part I my general thesis will be that the field of artificial intelligence exhibits a recurring pattern: early, dramatic success followed by sudden unexpected difficulties. This pattern occurs in all four areas, in two phases each lasting roughly five years. The work from 1957 to 1962 (Chapter 1), is concerned primarily with Cognitive Simulation (CS)—the use of heuristic programs to simulate human behavior by attempting to reproduce the steps by which human beings actually proceed. The second period (Chapter 2) is predominantly devoted to semantic information processing. This is artificial intelligence in a narrower sense than I have been using the term thus far. AI (for this restricted sense I shall use the initials) is the attempt to simulate human intelligent behavior using programming techniques which need bear little or no resemblance to human mental processes. The difficulties confronting this approach have just begun to emerge. The task of the rest of Part I is to discover the underlying common source of all these seemingly unconnected setbacks.

These empirical difficulties, these failures to achieve predicted progress, never, however, discourage the researchers, whose optimism seems to grow with each disappointment. We therefore have to ask what assumptions underlie this persistent optimism in the face of repeated failures. Part II attempts to bring to light four deeply rooted assumptions or prejudices which mask the gravity of the current impasse, and to lay bare the conceptual confusion to which these prejudices give rise.

But these prejudices are so deeply rooted in our thinking that the only alternative to them seems to be an obscurantist rejection of the possibility of a science of human behavior. Part III attempts to answer this objection, insofar as it can be answered, by presenting an alternative to these traditional assumptions, drawing on the ideas of twentieth-century thinkers whose work is an implicit critique of artificial reason, although it has not before been read in this light.

We shall then, in the Conclusion, be in a position to characterize artificial reason and indicate its scope and limits. This in turn will enable us to distinguish among various forms of intelligent behavior and to judge to what extent each of these types of intelligent behavior is programmable in practice and in principle.

If the order of argument presented above and the tone of my opening remarks seem strangely polemical for an effort in philosophical analysis, I can only point out that, as we have already seen, artificial intelligence is a field in which the rhetorical presentation of results often substitutes for research, so that research papers resemble more a debater's brief than a scientific report. Such persuasive marshaling of facts can only be answered in kind. Thus the accusatory tone of Part I. In Part II, however, I have tried to remain as objective as possible in testing fundamental assumptions, although I know from experience that challenging these assumptions will produce reactions similar to those of an insecure believer when his faith is challenged.

For example, the year following the publication of my first investigation of work in artificial intelligence, the RAND Corporation held a meeting of experts in computer science to discuss, among other topics, my report. Only an "expurgated" transcript of this meeting has been released to the public, but even there the tone of paranoia which pervaded the discussion is present on almost every page. My report is called "sinister," "dishonest," "hilariously funny," and an "incredible misrepresentation of history." When, at one point, Dr. J. C. R. Licklider, then of IBM, tried to come to the defense of my conclusion that work should be done on man-machine cooperation, Seymour Papert of M.I.T. responded:

I protest vehemently against crediting Dreyfus with any good. To state that you can associate yourself with one of his conclusions is unprincipled. Dreyfus' concept of coupling men with machines is based on thorough misunderstanding of the problems and has nothing in common with any good statement that might go by the same words.[50]

The causes of this panic-reaction should themselves be investigated, but that is a job for psychology, or the sociology of knowledge. However, in anticipation of the impending outrage I want to make absolutely clear from the outset that what I am criticizing is the implicit and explicit philosophical assumptions of Simon and Minsky and their co-workers, not their technical work. True, their philosophical prejudices and naïveté distort their own evaluation of their results, but this in no way detracts from the importance and value of their research on specific techniques such as list structures, and on more general problems such as data-base organization and access, compatibility theorems, and so forth. The fundamental ideas that they have contributed in these areas have not only made possible the limited achievements in artificial intelligence but have contributed to other more flourishing areas of computer science.

In some restricted ways even AI can have, and presumably will have practical value despite what I shall try to show are its fundamental limitations. (I restrict myself to AI because it is not clear that naïve Cognitive Simulation, as it is now practiced, can have any value at all, except perhaps as a striking demonstration of the fact that in behaving intelligently people do not process information like a heuristically programmed digital computer.) An artifact could replace men in some tasks —for example, those involved in exploring planets—without performing the way human beings would and without exhibiting human flexibility. Research in this area is not wasted or foolish, although a balanced view of what can and cannot be expected of such an artifact would certainly be aided by a little philosophical perspective.

P A R T I

TEN YEARS OF RESEARCH

IN ARTIFICIAL INTELLIGENCE

(1957–1967)

1

Phase I (1957–1962) Cognitive Simulation

I. Analysis of Work in Language Translation, Problem Solving, and Pattern Recognition

LANGUAGE TRANSLATION

The attempts at language translation by computers had the earliest success, the most extensive and expensive research, and the most unequivocal failure. It was soon clear that a mechanical dictionary could easily be constructed in which linguistic items, whether they were parts of words, whole words, or groups of words, could be processed independently and converted one after another into corresponding items in another language. Anthony Oettinger, the first to produce a mechanical dictionary (1954), recalls the climate of these early days: "The notion of . . . fully automatic high quality mechanical translation, planted by overzealous propagandists for automatic translation on both sides of the Iron Curtain and nurtured by the wishful thinking of potential users, blossomed like a vigorous weed."[1]§ This initial enthusiasm and the subsequent disillusionment provide a sort of paradigm for the field. It is aptly described by Bar-Hillel in his report "The Present Status of Automatic Translation of Languages."

§Notes begin on p. 307. [Citations are indicated by a superior figure. Substantive notes are indicated by a superior figure and an asterisk.]

During the first year of the research in machine translation, a considerable amount of progress was made. . . . It created among many of the workers actively engaged in this field the strong feeling that a working system was just around the corner. Though it is understandable that such an illusion should have been formed at the time, it was an illusion. It was created . . . by the fact that a large number of problems were rather readily solved. . . . It was not sufficiently realized that the gap between such output . . . and high quality translation proper was still enormous, and that the problems solved until then were indeed many but just the simplest ones whereas the "few" remaining problems were the harder ones—very hard indeed.[2]

During the ten years following the development of a mechanical dictionary, five government agencies spent about $20 million on mechanical translation research.[3] In spite of journalistic claims at various moments that machine translation was at last operational, this research produced primarily a much deeper knowledge of the unsuspected complexity of syntax and semantics. As Oettinger remarks, "The major problem of selecting an appropriate target correspondent for a source word on the basis of context remains unsolved, as does the related one of establishing a unique syntactic structure for a sentence that human readers find unambiguous."[4] Oettinger concludes: "The outlook is grim for those who still cherish hopes for fully automatic high-quality mechanical translation."[5]*

That was in 1963. Three years later, a government report, *Language and Machines,* distributed by the National Academy of Sciences National Research Council, pronounced the last word on the translation boom. After carefully comparing human translations and machine products the committee concluded:

We have already noted that, while we have machine-aided translation of general scientific text, we do not have useful machine translation. Furthermore, there is no immediate or predictable prospect of useful machine translation.[6]

Ten years have elapsed since the early optimism concerning machine translation. At that time, flight to the moon was still science fiction, and the mechanical secretary was just around the corner. Now we have landed on the moon, and yet machine translation of typed scientific texts

—let alone spoken language and more general material—is still over the horizon, and the horizon seems to be receding at an accelerating rate. Since much of the hope for robots like those of *2001,* or for more modest servants, depends on the sort of understanding of natural language which is also necessary for machine translation, the conclusion of the National Academy of Sciences strikes at *all* predictions—such as Minsky's—that within a generation the problem of creating artificial intelligence will be substantially solved.

PROBLEM SOLVING

Much of the early work in the general area of artificial intelligence, especially work on game playing and problem solving, was inspired and dominated by the work of Newell, Shaw, and Simon at the RAND Corporation and at Carnegie Institute of Technology.[7] Their approach is called Cognitive Simulation (CS) because the technique generally employed is to collect protocols from human subjects, which are then analyzed to discover the heuristics these subjects employ.[8]* A program is then written which incorporates similar rules of thumb.

Again we find an early success: in 1957 Newell, Shaw, and Simon's Logic Theorist, using heuristically guided trial-and-error search, proved 38 out of 52 theorems from *Principia Mathematica.* Two years later, another Newell, Shaw, and Simon program, the General Problem Solver (GPS), using more sophisticated means-ends analysis, solved the "cannibal and missionary" problem and other problems of similar complexity.[9]*

In 1961, after comparing a machine trace (see Figure 2, p. 95) with a protocol and finding that they matched to some extent, Newell and Simon concluded rather cautiously:

The fragmentary evidence we have obtained to date encourages us to think that the General Problem Solver provides a rather good *first approximation* to an information processing theory of *certain kinds* of thinking and problem-solving behavior. The processes of "thinking" can no longer be regarded as completely mysterious.[10]

Soon, however, Simon gave way to more enthusiastic claims:

Subsequent work has tended to confirm [our] initial hunch, and to demonstrate that heuristics, or rules of thumb, form the integral core of human problem-solving processes. As we begin to understand the nature of the heuristics that people use in thinking the mystery begins to dissolve from such (heretofore) vaguely understood processes as "intuition" and "judgment."[11]

But, as we have seen in the case of language translating, difficulties have an annoying way of reasserting themselves. This time, the "mystery" of judgment reappears in terms of the organizational aspect of the problem-solving programs. Already in 1961 at the height of Simon's enthusiasm, Minsky saw the difficulties which would attend the application of trial-and-error techniques to really complex problems:

The simplest problems, e.g., playing tic-tac-toe or proving the very simplest theorems of logic, can be solved by simple recursive application of all the available transformations to all the situations that occur, dealing with sub-problems in the order of their generation. This becomes impractical in more complex problems as the search space grows larger and each trial becomes more expensive in time and effort. One can no longer afford a policy of simply leaving one unsuccessful attempt to go on to another. For, each attempt on a difficult problem will involve so much effort that one must be quite sure that, whatever the outcome, the effort will not be wasted entirely. One must become selective to the point that no trial is made without a compelling reason. . . .[12]

This, Minsky claims, shows the need for a planning program, but as he goes on to point out:

Planning methods . . . threaten to collapse when the fixed sets of categories adequate for simple problems have to be replaced by the expressions of descriptive language.[13]

In "Some Problems of Basic Organization in Problem-Solving Programs" (December 1962), Newell discusses some of the problems which arise in organizing the Chess Program, the Logic Theorist, and especially the GPS with a candor rare in the field, and admits that "most of [these problems] are unsolved to some extent, either completely, or because the solutions that have been adopted are still unsatisfactory in one way or another."[14] No further progress has been reported toward the successful

```
L0   ~(~Q·P)
L1   (R⊃~P)·(~R⊃Q)

GOAL 1  TRANSFORM L1 INTO L0
       GOAL 2   DELETE R FROM L1
              GOAL 3  APPLY R8 TO L1
                     PRODUCES L2 R⊃~P

       GOAL 4  TRANSFORM L2 INTO L0
              GOAL 5  ADD Q TO L2
                     REJECT

       GOAL 2
              GOAL 6  APPLY R8 TO L1
                     PRODUCES L3  ~R⊃Q

       GOAL 7  TRANSFORM L3 INTO L0
              GOAL 8  ADD P TO L3
                     REJECT

       GOAL 2
              GOAL 9  APPLY R7 TO L1
                     GOAL 10  CHANGE CONNECTIVE TO V IN LEFT L1
                            GOAL 11  APPLY R6 TO LEFT L1
                                   PRODUCES L4  (~R V ~P)·(~R⊃Q)

                     GOAL 12  APPLY R7 TO L4
                            GOAL 13  CHANGE CONNECTIVE TO V IN RIGHT L4
                                   GOAL 14  APPLY R6 TO RIGHT L4
                                          PRODUCES L5  (~R V ~P)·(R V Q)

                            GOAL 15  APPLY R7 TO L5
                                   GOAL 16  CHANGE SIGN OF LEFT RIGHT L5
                                          GOAL 17  APPLY R6 TO RIGHT L5
                                                 PRODUCES L6  (~R V ~P)·(~R⊃Q)

                                   GOAL 18  APPLY R7 TO L6
                                          GOAL 19  CHANGE CONNECTIVE TO V
                                                 IN RIGHT L6
                                                 REJECT

                                   GOAL 16
                                          NOTHING MORE

                            GOAL 13
                                   NOTHING MORE

                     GOAL 10
                            NOTHING MORE
```

Figure 2

hierarchical organization of heuristic programs. (Significantly, the greatest achievement in the field of mechanical theorem-proving, Wang's theorem-proving program, which proved in less than five minutes all 52 theorems chosen by Newell, Shaw, and Simon, does not use heuristics.)

Public admission that GPS was a dead end, however, did not come until much later. In 1967, the tenth anniversary of Simon's predictions, Newell (and Ernst) soberly, quietly, and somewhat ambiguously announced that GPS was being abandoned. The preface to their paper reveals that peculiar mixture of impasse and optimism which we have begun to recognize as characteristic of the field:

We have used the term "final" in several places above. This does not indicate any feeling that this document marks a terminus to our research on general problem solvers; quite the contrary is true. However, we do feel that this particular aggregate of IPL–V code should be laid to rest.[15]

That GPS has collapsed under the weight of its own organization becomes clearer later in the monograph. The section entitled "History of GPS" concludes:

One serious limitation of the expected performance of GPS is the size of the program and the size of its rather elaborate data structure. The program itself occupies a significant portion of the computer memory and the generation of new data structures during problem solving quickly exhausts the remaining memory. Thus GPS is only designed to solve modest problems whose representation is not too elaborate. Although larger computers' memories would alleviate the extravagances of GPS's use of memory, conceptual difficulties would remain.[16]

This curve from success to optimism to failure can be followed in miniature in the case of Gelernter's Geometry Theorem Machine (1959). Its early success with theorems like the *pons asinorum* gave rise to the first prediction to be totally discredited. In an article published in 1960, Gelernter explains the heuristics of his program and then concludes: "Three years ago, the dominant opinion was that the geometry machine would not exist today. And today, hardly an expert will contest the assertion that machines will be proving interesting theorems in number theory three years hence," that is, in 1963.[17] There has been no further word from Gelernter and no further progress in purely mechanical mathematics. No more striking example exists of an "astonishing" early success and an even more astonishing failure to follow it up.

PATTERN RECOGNITION

This field is discussed last because the resolution of the difficulties which have arrested development in game playing, language translation, and problem solving presupposes success in the field of pattern recognition (which in turn suffers from each of the difficulties encountered in the other fields). As Selfridge and Neisser point out in their classic article "Pattern Recognition by Machine,"

a man is continually exposed to a welter of data from his senses, and abstracts from it the patterns relevant to his activity at the moment. His ability to solve problems, prove theorems and generally run his life depends on this type of perception. We suspect that until programs to perceive patterns can be developed, achievements in mechanical problem-solving will remain isolated technical triumphs.[18]

There has as usual been some excellent early work. For example, the Lincoln Laboratory group under Bernard Gold produced a program for transliterating hand-sent Morse code. More recently, programs have been written for recognizing a limited set of handwritten words and printed characters in various type fonts. These all operate by searching for predetermined topological features of the characters to be recognized, and checking these features against preset or learned "definitions" of each letter in terms of these traits. The trick is to find relevant features, that is, those that remain generally invariant throughout variations of size and orientation, and other distortions. This approach has been surprisingly successful where recognition depends on a small number of specific traits.

But none of these programs constitutes a breakthrough in pattern recognition. Each is a small engineering triumph, an *ad hoc* solution of a specific problem, without general applicability. As Murray Eden, who has done some of the best work in pattern recognition, summed up the situation in 1968:

Where there have been successes in performing pattern-recognition tasks by mechanical means, the successes have rested on rules that were prescribed *ad hoc,* in the literal sense of that phrase; that is to say, the successful methods classify *reliably* that particular set of patterns for which the methods were designed, but are likely to lack any significant value for classifying any other set of patterns.[19]

Even in these special cases, as Selfridge and Neisser remark, "The only way the machine can get an adequate set of features is from a human programmer."[20] They thus conclude their survey of the field with a challenge rather than a prediction:

The most important learning process of all is still untouched: No current program can generate test features of its own. The effectiveness of all of them is forever restricted by the ingenuity or arbitrariness of their programmers. We can barely guess how this restriction might be overcome. Until it is, 'artificial intelligence' will remain tainted with artifice.[21]

Even these remarks may be too optimistic, however, in their supposition that the present problem is *feature*-generation. The relative success of the Uhr-Vossler program, which generates and evaluates its own operators, shows that this problem is partially soluble.[22] But as long as recognition depends on a limited set of features, whether *ad hoc* or general, preprogrammed or generated, mechanical recognition has gone about as far as it can go. The number of traits that can be looked up in a reasonable amount of time is limited, and present programs have already reached this technological limit. In a paper presented at the Hawaii International Conference on the Methodologies of Pattern Recognition (1968), Laveen Kanal and B. Chandrasekaran summed up the impasse as follows:

Obviously, the engineering approach has built in limitations. There is a certain level of complexity above which the engineer's bag of tricks fails to produce results. As an example while even multifont printed character recognition has been successfully handled, a satisfactory solution of cursive script recognition defies all attempts. Similarly there seems to be a fairly big jump between isolated speech recognition and continuous speech recognition. Those who have been hoping to model human recognition processes have also reached an impasse. It is probable that those problems which the engineers have found difficult to handle are precisely those which have to await more detailed understanding of human recognition systems. In any case, these feelings of crisis are intimately related to those in other aspects of artificial intelligence: game playing and mechanical translation.[23]

Again we find the same pattern of optimism followed by disillusionment. Often the disillusioned do not even understand why their hopes have been dashed, and their questioning goes unheard amidst the promises and announcements of small technological advances. Such a dissenter is Vincent Giuliano, formerly of Arthur D. Little Corporation. If Giuliano had a more detailed and insightful account of what went wrong, he would be the Oettinger or Bar-Hillel of the pattern recognition field.

Like many of my colleagues, I was in hot pursuit of ways to develop something we sometimes refer to as artificial intelligence. . . . in the mid-fifties, many ambitious research projects were launched with the goal of clearly demonstrating the learning capabilities of computers so that they could translate idiomatically, carry on free and natural conversations with humans, recognize speech and print it out, and diagnose diseases. All of these activities involve the discovery and learning of complex patterns.

Only a few years ago we really believed that ultimately computers could be given the *entire* task of solving such problems, if only we could find the master key to making them do so.

Alas! I feel that many of the hoped-for objectives may well be porcelain eggs; they will never hatch, no matter how long heat is applied to them, because they require pattern discovery purely on the part of *machines* working alone. The tasks of discovery demand human qualities.[24]

Conclusion

By 1962, if we are to judge by published results, an overall pattern had begun to take shape, although in some cases it was not recognized until later: an early, dramatic success based on the easy performance of simple tasks, or low-quality work on complex tasks, and then diminishing returns, disenchantment, and, in some cases, pessimism. This pattern is not the result of overenthusiastic pressure from eager or skeptical outsiders who demand too much too fast. The failure to produce is measured solely against the expectations of those working in the field.

When the situation is grim, however, enthusiasts can always fall back on their own optimism. This tendency to substitute long-range for operational programs slips out in Feigenbaum and Feldman's claim that "the forecast for progress in research in human cognitive processes is most encouraging."[25] The *forecast* always has been, but one wonders: how encouraging are the *prospects?* Feigenbaum and Feldman claim that tangible progress is indeed being made, and they define *progress* very carefully as "displacement toward the ultimate goal."[26] According to this definition, the first man to climb a tree could claim tangible progress toward reaching the moon.

Rather than climbing blindly, it is better to look where one is going. It is time to study in detail the specific problems confronting work in artificial intelligence and the underlying difficulties that they reveal.

II. The Underlying Significance of Failure to Achieve Predicted Results

Negative results, provided one recognizes them as such, can be interesting. Diminishing achievement, instead of the predicted accelerating success, perhaps indicates some unexpected phenomenon. Perhaps we are pushing out on a continuum like that of velocity, where further acceleration costs more and more energy as we approach the speed of light, or perhaps we are instead facing a discontinuity, which requires not greater effort but entirely different techniques, as in the case of the tree-climbing man who tries to reach the moon.

It seems natural to take stock of the field at this point, yet surprisingly no one has done so. If someone had, he might have found that each of the four areas considered presupposes a specific form of human "information processing" that enables human subjects in that area to avoid the difficulties an artificial "subject" must confront. This section will isolate these four human forms of "information processing" and contrast them with their machine surrogates.

FRINGE CONSCIOUSNESS VS. HEURISTICALLY GUIDED SEARCH

It is common knowledge that certain games can be worked through on present-day computers with present-day techniques—games like nim and tic-tac-toe can be programmed so that the machine will win or draw every time. Other games, however, cannot be solved in this way on present-day computers, and yet have been successfully programmed. In checkers, for example, it turns out that there are reliable ways to determine the probable value of a move on the basis of certain parameters such as control of center position, advancement, and so forth. This, plus the fact that there are relatively few moves since pieces block each other and captures are forced, makes it possible to explore all plausible moves to a depth of as many as twenty moves, which proves sufficient for excellent play.

Chess, however, although decidable in principle by counting out all possible moves and responses, presents the problem inevitably connected with choice mazes: exponential growth. Alternative paths multiply so rapidly that we cannot even run through all the branching possibilities far enough to form a reliable judgment as to whether a given branch is sufficiently promising to merit further exploration. Newell notes that it would take much too long to find an interesting move if the machine had to examine the possible moves of each of the pieces on the board one after another. He is also aware that if this is not done, the machine may sometimes miss an important and original combination. "We do not want the machine to spend all its time examining the future actions of committed men; yet if it were never to do this, it could overlook real opportunities."[27]

Newell's first solution was "the random element": "The machine should rarely [that is, occasionally] search for combinations which sacrifice a Queen."[28] But this solution is unsatisfactory, as Newell himself, presumably, now realizes. The machine should not look just every once in a while for a Queen sacrifice but, rather, look in those situations in which such a sacrifice would be relevant. This is what the right heuristics are supposed to assure, by limiting the number of branches explored while retaining the more promising alternatives.

But no master-level heuristics have as yet been found. All current heuristics either exclude some moves masters would find or leave open the risk of exponential growth. Simon is nonetheless convinced, for reasons to be discussed in Part II, that chess masters use such heuristics, and so he is confident that if we listen to their protocols, follow their eye movements, perhaps question them under bright lights, we can eventually discover these heuristics and build them into our program—thereby pruning the exponential tree. But let us examine more closely the evidence that chess playing is governed by the use of heuristics.

Consider the following protocol quoted by Simon, noting especially how it begins rather than how it ends. The subject says,

Again I notice that one of his pieces is not defended, the Rook, and there must be ways of taking advantage of this. Suppose now, if I push the pawn up at Bishop four, if the Bishop retreats I have a Queen check and I can pick up the Rook. If, etc., etc.[29]

At the end we have an example of what I shall call "counting out"— thinking through the various possibilities by brute-force enumeration. We have all engaged in this process, which, guided by suitable heuristics, is supposed to account for the performance of chess masters. But how did our subject notice that the opponent's Rook was undefended? Did he examine each of his opponent's pieces and their possible defenders sequentially (or simultaneously) until he stumbled on the vulnerable Rook? That would use up too many considerations, for as Newell, Shaw, and Simon remark, "The best evidence suggests that a human player considers considerably less than 100 positions in the analysis of a move,"[30] and our player must still consider many positions in evaluating the situation once the undefended Rook has been discovered. We need not appeal to introspection to discover what a player in fact does before he begins to count out; the protocol itself indicates it: the subject "zeroed in" on the promising situation ("I notice that one of his pieces is not defended"). Only *after* the player has zeroed in on an area does he begin to count out, to test, what he can do from there.

An analysis of the MacHack program written by Richard Greenblatt will illustrate this difference between the way a human being sizes up a position and the machine's brute-force counting out. Even MacHack could not look at every alternative. The program contains a plausible move generator which limits the moves considered to the more promising ones. Yet in a tough spot during a tournament, the Greenblatt program once calculated for fifteen minutes and considered 26,000 alternatives, while a human player can consider only 100, or possibly 200, moves. MacHack came up with an excellent move, which is not to say a master could not have done even better; but what is significant here is not the quality of the move, but the difference between 26,000 and 200 possibilities. This order of difference suggests that when playing chess, human beings are doing something different than just considering alternatives, and the interesting question is: what are they doing that enables them, while considering 100 or 200 alternatives, to find more brilliant moves than the computer can find working through 26,000?

The human player whose protocol we are examining is not aware of having explicitly considered or explicitly excluded from consideration any of the hundreds of possibilities that would have had to have been enumerated in order to arrive at a particular relevant area of the board by counting out. Nonetheless, the specific portion of the board which finally attracts the subject's attention depends on the overall position. To understand how this is possible, we must consider what William James has called "the fringes of consciousness": the ticking of a clock which we notice only if it stops provides a simple example of this sort of marginal awareness. Our vague awareness of the faces in a crowd when we search for a friend is another, more complex and more nearly appropriate, case.

While suggesting an alternative to the explicit awareness of counting out, neither example is entirely appropriate, however. In neither of these cases does the subject make positive use of the information resting on the fringe. The chess case is best understood in terms of Michael Polanyi's general description of the power of the fringes of consciousness to concentrate information concerning our peripheral experience.

This power resides in the area which tends to function as a background because it extends indeterminately around the central object of our attention. Seen thus from the corner of our eyes, or remembered at the back of our mind, this area compellingly affects the way we see the object on which we are focusing. We may indeed go so far as to say that we are aware of this subsidiarily noticed area mainly in the appearance of the object to which we are attending.[31]*

Once one is familiar with a house, for example, to him the front *looks* thicker than a façade, because he is marginally aware of the house behind. Similarly, in chess, cues from all over the board, while remaining on the fringes of consciousness, draw attention to certain sectors by making them appear promising, dangerous, or simply worth looking into.

As Newell and Simon themselves note:

There are concepts in human chess playing that are much more global than those above; for example, a "developed position," "control of the center," "a won position," "a weak king side," "a closed position."[32]

Moreover, they admit that:

Sometimes de Groot's subject used very global phrases such as ". . . and it's a won position for White," where *it is not possible to see what structure or feature of the position leads to the evaluation.*[33]

This is Newell and Simon's way of saying that they see no way of analyzing this evaluation of the overall position in terms of heuristically guided counting out. And judiciously, but without seeming to realize what this does to the plausibility of Simon's predictions, Newell and Simon go on to note:

To date the work on chess programs has not shed much new light on these higher-level concepts.[34]*

The attitude of Newell and Simon is typically ambiguous here. Do they think that better static evaluators—that is, better heuristics for generating plausible moves—could simulate zeroing in? Their continued belief in the possibility of a mechanical chess master suggests they do. However, their analysis of master play, based on the work of de Groot, should be grounds for pessimism. (As we have seen, de Groot himself says he does not have much hope for substantial improvement of heuristic chess programs.)

Newell and Simon note that

De Groot finally succeeded in separating strong from weak players by using perceptual tests involving the reproduction of chess positions after brief exposure to them (3–7 seconds). The grandmaster was able to reproduce the positions perfectly, and performance degraded appreciably with decrease in chess ability. De Groot was led to propose that perceptual abilities and organization were an important factor in very good play.[35]

In the article we have already discussed, chess master Hearst casts some further light on this perceptual process and why it defies programming:

Apparently the master perceives the setup in large units, such as pawn structure of cooperating pieces. . . . When he does make an error, it is often one of putting a piece on a very desirable square for that type of position.[36]

Hearst sums up his view as follows:

Because of the large number of prior associations which an experienced player has acquired, he does not visualize a chess position as a conglomeration of scattered squares and wooden pieces, but as an organized pattern (like the "Gestalt," or integrated configuration, emphasized by the Gestalt psychologists).[37]

Applying these ideas to our original protocol, we can conclude that our subject's familiarity with the overall chess pattern and with the past moves of this particular game enabled him to recognize the lines of force, the loci of strength and weakness, as well as specific positions. He sees that his opponent looks vulnerable in a certain area (just as one familiar with houses in general and with a certain house sees it as having a certain sort of back), and zeroing in on this area he discovers the unprotected Rook. This move is seen as one step in a developing pattern.

There is no chess program which even tries to use the past experience of a particular game in this way. Rather, each move is taken up anew as if it were an isolated chess problem found in a book. This technique is forced upon programmers, since a program which carried along information on the past position of each piece would rapidly sink under the accumulating data. What is needed is a program which *selectively* carries over from the past just those features which were significant in the light of its present strategy and the strategy attributed to its opponent.[38]* But present programs embody no long-range strategy at all.

In general what is needed is an account of the way that the *background* of past experience and the history of the current game can determine what shows up as a *figure* and attracts a player's attention. But this gestaltist notion of figure and ground has no place in explicit step-by-step computation.

Since this global form of "information processing" in which information, rather than being explicitly considered remains on the fringes of consciousness and is implicitly taken into account, is constantly at work in organizing our experience, there is no reason to suppose that in order to discover an undefended Rook our subject must have counted out rapidly and unconsciously until he arrived at the area in which he began consciously counting out. Moreover, there are good reasons to reject this assumption, since it raises more problems than it solves.

If the subject has been unconsciously counting out thousands of alternatives with brilliant heuristics to get to the point where he focuses on that Rook, why doesn't he carry on with that unconscious process all the way to the end, until the best move just pops into his consciousness? Why, if the *unconscious* counting is rapid and accurate, does he resort to a cumbersome method of slowly, awkwardly, and consciously counting things out at the particular point where he spots the Rook? Or if, on the other hand, the unconscious counting is *inadequate,* what is the advantage of switching to a conscious version of the same process?

This sort of teleological consideration—while not a proof that unconscious processing is nonheuristic—does put the burden of proof on those who claim that it is or must be. And those who make this claim have brought forward no arguments to support it. There is no evidence, behavioral or introspective, that counting out is the only kind of "information processing" involved in playing chess, that "the essential nature of the task [is] search in a space of exponentially growing possibilities."[39] On the contrary, all protocols testify that chess involves two kinds of behavior: (1) *zeroing in,* by means of the overall organization of the perceptual field, on an area formerly on the fringes of consciousness, and which other areas still on the fringes of consciousness make interesting; and (2) *counting out* explicit alternatives.

This distinction clarifies the early success and the later failure of work in cognitive simulation. In all game-playing programs, early success is attained by working on those games or parts of games in which heuristically guided counting out is feasible; failure occurs at the point where complexity is such that global awareness would be necessary to avoid an overwhelming exponential growth of possibilities to be counted.

AMBIGUITY TOLERANCE VS. CONTEXT-FREE PRECISION

Work on game playing revealed the necessity of processing "information" which is not explicitly considered or excluded, that is, information on the fringes of consciousness. Work in language translation has been halted by the need for a second nonprogrammable form of "information processing": the ability to deal with situations which are ambiguous without having to transform them by substituting a precise description.

We have seen that Bar-Hillel and Oettinger, two of the most respected and best-informed workers in the field of automatic language translation, agree in their pessimistic conclusions concerning the possibility of further progress in the field. Each has realized that in order to translate a natural language, more is needed than a mechanical dictionary—no matter how complete—and the laws of grammar—no matter how sophisticated. The order of the words in a sentence does not provide enough information to enable a machine to determine which of several possible parsings is the appropriate one, nor do the surrounding words —the written context—always indicate which of several possible meanings is the one the author had in mind.

As Oettinger says in discussing systems for producing all parsings of a sentence acceptable to a given grammar:

The operation of such analyzers to date has revealed a far higher degree of legitimate *syntactic* ambiguity in English and in Russian than has been anticipated. This, and a related fuzziness of the boundary between the grammatical and the non-grammatical, raises serious questions about the possibility of effective fully automatic manipulations of English or Russian for any purpose of translation or information retrieval.[40]

Instead of claiming, on the basis of his early partial success with a mechanical dictionary, and later (with Kuno and others) with syntactic analyzers, that in spite of a few exceptions and difficulties, the mystery surrounding our understanding of language is beginning to dissolve, Oettinger draws attention to the "very mysterious semantic processes that enable most reasonable people to interpret most reasonable sentences unequivocally most of the time."[41]

Here is another example of the importance of fringe consciousness. Obviously, the user of a natural language is not aware of many of the cues to which he responds in determining the intended syntax and meaning. On the other hand, nothing indicates that he considers each of these cues unconsciously. In fact, two considerations suggest that these cues are not the sort that *could* be taken up and considered by a sequential or even a parallel program.[42]*

First, there is Bar-Hillel's argument, which we shall later study in detail (Chapter 6), that there is an infinity of possibly relevant cues. Second, this suggests that perhaps it is not primarily a question of cues at all. In any particular context most of the abstractly conceivable ambiguities do not arise. The sentence is heard in the appropriate way because the context organizes the perception; and since sentences are not perceived except in context they are always perceived with the narrow range of meanings the context confers. The common stream of sounds which is the same in each context and must be disambiguated is a problem for computers, not human beings.

Insofar as cues *are* relevant we must remember that natural language is used by people involved in situations in which they are pursuing certain goals. These extralinguistic goals, which need not themselves be precisely stated or statable, provide some of the cues which reduce the ambiguity of expressions as much as is necessary for the task at hand. A phrase like "stay near me" can mean anything from "press up against me" to "stand one mile away," depending upon whether it is addressed to a child in a crowd or a fellow astronaut exploring the moon. Its meaning is never unambiguous in all possible situations—as if this ideal of exactitude even makes sense—but the meaning can always be made sufficiently unambiguous in any *particular* situation so as to get the intended result. Wittgenstein makes this pragmatic point:

We are unable clearly to circumscribe the concepts we use; not because we don't know their real definition, but because there is no real "definition" to them. To suppose that there *must* be would be like supposing that whenever children play with a ball they play a game according to strict rules.[43]*

Our ability to use a global context to *reduce ambiguity sufficiently* without having to formalize (that is, eliminate ambiguity altogether) reveals a second fundamental form of human "information processing," which presupposes the first. Fringe consciousness takes account of cues in the context, and probably some possible parsings and meanings, all of which would have to be made explicit in the output of a machine. Our sense of the situation, however, allows us to exclude most possibilities without their ever coming up for consideration. We shall call the ability to narrow down the spectrum of possible meanings by ignoring what, out of context, would be ambiguities, "ambiguity tolerance."

Since a human being uses and understands sentences in familiar situations, the only way to make a computer that can understand actual utterances and translate a natural language may well be, as Turing suspected, to program it to learn about the world. Bar-Hillel remarks: "I do not believe that machines whose programs do not enable them to learn, in a sophisticated sense of this word, will ever be able to consistently produce high-quality translations."[44] When occasionally artificial intelligence enthusiasts admit the difficulties confronting present techniques, the appeal to learning is a favorite panacea. Seymour Papert of M.I.T., for example, has recently claimed that one cannot expect machines to perform like adults unless they are first taught, and that what is needed is a machine with the child's ability to learn. This move, however, as we shall see, only evades the problem.

In the area of language learning, the only interesting and successful program is Feigenbaum's EPAM (Elementary Perceiver and Memorizer). EPAM simulates the learning of the association of nonsense syllables, which Feigenbaum calls a simplified case of verbal learning.[45] The interesting thing about nonsense syllable learning, however, is that it is not a case of *language* learning at all. Learning to associate nonsense syllables is, in fact, acquiring something like a Pavlovian conditioned reflex. The experimenter could exhibit "DAX" then "JIR," or he could flash red and then green lights; as long as two such events were associated frequently enough, one would learn to anticipate the second member of the pair. In such an experiment, the subject is assumed to be completely passive. In a sense, he isn't really learning anything, but is having something done to him. Whether the subject is an idiot, a child, or an adult should ideally make no difference in the case of nonsense syllable learning. Ebbinghaus, at the end of the nineteenth century, proposed this form of conditioning precisely to eliminate any use of meaningful grouping or appeal to a context of previously learned associations.

It is no surprise that subject protocol and machine trace most nearly match in this area. But it is a dubious triumph: the only successful case of cognitive simulation simulates a process which does not involve comprehension, and so is not genuinely cognitive.

What is involved in learning a language is much more complicated and more mysterious than the sort of conditioned reflex involved in learning to associate nonsense syllables. To teach someone the meaning of a new word, we can sometimes point at the object which the word names. Augustine, in his *Confessions,* and Turing, in his article on machine intelligence, assume that this is the way we teach language to children. But Wittgenstein points out that if we simply point at a table, for example, and say "brown," a child will not know if brown is the color, the size, or the shape of the table, the kind of object, or the proper name of the object. If the child already uses language, we can *say* that we are pointing out the color; but if he doesn't already use language, how do we ever get off the ground? Wittgenstein suggests that the child must be engaged in a "form of life" in which he shares at least some of the goals and interests of the teacher, so that the activity at hand helps to delimit the possible reference of the words used.

What, then, can be taught to a machine? This is precisely what is in question in one of the few serious objections to work in artificial intelligence made by one of the workers himself. A. L. Samuel, who wrote the celebrated checkers program, has argued that machines cannot be intelligent because they can only do what they are instructed to do. Minsky dismisses this objection with the remark that we can be surprised by the performance of our machines.[46] But Samuel certainly is aware of this, having been beaten by his own checkers program. He must mean something else, presumably that the machine had to be given the program by which it could win, in a different sense than children are taught to play checkers. But if this is his defense, Samuel is already answered by Michael Scriven. Scriven argues that new strategies are " 'put into' the computer by the designer . . . in *exactly* the same metaphorical sense that we put into our children everything they come up with in their later life."[47] Still, Samuel should not let himself be bullied by the philosophers any more than by his colleagues. Data are indeed put into a machine but in an entirely different way than children are taught. We have just seen that when language is taught it is not, and, as we shall see in Chapter 6, cannot be, precisely defined. Our attempts to teach meaning must be disambiguated and assimilated in terms of a shared context. Learning as opposed to memorization and repetition requires this sort of judgment. Wittgenstein takes up this question as follows:

Can someone be a man's teacher in this? Certainly. From time to time he gives him the right *tip*. . . . This is what learning and teaching are like here. . . . What one acquires here is not a technique; one learns correct judgements. There are also rules, but they do not form a system, and only experienced people can apply them right. Unlike calculation rules.[48]*

It is this ability to grasp the point in a particular context which is true learning; since children can and must make this leap, they can and do surprise us and come up with something genuinely new.

The foregoing considerations concerning the essential role of context awareness and ambiguity tolerance in the use of a natural language should suggest why, after the success of the mechanical dictionary, progress has come to a halt in the translating field. Moreover, since, as we have seen, the ability to *learn* a language presupposes the same complex combination of the human forms of "information processing" needed to *understand* a language, it is hard to see how an appeal to learning can be used to bypass the problems this area must confront.

ESSENTIAL/INESSENTIAL DISCRIMINATION VS. TRIAL-AND-ERROR
SEARCH

Work in problem solving also encounters two functions of thought:
one, elementary and piecemeal, accounts for the early success in the field;
another, more complex and requiring insight, has proved intractable to
stepwise programs such as Simon's General Problem Solver. For simple
problems it is possible to proceed by simply trying all possible combinations until one stumbles on the answer. This trial-and-error search is
another example of a brute-force technique like counting out in chess.
But, just as in game playing, the possibilities soon get out of hand. In
problem solving one needs some systematic way to cut down the search
maze so that one can spend one's time exploring promising alternatives.
This is where people rely on insight and where programmers run into
trouble.

If a problem is set up in a simple, completely determinate way, with
an end and a beginning and simple, specifically defined operations for
getting from one to the other (in other words, if we have what Simon calls
a "simple formal problem"), then Simon's General Problem Solver can,
by trying many possibilities, bring the end and the beginning closer and
closer together until the problem is solved. This would be a successful
example of means-ends analysis. But even this simple case presents many
difficulties. Comparing the machine print-out of the steps of a GPS
solution with the transcript of the verbal report of a human being solving
the same problem reveals steps in the machine trace (explicit searching)
which do not appear in the subject's protocol. And Simon asks us to
accept the methodologically dubious explanation of the missing steps in
the human protocol that "many things concerning the task surely occurred without the subject's commenting on them (or being aware of
them)"[49] and the even more arbitrary assumption that these further
operations were of the same elementary sort as those verbalized. In fact,
certain details of Newell and Simon's article, "GPS: A Program That
Simulates Human Thought," suggest that these further operations are
not like the programmed operations at all.

In one of Simon's experiments, subjects were given problems in formal logic and a list of rules for transforming symbolic expressions and asked to verbalize their attempt to solve the problems. The details of the rules are not important; what is important is that at a point in the protocol the subject notes that he applies the rule $(A \cdot B \longrightarrow A)$ and the rule $(A \cdot B \longrightarrow B)$, to the conjunction $(-R \vee -P) \cdot (R \vee Q)$. Newell and Simon comment:

> The subject handled both forms of rule 8 together, at least as far as his comment is concerned. GPS, on the other hand, took a separate cycle of consideration for each form. Possibly the subject followed the program covertly and simply reported the two results together.[50]

Possibly, however, the subject grasped the conjunction as symmetric with respect to the transformation operated by the rule, and so in fact applied both forms of the rule at once. Even Newell and Simon admit that they would have preferred that GPS apply both forms of the rule in the same cycle. Only then would their program provide a psychological theory of the steps the subject was going through. They wisely refrain, however, from trying to write a program which could discriminate between occasions when it was appropriate to apply both forms of the rule at once and those occasions when it was not. Such a program, far from eliminating the above divergence, would require further processing not reported by the subject, thereby increasing the discrepancy between the program and the protocol. Unable thus to eliminate the divergence and unwilling to try to understand its significance, Newell and Simon dismiss the discrepancy as "an example of parallel processing."[51]*

Another divergence noted by Newell and Simon, however, does not permit such an evasion. At a certain point, the protocol reads: ". . . I should have used rule 6 on the left-hand side of the equation. So use 6, but only on the left-hand side." Simon notes:

> Here we have a strong departure from the GPS trace. Both the subject and GPS found rule 6 as the appropriate one to change signs. At this point GPS simply applied the rule to the current expression; whereas the subject went back and corrected the previous application. Nothing exists in the program that corre-

sponds to this. The most direct explanation is that the application of rule 6 in the inverse direction is perceived by the subject as undoing the previous application of rule 6.[52]

This is indeed the most direct explanation, but Newell and Simon do not seem to realize that this departure from the trace, which cannot be explained away by parallel processing, is as detrimental to their theory as were the discrepancies in the movements of the planets to the Ptolemaic system. Some form of thinking other than searching is taking place!

Newell and Simon note the problem: "It clearly implies a mechanism (maybe a whole set of them) that is not in GPS,"[53] but, like the ancient astronomers, they try to save their theory by adding a few epicycles. They continue to suppose, without any evidence, that this mechanism is just a more elaborate search technique which can be accommodated by providing GPS with "a little continuous hindsight about its past actions."[54] They do not realize that their assumption that intelligent behavior is always the result of following heuristic rules commits them to the implausible view that their subject's decision to backtrack must be the result of a very *selective* checking procedure. Otherwise, all past steps would have to be rechecked at each stage, which would hopelessly encumber the program.

A more scientific approach would be to explore further the implications of the five discrepancies noted in the article, in order to determine whether or not a different form of "information processing" might be involved. For example, Gestalt pyschologist Max Wertheimer points out in his classic work, *Productive Thinking,* that the trial-and-error account of problem solving excludes the most important aspect of problem-solving behavior, namely a grasp of the essential structure of the problem, which he calls "insight."[55] In this operation, one breaks away from the surface structure and sees the basic problem—what Wertheimer calls the "deeper structure"—which enables one to organize the steps necessary for a solution. This gestaltist conception may seem antithetical to the operational concepts demanded by artificial intelligence, but Minsky recognizes the same need in different terms:

The ability to solve a difficult problem hinges on the ability to split or transform it into problems of a lower order of difficulty. To do this, without total reliance on luck, requires some understanding of the situation. One must be able to deduce, or guess, enough of the consequences of the problem statement to be able to set up simpler models of the problem situation. The models must have enough structure to make it likely that there will be a way to extend their solutions to the original problem.[56]

Since insight is necessary in solving complex problems and since what Minsky demands has never been programmed, we should not be surprised to find that in the work of Newell and Simon this insightful restructuring of the problem is surreptitiously introduced by the programmers themselves. In *The Processes of Creative Thinking,* Newell, Shaw, and Simon introduce "the heuristics of planning" to account for characteristics of the subject's protocol lacking in a simple means-ends analysis.

We have devised a program . . . to describe the way some of our subjects handle O. K. Moore's logic problems, and perhaps the easiest way to show what is involved in planning is to describe that program. On a purely pragmatic basis, the twelve operators that are admitted in this system of logic can be put in two classes, which we shall call "essential" and "inessential" operators, respectively. Essential operators are those which, when applied to an expression, make "large" changes in its appearance—change "P ∨ P" to "P," for example. Inessential operators are those which make "small" changes—e.g., change "P ∨ Q" to "Q ∨ P." As we have said, the distinction is purely pragmatic. Of the twelve operators in this calculus, we have classified eight as essential and four as inessential. . . .

Next, we can take an expression and abstract from it those features that relate only to essential changes. For example, we can abstract from "P ∨ Q" the expression (PQ), where the order of the symbols in the latter expression is regarded as irrelevant. Clearly, if inessential operations are applied to the abstracted expressions, the expressions will remain unchanged, while essential operations can be expected to change them. . . .

We can now set up a correspondence between our original expressions and operators, on the one hand, and the abstracted expressions and essential operators, on the other. Corresponding to the original problem of transforming a into b, we can construct a new problem of transforming a' into b', where a' and b' are the expressions obtained by abstracting a and b respectively. Suppose that we solve the new problem, obtaining a sequence of expressions, $a'c'd' \ldots b'$.

We can now transform back to the original problem space and set up the new problems of transforming *a* into *c, c* into *d,* and so on. Thus, the solution of the problem in the planning space provides a plan for the solution of the original problem.[57]

No comment is necessary. One merely has to note that the actual program description begins in the second paragraph. The classification of the operators into essential and inessential, the function Wertheimer calls "finding the deeper structure" or "insight," is *introduced by the programmers before the actual programming begins.*

This sleight of hand is overlooked by Miller, Galanter, and Pribram in *Plans and the Structure of Behavior,* a book which presents a psychological theory influenced by Newell, Shaw, and Simon's work. Miller et al. begin by quoting Polya, who is fully aware of the necessary role insight plays in problem solving:

In his popular text, *How to Solve It,* Polya distinguishes . . . phases in the heuristic process:
  —First, we must understand the problem. We have to see clearly what the data are, what conditions are imposed, and what the unknown thing is that we are searching for.
  —Second, we must devise a plan that will guide the solution and connect the data to the unknown.[58]

Miller et al. then minimize the importance of phase I, or rather simply decide not to worry about it.

Obviously, the second of these is most critical. The first is what we have described in Chapter 12 as the construction of a clear Image of the situation in order to establish a test for the solution of the problem; it is indispensable, of course, but in the discussion of well-defined problems we assume that it has already been accomplished.[59]

Still the whole psychological theory of problem solving will not be worth much if there is no way to bring step one into the computer model. Therefore, it is no surprise that ten pages later, after adopting Simon's means-ends analysis, we find Miller et al. referring with relief to Simon's "planning method,"[60] presumably the very paragraphs we have just discussed:

A second very general system of heuristics used by Newell, Shaw, and Simon consists in omitting certain details of the problem. This usually simplifies the task and the simplified problem may be solved by some familiar plan. The plan used to solve the simple problem is then used as the strategy for solving the original, complicated problem. In solving a problem in the propositional calculus, for example, *the machine can decide to ignore differences among the logical connectives and the order of the symbols. . . .*[61]

But, as we have seen, it is not the *machine* that decides, but Newell, Shaw, and Simon, themselves. To speak of heuristics here is completely misleading, since no one has succeeded in formulating the rules which guide this preliminary choice or even in showing that at this stage, where insight is required, people follow rules. Thus we are left with no computer theory of the fundamental first step in all problem solving: the making of the essential/inessential distinction. Only those with faith such as that of Miller et al. could have missed the fact that Simon's "planning method," with its predigesting of the material, poses the problem for computer simulation rather than provides the solution.

This human ability to distinguish the essential from the inessential in a specific task accounts for the divergence of the protocol of the problem-solving subjects from the GPS trace. We have already suggested that the subject applies both forms of rule 8 together because he realizes at this initial stage that both sides of the conjunction are functionally equivalent. Likewise, because he has grasped the essential function of rule 6, the subject can see that a second application of the rule simply neutralizes the previous one. As Wertheimer notes:

The process [of structuring a problem] does not involve merely the given parts and their transformations. It works in conjunction with material that is structurally relevant but is selected from past experience. . . .[62]

Since game playing is a form of problem solving we should expect to find the same process in chess playing, and indeed we do. To quote Hearst:

De Groot concluded from his study that differences in playing strength depend much less on calculating power than on "skill in problem conception." Grandmasters seem to be superior to masters in isolating the most significant features of a position, rather than in the total number of moves that they consider.

Somewhat surprisingly, de Groot found that grandmasters do not examine more possibilities on a single move than lower-ranked experts or masters (an average of two to four first moves per position) nor do they look further ahead (usually a maximum of six to seven moves ahead for each). The grandmaster is somehow able to "see" the core of the problem immediately, whereas the expert or lesser player finds it with difficulty, or misses it completely, even though he analyzes as many alternatives and looks as many moves ahead as the grandmaster.[63]

In 1961, as we have seen, Minsky was already aware of these problems. But his only hope was that one would discover a planning program which would use more of the same sort of heuristic searching on a higher level:

When we call for the use of "reasoning," we intend no suggestion of giving up the game by invoking an intelligent subroutine. The program that administers the search will be just another heuristic program. Almost certainly it will be composed largely of the same sorts of objects and processes that will comprise the subject-domain programs.[64]

But such a planning program itself would require a distinction between essential and inessential operators. Unless at some stage the programmer himself introduces this distinction, he will be forced into an infinite regress of planning programs, each one of which will require a higher-order program to structure its ill-structured data. At this point, the transition from the easy to the difficult form of "information processing," Minsky makes the typical move to learning.

The problem of making useful deductions from a large body of statements (e.g. about the relevance of different methods to different kinds of problems) raises a new search problem. One must restrict the logical exploration to data likely to be relevant to the current problem. This selection function could hardly be completely built in at the start. It must develop along with other data accumulated by experience.[65]

But thus far no one has even tried to suggest how a machine could perform this selection operation, or how it could be programmed to learn to perform it, since it is one of the conditions for learning from past experience.

Feigenbaum, in a recent appraisal of work done since *Computers and Thought,* notes the glaring lack of learning programs:

The AI field still has little grasp of the machine learning problem for problem solvers. For many years, almost the only citation worth making was to Samuel's famed checker playing program and its learning system. (Great interest arose once in a scheme proposed by Newell, Shaw, and Simon for learning in GPS, but the scheme was never realized.) Surprisingly, today we face the same situation.[66]

This lack of progress is surprising only to those, like Feigenbaum, who do not recognize the ability to distinguish the essential from the inessential as a human form of "information processing," necessary for learning and problem solving, yet not amenable to the mechanical search techniques which may operate once this distinction has been made. It is precisely this function of intelligence which resists further progress in the problem-solving field.

It is an illusion, moreover, to think that the planning problem can be solved in isolation; that essential/inessential operations are given like blocks and one need only sort them out. It is easy to be hypnotized by oversimplified and *ad hoc* cases—like the logic problem—into thinking that some operations are essential or inessential in themselves. It then looks as if we can find them because they are already there, so that we simply have to discover a heuristic rule to sort them out. But normally (and often even in logic) essential operations are not around to be found because they do not exist independently of the pragmatic context.

In the light of their frank inevitable recourse to the insightful predigesting of their material, there seems to be no foundation for Newell, Shaw, and Simon's claim that the behavior vaguely labeled cleverness or keen insight in human problem solving is really just the result of the judicious application of certain heuristics for narrowing the search for solutions. Their work with GPS, on the contrary, demonstrates that all searching, unless directed by a preliminary structuring of the problem, is merely muddling through.

Ironically, research in Cognitive Simulation is a perfect example of so-called intelligent behavior which proceeds like the unaided GPS. Here one finds the kind of tinkering and *ad hoc* patchwork characteristic of a fascination with the surface structure—a sort of tree-climbing with one's eyes on the moon. Perhaps it is just because the field provides no example of insight that some people in Cognitive Simulation have mistaken the operation of GPS for intelligent behavior.

PERSPICUOUS GROUPING VS. CHARACTER LISTS

A computer must recognize all patterns in terms of a list of specific traits. This raises problems of exponential growth which human beings are able to avoid by proceeding in a different way. Simulating recognition of even simple patterns may thus require recourse to each of the fundamental forms of human "information processing" discussed this far. And even if in these simple cases artificial intelligence workers have been able to make some headway with mechanical techniques, patterns as complex as artistic styles and the human face reveal a loose sort of resemblance which seems to require a special combination of insight, fringe consciousness, and ambiguity tolerance beyond the reach of digital machines. It is no wonder, then, that work in pattern recognition has had a late start and an early stagnation.

In Chapter 1 we noted that a weakness of current pattern recognition programs (with the possible exception of the Uhr-Vossler program, the power of whose operators—since it only recognizes five letters—has not yet been sufficiently tested) is that they are not able to determine their own selection operators. Now, however, we shall see that this way of presenting the problem is based on assumptions that hide deeper and more difficult issues.

Insight. A first indication that human pattern recognition differs radically from mechanical recognition is seen in human (and animal) tolerance for changes in orientation and size, degrees of incompleteness and distortion, and amount of background noise.

An early artificial intelligence approach was to try to normalize the pattern and then to test it against a set of templates to see which it matched. Human recognition, on the other hand, seems to simply disregard changes in size and orientation, as well as breaks in the figure, and so on. Although certain perceptual constants do achieve some normalization (apparent size and brightness do not vary as much as corresponding changes in the signal reaching the retina), it seems clear that we do not need to fully normalize and smooth out the pattern, since we can perceive the pattern as skewed, incomplete, large or small, and so on, at the same time we recognize it.

More recent programs, rather than normalizing the pattern, seek powerful operators which pick out discriminating traits but remain insensitive to distortion and noise. But human beings, when recognizing patterns, do not seem to employ these artificial expedients either. In those special cases where human beings can articulate their cues, these turn out not to be powerful operators which include sloppy patterns and exclude noise, but rather a set of ideal traits which are only approximated in the specific instances of patterns recognized. Distorted patterns are recognized not as falling under some looser and more ingenious set of traits, but as exhibiting the same simple traits as the undistorted figures, along with certain accidental additions or omissions. Similarly, noise is not tested and excluded; it is ignored as inessential.[67]* Here again, we note the human ability to distinguish the essential from the inessential.

Fringe Consciousness. To determine which of a set of already analyzed patterns a presented pattern most nearly resembles, workers have proposed analyzing the presented pattern for a set of traits by means of a decision tree; or by combining the probabilities that each of a set of traits is present, as in Selfridge's Pandaemonium program. Either method uncritically assumes that a human being, like a mechanical pattern recognizer, must classify a pattern in terms of a specific list of traits. It seems self-evident to Selfridge and Neisser that "a man who abstracts a pattern from a complex of stimuli has essentially classified the possible inputs."[68] Earl Hunt makes the same assumption in his review of pattern recognition work: "Pattern recognition, like concept learning, involves the learning of a classification rule."[69]

Yet, if the pattern is at all complicated and sufficiently similar to many other patterns so that many traits are needed for discrimination, the problem of exponential growth threatens. Supposing that a trait-by-trait analysis is the way any pattern recognizer, human or artificial, must proceed thus leads to the assumption that there must be certain crucial traits—if one could only find them, or program the machine to find them for itself—which would make the processing manageable.

One is led to look for a sort of perceptual heuristic, the "powerful operators" which no one as yet has been able to find. And just as the chess masters are not able to provide the programmer with the heuristic shortcuts they are supposed to be using, Selfridge and Neisser note in the case of pattern recognition that "very often the basis of classification is unknown, even to [the analyzer]." Nevertheless, Selfridge and Neisser assume, like Newell and Simon, that unconsciously a maze is being explored—in this case, that a list of traits is being searched. They are thus led to conclude that "it [the basis of classification] is too complex to be specified explicitly."[70]

But the difficulties involved in searching such a list suggest again that, for human beings at least, not all possibly relevant traits are taken up in a series or in parallel and used to make some sort of decision, but that many traits crucial to discrimination are never taken up explicitly at all but do their work while remaining on the fringe of consciousness.

Whereas in chess we begin with a global sense of the situation and have recourse to counting out only in the last analysis, in perception we need never appeal to *any* explicit traits. We normally recognize an object as similar to other objects without being aware of it as an example of a type or as a member of a class defined in terms of specific traits. As Aron Gurwitsch puts it in his analysis of the difference between perceptual and conceptual consciousness:

Perceived objects appear to us with generic determinations. . . . But—and this is the decisive point—*to perceive an object of a certain kind is not at all the same thing as grasping that object as representative or as a particular case of a type.*[71]

Of course, we can sometimes make the defining traits explicit:

The first step in the constituting of conceptual consciousness consists in effecting a dissociation within the object perceived in its typicality. The generic traits which until then were immanent and inherent in the perceived thing are detached and disengaged from it. Rendered explicit, these traits can be seized in themselves. . . . Consequent upon this dissociation, *the generic becomes the general.* From this aspect it opposes itself to the thing perceived from which it has just been disengaged, and which now is transformed into an example, a particular instance. . . .

[Thus, cues] can be grasped and become themes [specific traits we are aware of] . . . , whereas previously they only contributed to the constitution of another theme [the pattern] within which they played only a mute role.[72]

This shift from perceptual to conceptual consciousness (from the perceptive to the mathematical frame of mind, to use Pascal's expression), is not necessarily an improvement. Certain victims of aphasia, studied by Gelb and Goldstein, have lost their capacity for perceptual recognition. All recognition for the patient becomes a question of classification. The patient has to resort to checklists and search procedures, like a digital computer. Some such aphasics can only recognize a figure such as a triangle by listing its traits, that is, by counting its sides and then thinking: "A triangle has three sides. Therefore, this is a triangle."[73] Such conceptual recognition is time consuming and unwieldy; the victims of such brain injuries are utterly incapable of getting along in the everyday world.

Evidently, in pattern recognition, passing from implicit perceptual grouping to explicit conceptual classification—even at some final stage, as in chess—is usually disadvantageous. The fact that we need not conceptualize or thematize the traits common to several instances of the same pattern in order to recognize that pattern distinguishes human recognition from machine recognition, which only occurs on the explicit conceptual level of class membership.

Context-Dependent Ambiguity Reduction. In the cases thus far considered, the traits defining a member of a class, while generally too numerous to be useful in practical recognition, could at least in principle always be made explicit. In some cases, however, such explicitation is not even possible. To appreciate this point we must first get over the idea, shared by traditional philosophers and workers in artificial intelligence alike, that pattern recognition can always be understood as a sort of classification. In this overhasty generalization three distinct kinds of pattern recognition are lumped together, none of which has the characteristics philosophers and digital computers demand.

First there is the recognition of what Gurwitsch calls the generic. An example of such recognition would be the recognition of a certain object as a pencil. As Gurwitsch has pointed out, this form of recognition, while not explicit, lends itself to explicitation in terms of a set of features. It might thus seem adapted to being programmed. But what Gurwitsch overlooks in his account is that in this form of recognition our purposes serve to select which features are significant, and, among these, certain features which are crucial. For example, it is significant for our purposes that a pen have a point. However, when a writing instrument with a ball at the end was introduced, the end was nonetheless called a point (not a tip), and the instrument a ball-point pen (not a pencil), presumably because it was crucial to the users that the mark this instrument made could not be erased.

We might conclude that making an indelible mark is a defining criterion for being a pen, whereas having a point is only what Wittgenstein calls a symptom—". . . a phenomenon of which the experience has taught us that it coincided, in some way or other, with the phenomenon which is our defining criterion." We might even try to introduce this distinction between symptom and criterion into our program. But Wittgenstein's essential point in distinguishing between symptom and criterion is that the distinction is not fixed once and for all but changes with our changing purposes and knowledge:

> In practice, if you were asked which phenomenon is the defining criterion and which is a symptom, you would in most cases be unable to answer this question except by making an arbitrary decision *ad hoc*. It may be practical to define a word by taking one phenomenon as the defining criterion, but we shall easily be persuaded to define the word by means of what, according to our first use, was a symptom. Doctors will use names of diseases without ever deciding which phenomena are to be taken as criteria and which as symptoms; and this need not be a deplorable lack of clarity.[74]

Indeed, it is one way our concepts gain the openness crucial to human pattern recognition, a flexibility lacking in a computer using a fixed set of essential features.

A second sort of pattern recognition is the recognition of resemblance. In this sort of recognition, as in "narrowing down"[75]* the meaning of words or sentences, the context plays a determining role. The context may simply lead us to notice those resemblances which we can subsequently recognize in isolation—as in the case of ambiguous figures such as Wittgenstein's duck-rabbit, which resembles a duck when surrounded by pictures of ducks and a rabbit when surrounded by rabbits—or it may lead us to focus on certain aspects of the pattern, as in Pudovkin's famous experiment:

One day Pudovkin took a close-up of Mosjoukin with a completely impassive expression and projected it after showing: first, a bowl of soup, then, a young woman lying dead in her coffin, and last, a child playing with a teddy-bear. The first thing noticed was that Mosjoukin seemed to be looking at the bowl, the young woman, and the child, and next one noted that he was looking pensively at the dish, that he wore an expression of sorrow when looking at the woman, and that he had a glowing smile for the child. The audience was amazed at his variety of expression, although the same shot had actually been used all three times and was, if anything, remarkably inexpressive.[76]

Here, in a striking way, the meaning of the context determines what expression is seen on the face in a situation in which no traits of the face as projected on the screen could account for these differences. Still one might say that the expressive face, the one that the viewers thought they saw, had certain traits, like sad eyes, or a happy smile, which led the viewer to recognize the expression. But the expression of a person's eyes, for example, may depend on the whole face in such a way as to be unrecognizable if viewed through a slit. Moreover, a certain expression of the eyes may bring out a certain curve of the nose which would not be noticed if the nose were in another face; the nose in turn may give a certain twist to the smile which may affect the appearance of the eyes. As Wittgenstein remarks: "A human mouth smiles only in a human face."[77] In such cases, the traits necessary for recognizing a resemblance (dancing eyes, mocking smile, etc.) cannot, even when thematized, be isolated and defined in a neutral, context-free way. Moreover, as in the case of linguistic disambiguation, the context—in this example the whole face—not only determines the features essential for recognition, but is reciprocally determined by them. The expression is not *deduced from* the traits; it is simply the organization of the eyes, the mouth, and so forth, just as a melody is made up of the very notes to which it gives their particular values. In this sort of resemblance, the notion of recognizing the pattern in terms of isolated traits makes no sense.

In another case of resemblance, objects recognized as belonging together need not have any traits in common at all—not even context-dependent ones. Wittgenstein, in his study of natural language, was led to investigate this type of nonclassifactory recognition:

We see a complicated network of similarities overlapping and criss-crossing: Sometimes overall similarities, sometimes similarities of detail.

I can think of no better expression to characterize these similarities than "family resemblances"; for the various resemblances between members of a family: build, features, color of eyes, gait, temperament, etc. etc., overlap and criss-cross in the same way. . . . We extend our concept . . . as in spinning a thread we twist fiber on fiber.[78]

Family resemblance differs from class membership in several important ways: classes can be defined in terms of traits even if they have no members, whereas family resemblances are recognized only in terms of real or imaginary examples.[79]* Moreover, whereas class membership is all or nothing,[80]* family resemblance allows a spectrum ranging from the typical to the atypical. An atypical member of a family, for example, may be recognized by being placed in a series of faces leading from a typical member to the atypical one. Similarly, certain concepts like graceful, garish, and crude can not be defined in terms of necessary and sufficient conditions, but only by exhibiting a typical case. Since this sort of recognition of a member of a "family" is accomplished not by a list of traits, but by seeing the case in question in terms of its proximity to a paradigm (i.e., typical) case, such recognition gives us another kind of openness and flexibility.

Finally Wittgenstein goes even further and suggests that in some kinds of recognition there may be no common traits, even overlapping ones. Wittgenstein continues the above remarks rather obscurely:

. . . If someone wishes to say: "There is something common to all these constructions—namely the disjunction of all their common properties"—I should reply: Now you are only playing with words. One might as well say: "Something runs through the whole thread—namely the continuous overlapping of these fibres."[81]

Wittgenstein here may be suggesting a third kind of recognition which he does not clearly distinguish from resemblance, but which we might call the recognition of similarity.

Wittgenstein, on this interpretation, should not be taken to mean that recognition involves so many overlapping traits, but that one cannot use such an unwieldy disjunction. A more consistent way of understanding his analysis would be to conclude that each of the traits he mentions in discussing family resemblance—the build, color of eyes, gait, etc.—is not identical in any two members of the family, but in turn consists of a network of crisscrossing similarities. To follow the analogy, each fiber is made of fibers all the way down. Thus, no two members of a family need have *any* identical features for them all to share a family resemblance. Similarity is the ultimate notion in Wittgenstein's analysis and it cannot be reduced—as machine-thinking would require—to a list or disjunction of identical, determinate features.[82]

Those capable of recognizing a member of a "family" need not be able to list *any* exactly similar traits common to even two members, nor is there any reason to suppose such traits exist. Indeed, formalizing family resemblance in terms of exactly similar traits would eliminate a kind of openness to new cases which is the most striking feature of this form of recognition. No matter what disjunctive list of traits is constructed, one can always invent a new "family" member whose traits are similar to those of the given members without being *exactly* similar to any of the traits of any of them, and which in some situation would be recognized as belonging with the others.

This sophisticated but nonetheless very common form of recognition employs a special combination of the three forms of "information processing" discussed thus far: fringe consciousness, insight, and context dependence. To begin with, the process is implicit. It uses information which, in a manner of speaking, remains on the fringes of consciousness. To see the role of insight we must first distinguish the generic from the typical, although Gurwitsch uses these two terms interchangeably. As Gurwitsch defines it, recognition of the *generic* depends on implicit cues which can always be made explicit. Recognition of the *typical,* as we have been using the term, depends on similarities which cannot be thematized. Recognition of the typical, then, unlike recognition of the generic, requires insightful ordering around a paradigm. A paradigm case serves its function insofar as it is the clearest manifestation of what (essentially) makes all members, members of a given group. Finally, recognition in terms of proximity to the paradigm is a form of context dependence.

Wittgenstein remarks that "a perspicuous representation produces just that understanding which consists in seeing connections."[83] Following Wittgenstein, we have called this combination of fringe consciousness, insight, and context determination "perspicuous grouping." This form of human "information processing" is as important as the three fundamental forms of information processing from which it is derived.

Summary. Human beings are able to recognize patterns under the following increasingly difficult conditions:

1. The pattern may be skewed, incomplete, deformed, and embedded in noise;
2. The traits required for recognition may be "so fine and so numerous" that, even if they could be formalized, a search through a branching list of such traits would soon become unmanageable as new patterns for discrimination were added;
3. The traits may depend upon external and internal context and are thus not amenable to context-free specification;
4. There may be no common traits but a "complicated network of overlapping similarities," capable of assimilating ever new variations.

Any system which can equal human performance, must therefore, be able to

1. Distinguish the essential from the inessential features of a particular instance of a pattern;
2. Use cues which remain on the fringes of consciousness;
3. Take account of the context;
4. Perceive the individual as typical, i.e., situate the individual with respect to a paradigm case.

Since the recognition of patterns of even moderate complexity may require these four forms of human "information processing," work in pattern recognition has not progressed beyond the laborious recognition of simple alphanumeric patterns such as typewriter fonts and zip code figures. Moreover, it is generally acknowledged that further progress in game playing, language translation, and problem solving awaits a breakthrough in pattern recognition research.

Conclusion

The basic problem facing workers attempting to use computers in the simulation of human intelligent behavior should now be clear: all alternatives must be made explicit. In game playing, the exponential growth of the tree of these alternative paths requires a restriction on the paths which can be followed out; in complicated games such as chess, programs cannot now select the most promising paths. In problem solving, the issue is not only how to direct a selective search among the explicit alternatives, but how to structure the problem so as to begin the search process. In language translation, even the elements to be manipulated are not clear due to the intrinsic ambiguities of a natural language; in pattern recognition, all three difficulties are inextricably intertwined, as well as the fact that similarity and typicality seem to be irreducible characteristics of perception. These difficulties have brought to a standstill the first five years of work on Cognitive Simulation.

None of Simon's predictions has been fulfilled. The failure to fulfill the first two, about how well machines could do in chess and mathematics, gave the lie to Simon's third prediction concerning a psychological theory of human behavior. In spite of the eagerness and gullibility of psychologists, within the past ten years most theories in psychology have not taken the form of computer programs.

Instead of these triumphs, an overall pattern has emerged: success with simple mechanical forms of information processing, great expectations, and then failure when confronted with more complicated forms of behavior. Simon's predictions fall into place as just another example of the phenomenon which Bar-Hillel has called the "fallacy of the successful first step."[84]* Simon himself, however, has drawn no such sobering conclusions. In his latest prediction, made in 1965, Simon now affirms that "machines will be capable, within twenty years, of doing any work that a man can do."[85]

We shall devote Part II to the reasons for this imperturbable optimism, but first we must consider the work in AI which has taken up where work in Cognitive Simulation gave out.

2

Phase II (1962–1967) Semantic Information Processing

To place Phase I in perspective and to form an idea of what was expected and accomplished in Phase II, it is helpful to begin by quoting Minsky's brief account of the history of work on machine intelligence:

In the early 1950's, as general-purpose computers became available to the scientific community, Cybernetics divided . . . into three chief avenues: The first was the continuation of the search for simple basic principles. This became transformed into the goal of discovering what we might call minimal, Self-Organizing Systems. A paradigm of this approach is to find large collections of generally similar components that, when arranged in a very weakly specified structure and placed in an appropriate environment, would eventually come to behave in an "adaptive" fashion. Eventually, it was hoped, intelligent behavior would emerge from the evolution of such a system.[1]

Since those still pursuing this course, sometimes called cybernetics, have produced no interesting results—although their spokesman, Frank Rosenblatt, has produced some of the most fantastic promises and claims[2]*—they will not be dealt with here.

The second important avenue was an attempt to build working models of human behavior, . . . requiring the machine's behavior to match that of human subjects. . . .[3]

The book, *Computers and Thought,* edited by E. Feigenbaum and J. Feldman who did their graduate work in the Carnegie group, gives a good view of the state of affairs as it stood by about the end of 1961.[4]

This is the research in Cognitive Simulation, led by Newell and Simon, which we have criticized in Chapter 1. Minsky is similarly critical of this work in a paper delivered at the time Phase I was nearing its end:

Methods that worked quite well on easy problems did not extend smoothly to the difficult ones. Continued progress will require implementation of new ideas, for there are some very tough problems in our immediate path.[5]

This is Minsky's way of recognizing the stagnation we have noted. At the same time Minsky and his group at M.I.T. undertook to provide new ideas and their implementation:

The third approach, the one we call *Artificial Intelligence,* was an attempt to build intelligent machines without any prejudice toward making the system simple, biological, or humanoid. Workers taking this route regarded the self-organizing systems as unpromising or, perhaps, premature. Even if simplicity of initial organization was to be an ultimate goal, one might first need experience with working intelligent systems (based if necessary on *ad hoc* mechanisms) if one were eventually to be able to design more economical schemes.[6]

We shall now turn to this third and most recent approach, the results of which are reported in Minsky's book *Semantic Information Processing,* to see just what has actually been accomplished. Minsky once suggested that in evaluating the programs presented in his book one might ask five questions:

1. Why were these particular problems selected?
2. How do these programs work?
3. What are their limitations?
4. What do the programs actually achieve?
5. How can they be extended to larger domains of competence?

If, following this method, we analyze the programs which Minsky presents as the best work since 1962, we shall find that unlike work done before 1961, which tended to give the impression of intelligence by simulating simple, mechanical aspects of intelligent behavior, *the current approach is characterized by* ad hoc *solutions of cleverly chosen problems, which give the illusion of complex intellectual activity.* In fact, however, problems which arrested work in 1961 still remain unsolved. We shall also find again that only an unquestioned underlying faith enables workers such as Minsky to find this situation encouraging.

Let us look at the programs in detail.

I. Analysis of Semantic Information Processing Programs

ANALYSIS OF A PROGRAM WHICH "UNDERSTANDS ENGLISH"— BOBROW'S STUDENT

Of the five semantic information processing programs collected in Minsky's book, Daniel Bobrow's STUDENT—a program for solving algebra word problems—is put forward as the most successful. It is, Minsky tells us, "a demonstration *par excellence* of the power of using meaning to solve linguistic problems."[7] Indeed, Minsky devotes a great deal of his *Scientific American* article to Bobrow's program and goes so far as to say that "it understands English."[8]

Since this program is presented as the best so far, we shall begin by analyzing it in detail, according to Minsky's suggested five questions.

First: *Why was this particular problem selected?*

Bobrow himself tells us:

In constructing a question-answering system many problems are greatly simplified if the problem context is restricted.[9]

Moreover,

There are a number of reasons for choosing the context of algebra story problems in which to develop techniques which would allow a computer problem solving system to accept a natural language input. First, we know a good type of data structure in which to store information needed to answer questions in this context, namely, algebraic equations.[10]

It is important to note that the problem was chosen because the restricted context made it easier. The full significance of this restriction, however, will only be evident after we have answered the next two questions.

How does the program work?

The program simply breaks up the sentences of the story problem into units on the basis of cues such as the words "times," "of," "equals," etc.; equates these sentence chunks with x's and y's; and tries to set up simultaneous equations. If these equations cannot be solved, it appeals to further rules for breaking up the sentences into other units and tries again. The whole scheme works only because there is the constraint, not present in understanding ordinary discourse, that the pieces of the sentence, when represented by variables, will set up soluble equations. As Minsky puts it: ". . . some possibly syntactic ambiguities in the input are decided on the overall basis of algebraic consistency. . . ."[11]

Choosing algebra problems also has another advantage:

> In natural language, the ambiguities arise not only from the variety of structural groupings the words could be given, but also from the variety of meanings that can be assigned to each individual word. In STUDENT the strong semantic constraint (that the sentences express algebraic relations between the designated entities) keeps the situation more or less under control.[12]

What are the limitations of the program?

The advantage of using algebraic constraints is also a serious limitation on the generality of the program, however, for such a "strong constraint" eliminates just that aspect of natural language, namely its ambiguity, which makes machine processing of natural language difficult, if not impossible. Such a program is so far from semantic understanding that, as Bobrow admits, ". . . the phrase 'the number of times I went to the movies' which should be interpreted as a variable string will be interpreted incorrectly as the product of the two variables 'number of' and 'I went to the movies,' because 'times' is always considered to be an operator."[13]

What, then, has been achieved?

Bobrow is rather cautious. Although his thesis is somewhat misleadingly entitled "Natural Language Input for a Computer Problem Solving

Program," Bobrow makes clear from the outset that the program "accepts as input a comfortable but *restricted subset of English.*"[14] He adds:

In the following discussion, I shall use phrases such as "the computer understands English." In all such cases, the "English" is just the restricted subset of English allowable as input for the computer program under discussion.[15]

This is straightforward enough, and seems an admirable attempt to claim no more than is justified by the restricted choice of material. In the course of the work, Bobrow even makes clear that "The STUDENT program considers words as symbols, and makes do with as little knowledge about the meaning of words as is compatible with the goal of finding a solution of the particular problem."[16]

In other words this program embodies a minimum of semantic understanding. Bobrow is proud that he can get so much for so little: "The semantic model in the STUDENT system is based on one relationship (equality) and five basic arithmetic functions."[17]

Bobrow is equally careful in noting he has given a special meaning to "understands."

For purposes of this report I have adopted the following operational definition of "understanding." A computer *understands* a subset of English if it accepts input sentences which are members of this subset, and answers questions based on information contained in the input. The STUDENT system understands English in this sense.[18]*

Bobrow concludes cautiously: "I think we are far from writing a program which can understand all, or even a very large segment, of English. However, within its narrow field of competence, STUDENT has demonstrated that 'understanding' machines can be built."[19]

Yet Minsky says in his *Scientific American* article that "STUDENT . . . understands English." What has happened?

Bobrow's quotation marks around "understanding" are the key. If we remember that "understands" merely means "answers questions in a restricted subset of English subject to algebraic constraints," then we will also remember that although the words in quotation marks have nothing to do with what human understanding normally means, they are nonetheless accurate. However, one can't help being misled into feeling that if Bobrow uses "understands" rather than "processes," it must be because his program has something to do with human understanding. Minsky exploits this ambiguity in his rhetorical article simply by dropping the quotation marks.

Minsky makes even more surprising and misleading claims concerning the "enormous 'learning potential' " of Bobrow's program:

> Consider the qualitative effect, upon the subsequent performance of Bobrow's STUDENT, of telling it that *"distance equals speed times time!"* That one experience alone enables it to handle a large new portion of "high-school algebra"; the physical position-velocity-time problems. It is important not to fall into the habit . . . of concentrating only on the kind of "learning" that appears as slow-improvement-attendant-upon-sickeningly-often-repeated experience!
>
> Bobrow's program does not have any cautious statistical devices that have to be told something over and over again, so its *learning* is too brilliant to be called so.[20]

Again it is easy to show that what has been acquired by the machine can in no way be called "understanding." The machine has indeed been given another *equation,* but it does not understand it as a *formula.* That is, the program can now plug one distance, one rate, and one time into the equation $d = rt;$ but that it does not understand anything is clear from the fact that it cannot use this equation twice in one problem, for it has no way of determining which quantities should be used in which equation. As Bobrow admits: "the same phrase must always be used to represent the same variable in a problem."[21] *No learning has occurred.*

Once he has removed the quotation marks from "understand" and interpreted the quotation marks around "learning" to mean superhuman learning, Minsky is free to engage in the usual riot of speculation.

> In order for a program to improve itself substantially it would have to have at least a rudimentary understanding of its own problem-solving process and some ability to recognize an improvement when it found one. There is no inherent reason why this should be impossible for a machine. Given a model of its own

workings, it could use its problem-solving power to work on the problem of self-improvement. . . .

Once we have devised programs with a genuine capacity for self-improvement a rapid evolutionary process will begin. As the machine improves both itself and its model of itself, we shall begin to see all the phenomena associated with the terms "consciousness," "intuition" and "intelligence" itself. It is hard to say how close we are to this threshold, but once it is crossed the world will not be the same.[22]

It is not as hard to say how close we are to this threshold as Minsky would like us to believe. Since the success of Bobrow's program has allegedly given us the rudiments of understanding and learning that Minsky is relying on, we need only ask: to what extent can Bobrow's techniques be generalized and extended?

Which leads us to question five: *How can the program in question be extended to larger domains of competence?*

Here even Bobrow throws his caution to the winds and—in spite of his earlier remark that the semantic model is based on one relationship (equality); that is, only sets up and solves equations where it can use the algebraic constraint—claims that his "semantic theory of discourse can be used as a basis for a much more general language processing system."[23] And Bobrow concludes the abstract of his thesis with the now familiar first-step fallacy: "The STUDENT system is a first step toward natural language communication with computers. Further work on the semantic theory proposed should result in much more sophisticated systems."[24]

Five years have passed since Bobrow made this claim, and no more sophisticated semantic theory has been forthcoming. Why Bobrow and Minsky think, in the face of the peculiar restrictions necessary to the function of the program, that such a generalization must be possible is hard to understand. Nothing, I think, can justify or even explain their optimism concerning *this* admittedly limited and *ad hoc* approach. Their general optimism that *some* such computable approach must work, however, can be seen to follow from a fundamental metaphysical assumption concerning the nature of language and of human intelligent behavior, namely that whatever orderly behavior people engage in can in principle be formalized and processed by digital computers. (See Chapter 5.) This leads Minsky and Bobrow to shrug off all current difficulties as technological limitations, imposed, for example, by the restricted size of the storage capacity of present machine memories.[25]*

Were it not for such an assumption, Bobrow's limited success, heralded by Minsky as the most promising work thus far, would be recognized as a trick which says nothing either for or against the possibility of machine understanding, and the fact that this is the best that an intelligent person like Bobrow could do would lead to discouragement as to the possibility of ever reaching the threshold of self-improving machines.

EVANS' ANALOGY PROGRAM

The same pattern occurs throughout Minsky's collection: an *ad hoc* solution of a restricted problem, first reported with caution, and then interpreted as being the first step to more general methods. Yet all the work presented in Minsky's book was completed by 1964, and although seven more years have elapsed, none of the promised generalizations has been produced.

Evans' analogy-finding program, for example, is a masterful complex program for solving the sort of analogy problems used in intelligence testing. (See Figure 3.) It performs its particular restricted task as well as an average tenth grader, which, granted the state of the art, is an impressive performance. Evans, moreover, realizes that this success as such has little value unless the techniques he employs can be generalized. But, unlike Bobrow, he does not content himself with the assertion that such a generalization is possible. Rather, he attempts at the end of his paper to sketch the form such a generalization would take, and the contribution it would make to problem-solving programs such as GPS and work in pattern recognition.

In the final pages of this chapter we describe a "pattern recognition" process of which the main outlines are based on the conception of ANALOGY described. It is more ambitious chiefly in that a more powerful and more general-purpose descriptive framework for the "objects" is introduced.[26]

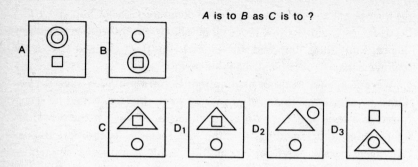

Figure 3

GPS treats sub-objects of a given object through its goal-subgoal organization. That is, GPS avoids looking at complex structures on a given level by decomposing them into smaller structures tied to subgoals. So GPS never sees a single complex structure as such; when a substructure is handled at some deeper subgoal level it is "out of context" in that the necessary information as to how the achievement of this subgoal contributes to the achievement of larger goals is lacking. Newell discusses a form of this "lack of context" problem and several rather unsatisfactory attempts at solving it. The mechanism we have sketched provides a pattern-recognition device capable of taking a look at the problem which is "global" yet has access to the full structure. Such "global" guidance could be expected to save GPS a large amount of the time now spent in setting up and pursuing subgoals that do not contribute to achieving goals at or near the top level. This alone would be a worthwhile contribution.[27]

Evans also has proposals for learning:

Certainly the study of these problems in the relatively well-understood domain of phrase-structure languages is a natural next step toward the development of genuine "generalization learning" by machines and a prerequisite to consideration of learning in still more complex descriptive language environments. One interesting possibility, since the transformation rules themselves can be described in phrase-structure terms, would be to apply the entire "phrase-structure + GPS" apparatus to improving its own set of transformation rules.[28]

Evans realizes that "this may, of course, turn out to be very difficult."[29] Presumably it has so turned out, because no more has been published concerning this scheme since this work was completed in 1963, and, as we have seen, since then Newell has abandoned GPS and Murray Eden has reported that in 1968 pattern recognition was as *ad hoc* as ever. Which, of course, raises the usual question: Why do Minsky and Evans so confidently expect that the *ad hoc* techniques used to solve this specific and rather complex analogy problem can be generalized? A hint as to the assumptions underlying this confidence can be found in Minsky's surprising comparison of Evans' program to human analogy solving. In spite of his disclaimers that AI is not interested in cognitive simulation, Minsky gives the following "mentalistic" description of Evans' program.

To explain the spirit of this work, it is best to describe the program in mentalistic form. Given a set of figures, it constructs a set of hypotheses or theories as follows:

1. Based on the descriptions D(A) and D(B) of Figures A and B [see Figure 3] there are many ways in which D(A) can be transformed into D(B); choose one of these.
2. There are also many ways in which the parts of A can be put into correspondence with the parts of C: each such correspondence *suggests* a relation like that proposed in (1), but which now relates Fig. C and some other figures.
3. It is unlikely that any of the relations found in (2) will apply perfectly to any of the answer-figures. (If just one does, then that will be the program's answer.) For each answer figure, "weaken," i.e., generalize each relation just enough so that it will apply to the figure.
4. Finally, the program measures how much it had to weaken each relation. It chooses the one that required the least change, and gives the corresponding answer figure as its answer.

By choosing that hypothesis which involved the least "weakening" of the original A⟶B transformation hypothesis, the program selects that explanation that contains the most information common to both A ⟶ B and C ⟶ D relations. The details of the selection rules in steps (1), (2), (3), and (4), amount, in effect to *Evans' theory of human behavior in such situations. I feel sure that something of this general character is involved in any kind of analogical reasoning.*[30]

This "something" is put more clearly in Minsky's *Scientific American* article. There he says: "I feel sure that *rules or procedures* of the same general character are involved in any kind of analogical reasoning."[31] This is the same assumption which, as we have seen, underlies Newell and Simon's work in CS. In fact, Evans uses a quotation from Newell to describe the problem-solving procedure involved:

"These programs are all rather similar in nature. For each the task is difficult enough to allow us to assert that the programs problem-solve, rather than simply carry out the steps of a procedure for a solution invented by the programmer. They all operate on formalized tasks, which, although difficult, are not unstructured. All the programs use the same conceptual approach: they interpret the problem as combinatorial, involving the discovery of the right sequence of operations out of a set of possible sequences. All of the programs generate some sort of tree of possibilities to gradually explore the possible sequences. The set of all sequences is much too large to generate and examine *in toto*, so that various devices, called heuristics, are employed to narrow the range of possibilities to a set that can be handled within the available limits of processing effort."

Evans then concludes:

The geometric-analogy program also fits this description. Stated very briefly, given a problem of this type, *the program uses various heuristics to select a "correct" rule* (in a reasonable time) *from a very extensive class of possible rules.* [32]

It is true that if human beings did solve analogy problems in this way, there would be every reason to expect to be able to improve and generalize Evans' program, since human beings certainly surpass the machines' present level of performance. But, as in the case of GPS, there is no evidence that human beings proceed in this way, and descriptive, psychological evidence suggests that they do not.

Rudolph Arnheim, professor of psychology at Harvard University, in discussing Evans' work, has described the different way in which human beings approach the same sort of problem. His description is worth quoting in full:

What happens when a person is confronted with a figure such as Figure [3]? The reaction will vary somewhat from individual to individual as long as no particular context calls for concentration on specific structural features. By and large, however, the observer is likely to notice a vertical arrangement, made up of two units, of which the upper is larger and more complex than the lower; he may also notice a difference in shape. In other words, he will perceive qualitative characteristics of placement, relative size, shape; whereas he is unlikely to notice much of the metric properties from which the computer's reading of the pattern must set out, namely, absolute size and the various lengths and distances by which this individual figure is constructed. If one asks observers to copy such a figure, their drawings will show concentration on the topological characteristics and neglect of specific measurements.

Confronted now with a pairing of A and B, the human observer may have a rather rich and dazzling experience. He may see, at first, fleeting, elusive resemblances among basically different patterns. The over-all figure, made up of the pairing of the two, may look unstable, ungraspable, irrational. There are two vertical arrangements, combining in a sort of symmetry; but these two columns are crossed and interfered with by diagonal relations between the two "filled" large circles and the two smaller, unfilled shapes. The various structural features do not add up to a unified, stable, understandable whole. Suddenly, however, the observer may be struck by the simple rectangular arrangement of the four smaller figures: two equal circles on top, two equal squares at the bottom. As soon as this group becomes the dominant theme or structural skeleton of the whole, the remainder—the two large circles—joins the basic pattern as a secondary, diagonal embellishment. A structural hierarchy has been established. Now the double figure is stable, surveyable, understandable, and therefore ready for comparison with other figures. A first act of problem solving has taken place.

If the observer turns to Figure C, his view of this new pattern is determined from the outset by his preceding concern with A and B. Perceived from the viewpoint of A, C reveals a similar vertical structure, distinguished from A mainly by a secondary contrast of shapes. The family resemblance is great, the relation comes easily. But if C is now paired with D_1, the resemblance looks excessive, the symmetry too complete. On the contrary, a comparison with D_2 offers too little resemblance. D_3 is recognized immediately as the correct partner, the missing fourth element of the analogy, if the relation between A and B had been properly grasped before.

This episode of perceptual problem solving has all the aspects of genuine thinking: the challenge, the productive confusion, the promising leads, the partial solutions, the disturbing contradictions, the flash appearance of a stable solution whose adequacy is self-evident, the structural changes brought about by the pressure of changing total situations, the resemblance discovered among different patterns. It is, in a small way, an exhilarating experience, worthy of a creature endowed with reason; and when the solution has been found, there is a sense of dis-tension, of pleasure, of rest.

None of this is true for the computer, not because it is without consciousness, but because it proceeds in a fundamentally different fashion. We are shocked to learn that in order to make the machine solve the analogy problem the experimenter "had to develop what is certainly one of the most complex programs ever written." For us the problem is not hard; it is accessible to the brain of a young student. The reason for the difference is that the task calls for the handling of topological relations, which require the neglect of purely metric ones. The brain is geared to precisely such topographical features because they inform us of the typical character of things, rather than of their particular measurements.[33]

As in the case of chess, it turns out that global perceptual grouping is a prior condition for the rule-governed counting out—the only kind of procedure available to the machine. As Arnheim puts it, "Topology was discovered by, and relies on, the perceptual powers of the brain, not the arithmetical ones."[34]

Obviously Minsky and Evans think that analogies are solved by human beings by applying transformation rules, because the prospects for AI are only encouraging if this is how humans proceed. But it is clearly circular to base one's optimism on an hypothesis which, in turn, is only justified by the fact that if the hypothesis were true, one's optimism would be justified.

QUILLIAN'S SEMANTIC MEMORY PROGRAM

The final program we shall consider from Phase II, Ross Quillian's Semantic Memory Program, is the most interesting, because most general; and the most modest, in that its author (working under Simon rather than Minsky) has made no sweeping promises or claims.[35]* This program confirms a general evaluation heuristic already apparent in Samuel's modesty and success and Simon's and Gelernter's claims and setbacks, namely that the value of a program is often inversely proportional to its programmer's promises and publicity.

Quillian, like Bobrow, is interested in simulating the understanding of natural language; but, unlike Bobrow and Minsky, he sees that this problem cannot be dealt with by *ad hoc* solutions.

In the first place, we do not believe that performance theories or computer models can ignore or put off semantics, as most language processing programs so far have done, and yet hope to achieve success. Whether a program is intended to parse sentences, to translate languages, or to answer natural language questions, if it does not take account of semantic facts both early and often, I do not think it has a chance of approaching the level of human competence.[36]

After reviewing all work in the field, including that of Bobrow, Quillian remarks:

Programs such as Bobrow's have been able to set up the equations corresponding to certain algebra word problems by an almost entirely "syntactic" procedure. . . . However, if one attempts to extend the range of language that such a program can handle, it becomes necessary to incorporate increasing numbers of semantic facts.[37]

Quillian concludes that

the problems of what is to be contained in an overall, human-like permanent memory, what format this is to be in, and how this memory is to be organized have not been dealt with in great generality in prior simulation programs. . . . Further advances in simulating problem-solving and game playing, as well as language performance, will surely require programs that develop and interact with large memories.[38]

Quillian then proceeds to propose a complex heuristic program for storing and accessing the meaning of words and "anything that can be stated in language, sensed in perception, or otherwise known and remembered"[39] in one "enormous interlinked net."[40] Quillian proposes this program as "a reasonable view of how semantic information is organized within a person's memory."[41] He gives no argument to show that it is reasonable except that if a *computer* were to store semantic information, this would be a reasonable model for *it*. People, indeed, are not aware of going through any of the complex storage and retrieval process Quillian outlines, but this does not disturb Quillian, who, like his teacher, Simon, in similar trouble can always claim that these processes are nonetheless unconsciously taking place:

While the encoding process is of course not identical to the covert processing that constitutes the understanding of the same text during normal reading, it is . . . in some ways a slowed-down, overt version of it.[42]

That such unconscious processing is going on, and moreover, that such processing follows heuristic rules is by no means obvious. We have seen in the cases of chess playing and analogy solving that gestalt grouping plays a crucial role, and it may well do so here. Yet Quillian seems to have inherited Newell and Simon's unquestioned assumption that human beings operate by heuristic programs.

The heuristic methods by which one particular comprehension of text is selected is the central problem for anyone who would explain "understanding," just as the heuristic methods by which one particular chess move is selected from all those possible is the central problem for anyone who would explain chess playing.[43]

In terms of this assumption Quillian must assume that the task of the program involves working from parts to wholes.

In selecting a task to perform with a model memory, one thinks first of the ability to understand unfamiliar sentences. It seems reasonable to suppose that people must necessarily understand new sentences by retrieving *stored* information about the meaning of isolated words and phrases, and then combining and perhaps altering these retrieved word meanings to build up the meanings of sentences. Accordingly, one should be able to take a model of stored semantic knowledge, and formulate rules of combination that would describe how sentence meanings get built up from stored word meanings.[44]

Quillian also has great hopes for his system:

It further seems likely that if one could manage to get even a few word meanings adequately encoded and stored in a computer memory, and a workable set of combination rules formalized as a computer program, he could then bootstrap his store of encoded word meanings by having the computer itself "understand" sentences that he had written to constitute the definitions of *other* single words. That is, whenever a new, as yet uncoded, word could be defined by a sentence using only words whose meanings had already been encoded, then the representation of this sentence's meaning, which the machine could build by using its previous knowledge together with its combination rules, would be the appropriate representation to *add* to its memory as the meaning of the new word.[45]

But with a frankness, rare in the literature, Quillian also reports his disappointments:

Unfortunately, two years of work on this problem led to the conclusion that the task is much too difficult to execute at our present stage of knowledge. The processing that goes on in a person's head when he "understands" a sentence and incorporates its meaning into his memory is very large indeed, practically all of it being done without his conscious knowledge.[46]

The magnitude of the problem confronting Quillian becomes clear when we note that

the definition of eight hundred and fifty words comprise far more information than can be modeled in the core of today's computers. . . .[47]

These difficulties suggest that the model itself—the idea that our understanding of a natural language involves building up a structured whole out of an enormous number of explicit parts—may well be mistaken. Quillian's work raises rather than resolves the question of storing the gigantic number of facts resulting from an analysis which has no place for perceptual gestalts. If this data structure grows too rapidly with the addition of new definitions, then Quillian's work, far from being encouraging, would be a *reductio ad absurdum* of the whole computer-oriented approach. Before taking a stand on whether Quillian's work is grounds for optimism, one would expect an answer to the basic question: Does Quillian's data base grow linearly or exponentially with additional entries?

On this crucial point it is surprising to find much hope but little information. Quillian's program contains definitions of only from 50 to 60 words, and, in describing Quillian's work, in his book written in 1968, three years after the work was completed, Minsky has to admit that "we simply do not know enough about how powerful Quillian's methods would be when provided with a more substantial knowledge bank."[48] Again, no further progress has been reported.

II. Significance of Current Difficulties

What would be reasonable to expect? Minsky estimates that Quillian's program now contains a few hundred facts. He estimates that "a million facts would be necessary for great intelligence."[49] He also admits that each of "the programs described [in this book] will work best when given exactly the necessary facts, and will bog down inexorably as the information files grow."[50]

Is there, thus, any reason to be confident that these programs are approaching the "superior heuristics for managing their knowledge structure" which Minsky believed human beings must have; or, as Minsky claims in another of his books, that

within a generation . . . few compartments of intellect will remain outside the machine's realm—the problem of creating "artificial intelligence" will be substantially solved.[51]

Certainly there is nothing in *Semantic Information Processing* to justify this confidence. As we have seen, Minsky criticizes the early programs for their lack of generality. "Each program worked only on its restricted specialty, and there was no way to combine two different problem-solvers."[52] But Minsky's solutions are as *ad hoc* as ever. Yet he adds jauntily:

The programs described in this volume may still have this character, but they are no longer ignoring the problem. In fact, their chief concern is finding methods of solving it.[53]

But there is no sign that any of the papers presented by Minsky have solved anything. They have not discovered any *general* feature of the human ability to behave intelligently. All Minsky presents are clever special solutions, like Bobrow's and Evans', or radically simplified models such as Quillian's, which work because the real problem, the problem of how to structure and store the mass of data required has been put aside. Minsky, of course, has already responded to this apparent shortcoming with a new version of the first step fallacy:

The fact that the present batch of programs still appear to have narrow ranges of application does not indicate lack of progress toward generality. *These programs are steps toward* ways to handle knowledge.[54]

In Phase II the game seems to be to see how far one can get with the *appearance* of complexity before the real problem of complexity has to be faced, and then when one fails to generalize, claim to have made a first step.

Such an approach is inevitable as long as workers in the field of AI are interested in producing striking results but have not solved the practical problem of how to store and access the large body of data necessary, if perhaps not sufficient, for full-scale, flexible, semantic information processing. Minsky notes with satisfaction, looking over the results, "one cannot help being astonished at how far they did get with their feeble semantic endowment."[55] Bar-Hillel in a recent talk to SIGART (Special Interest Group in Artificial Intelligence of the Association for Computing Machinery) calls attention to the misleading character of this sort of claim.

There are very many people—in all fields but particularly in the field of AI—who, whenever they themselves make a first step towards letting the computer do certain things it has never done before, then believe that the remaining steps are nothing more than an exercise in technical ability. Essentially, this is like saying that as soon as anything can be done *at all* by a computer, it can also be done *well.* On the contrary, the step from not being able to do something at all to being able to do it a little bit is very much smaller than the next step— being able to do it well. In AI, this fallacious thinking seems to be all pervasive.[56]

But Bar-Hillel is too generous in suggesting that the fallacy is simply overestimation of the ease of progress. To claim to have taken even an easy first step one must have reason to believe that by further such steps one could eventually reach one's goal. We have seen that Minsky's book provides no such reasons. In fact these steps may well be strides in the opposite direction. The restricted character of the results reported by Minsky, plus the fact that during the last five years none of the promised generalizations has been produced, suggests that human beings do not deal with a mass of isolated facts as does a digital computer, and thus do not have to store and retrieve these facts by heuristic rules. Judging from their behavior, human beings avoid rather than resolve the difficulties confronting workers in Cognitive Simulation and Artificial Intelligence by avoiding the discrete information-processing techniques from which these difficulties arise. Thus it is by no means obvious that Minsky's progress toward handling "knowledge" (slight as it is) is progress toward artificial intelligence at all.

Conclusion

We have seen how Phase I, heralded as a first step, ends with the abandonment of GPS and the general failure to provide the theorem proving, chess playing, and language translation programs anticipated. Minsky himself recognizes this failure, and while trying to minimize it, diagnoses it accurately:

A few projects have not progressed nearly as much as was hoped, notably projects in language translation and mathematical theorem-proving. Both cases, I think, represent premature attempts to handle complex formalisms without also representing their meaning.[1]

Phase II—a new first step—begins around 1961 with Minsky's graduate students at M.I.T. undertaking theses aimed at overcoming this difficulty. It ends in 1968 with the publication of Minsky's book *Semantic Information Processing,* which reports these attempts, all completed by 1964. After analyzing the admittedly *ad hoc* character of those programs which Minsky considers most successful, and noting the lack of follow-up during the last five years, we can only conclude that Phase II has also ended in failure.

Most reports on the state of the art try to cover up this failure. In a report undertaken for the IEEE in 1966, covering work in AI since 1960, R. J. Solomonoff devotes his first three pages to speaking of GPS and other past achievements, already completed by 1960, and the next three pages to talking of the glorious future of work on induction by S. Amarel: "Although Amarel hasn't programmed any of his theories, his ideas and his analysis of them are important."[2] There is little mention of the semantic information processing programs touted by Minsky. All hope is placed in induction and learning. Unfortunately, "in all the learning systems mentioned, the kinds of self improvement accessible to the machines have been quite limited. . . . We still need to know the kind of heuristics we need to find heuristics, as well as what languages can *readily* describe them."[3]

Since no one has made any contribution to finding these heuristics, Solomonoff's final hope is placed in artificial evolution:

The promise of artificial evolution is that many things are known or suspected about the mechanisms of natural evolution, and that those mechanisms can be used directly or indirectly to solve problems in their artificial counterparts. For artificial intelligence research, simulation of evolution is incomparably more promising than simulation of neural nets, since we know practically nothing about natural neural nets that would be at all useful in solving difficult problems.[4]

This work in artificial evolution, however, has hardly begun. "Research in simulation of evolution has been very limited in both quantity and quality."[5]

When an article supposed to sum up work done since 1960 begins with earlier accomplishments and ends in speculations, without presenting a single example of actual progress, stagnation can be read between the lines.

Occasionally one catches hints of disappointment in the lines themselves. For example, Fred Tonge, whose solid, unpretentious paper on a heuristic line-balancing procedure was reprinted in *Computers and Thought,* after reviewing progress in AI, concluded in 1968:

While many interesting programs (and some interesting devices) have been produced, progress in artificial intelligence has not been exciting or spectacular. . . . This is due at least in part to lack of a clear separation between accomplishment and conjecture in many past and current writings. In this field, as in many others, there is a large difference between saying that some accomplishment "ought to" be possible and doing it.

Identifiable, significant, *landmarks* of accomplishment are scarce.[6]

Tonge then gives his list of "landmarks." They are Newell, Shaw, and Simon's Logic Theory Machine, Samuel's Checker Program, and the Uhr-Vossler pattern recognition program—all completed long before 1961, and all dead ends if we are to judge from subsequent work.

That mine is no unduly prejudiced reaction to Tonge's summary of the work done thus far can be seen by comparing P. E. Greenwood's review of Tonge's article for *Computing Reviews:* "From this brief summary of the state of the art of artificial intelligence, one would conclude that little significant progress has been made since about 1960 and the prospects for the near future are not bright."[7]

Why, in the light of these difficulties, do those pursuing Cognitive Simulation assume that the information processes of a computer reveal the hidden information processes of a human being, and why do those working in Artificial Intelligence assume that there must be a digital way of performing human tasks? To my knowledge, no one in the field seems to have asked himself these questions. In fact, artificial intelligence is the least self-critical field on the scientific scene. There must be a reason why these intelligent men almost unanimously mimimize or fail to recognize their difficulties, and continue dogmatically to assert their faith in progress. Some force in their assumptions, clearly not their success, must allow them to ignore the need for justification. We must now try to discover why, in the face of increasing difficulties, workers in artificial intelligence show such untroubled confidence.

PART II

ASSUMPTIONS UNDERLYING

PERSISTENT OPTIMISM

Introduction

In spite of grave difficulties, workers in Cognitive Simulation and Artificial Intelligence are not discouraged. In fact, they are unqualifiedly optimistic. Underlying their optimism is the conviction that human intelligent behavior is the result of information processing by a digital computer, and, since nature has produced intelligent behavior with this form of processing, proper programming should be able to elicit such behavior from digital machines, either by imitating nature or by out-programming her.

This assumption, that human and mechanical information processing ultimately involve the same elementary processes, is sometimes made naïvely explicit. Newell and Simon introduce one of their papers with the following remark:

It can be seen that this approach makes no assumption that the "hardware" of computers and brains are similar, beyond the assumptions that both are general-purpose symbol-manipulating devices, and that the computer can be programmed to execute *elementary information processes* functionally quite like those executed by the brain.[1]

But this is no innocent and empty assumption. What is a general-purpose symbol-manipulating device? What are these "elementary information processes" allegedly shared by man and machine? All artificial intelligence work is done on digital computers because they are the only neral-purpose information-processing devices which we know how to design or even conceive of at present. All information with which these computers operate must be represented in terms of discrete elements. In the case of present computers the information is represented by binary digits, that is, in terms of a series of yeses and noes, of switches being open or closed. The machine must operate on finite strings of these determinate elements as a series of objects related to each other only by rules. Thus the assumption that man functions like a general-purpose symbol-manipulating device amounts to

1. A biological assumption that on some level of operation—usually supposed to be that of the neurons—the brain processes information in discrete operations by way of some biological equivalent of on/off switches.

2. A psychological assumption that the mind can be viewed as a device operating on bits of information according to formal rules. Thus, in psychology, the computer serves as a model of the mind as conceived of by empiricists such as Hume (with the bits as atomic impressions) and idealists such as Kant (with the program providing the rules). Both empiricists and idealists have prepared the ground for this model of thinking as data processing—a third-person process in which the involvement of the "processor" plays no essential role.

3. An epistemological assumption that all knowledge can be formalized, that is, that whatever can be understood can be expressed in terms of logical relations, more exactly in terms of Boolean functions, the logical calculus which governs the way the bits are related according to rules.

4. Finally, since all information fed into digital computers must be in bits, the computer model of the mind presupposes that all relevant information about the world, everything essential to the production of intelligent behavior, must in principle be analyzable as a set of situation-free determinate elements. This is the ontological assumption that what there is, is a set of facts each logically independent of all the others.

In the following chapters we shall turn to an analysis of the plausibility of each of these assumptions. In each case we shall see that the assumption is taken by workers in CS or AI as an axiom, guaranteeing results, whereas it is, in fact, only one possible hypothesis among others, to be tested by the success of such work. Furthermore, none of the four assumptions is justified on the basis of the empirical and *a priori* arguments brought forward in its favor. Finally, the last three assumptions, which are philosophical rather than empirical, can be criticized on philosophical grounds. They each lead to conceptual difficulties when followed through consistently as an account of intelligent behavior.

After we have examined each of these assumptions we shall be in a better position to understand the persistent optimism of workers in artificial intelligence and also to assess the true significance of results obtained thus far.

3

The Biological Assumption

In the period between the invention of the telephone relay and its apotheosis in the digital computer, the brain, always understood in terms of the latest technological inventions, was understood as a large telephone switchboard or, more recently, as an electronic computer. This model of the brain was correlated with work in neurophysiology which found that neurons fired a somewhat all-or-nothing burst of electricity. This burst, or spike, was taken to be the unit of information in the brain corresponding to the bit of information in a computer. This model is still uncritically accepted by practically everyone not directly involved with work in neurophysiology, and underlies the naïve assumption that man is a walking example of a successful digital computer program.

But to begin with, even if the brain did function like a digital computer at some level it would not necessarily provide encouragement for those working in CS or AI. For the brain might be wired like a very large array of randomly connected neurons, such as the perceptrons proposed by the group Minsky dismisses as the early cyberneticists.[1]* Such a neural net can be simulated using a program, but such a program is in no sense a heuristic program. Thus the mere fact that the brain might be a digital computer is in no way ground for optimism as to the success of artificial intelligence as defined by Simon or Minsky.

Moreover, it is an empirical question whether the elementary information processing in the brain can best be understood in terms of a digital model. The brain might "process information" in an entirely different way than a digital computer does. Information might, for example, be processed globally the way a resistor analogue solves the problem of the minimal path through a network. Indeed, current evidence suggests that the neuron-switch model of the brain is no longer empirically tenable. Already in 1956 John von Neumann, one of the inventors of the modern digital computer, had his doubts:

Now, speaking specifically of the human nervous system, this is an enormous mechanism—at least 10^6 times larger than any artifact with which we are familiar —and its activities are correspondingly varied and complex. Its duties include the interpretation of external sensory stimuli, of reports of physical and chemical conditions, the control of motor activities and of internal chemical levels, the memory function with its very complicated procedures for the transformation of and the search for information, and of course, the continuous relaying of coded orders and of more or less quantitative messages. It is possible to handle all these processes by digital methods (i.e., by using numbers and expressing them in the binary system—or, with some additional coding tricks, in the decimal or some other system), and to process the digitalized, and usually numericized, information by algebraical (i.e., basically arithmetical) methods. This is probably the way a human designer would at present approach such a problem. *The available evidence,* though scanty and inadequate, rather *tends to indicate that the human nervous system uses different principles and procedures.* Thus message pulse trains seem to convey meaning by certain analogic traits (within the pulse notation— i.e., this seems to be a mixed, part digital, part analog system), like the time density of pulses in one line, correlations of the pulse time series between different lines in a bundle, etc.[2]

Von Neumann goes on to spell out what he takes to be the "mixed character of living organisms."

The neuron transmits an impulse. . . . The nerve impulse seems in the main to be an all-or-none affair, comparable to a binary digit. Thus a digital element is evidently present, but it is equally evident that this is not the entire story. . . . It is well known that there are various composite functional sequences in the organism which have to go through a variety of steps from the original stimulus to the ultimate effect—some of the steps being neural, that is, digital, and others humoral, that is, analog.

But even this description grants too much to the digital model. It does not follow from the fact that the nerve impulse is an all-or-none affair that any digital processing at all is taking place. The distinction between digital and analogue computation is a logical distinction, not a distinction based on the hardware or the sort of electrical impulses in the system. The essential difference between digital and analogue information processing is that in digital processing a single element represents a symbol in a descriptive language, that is, carries a specific bit of information; while in a device functioning as an analogue computer, continuous physical variables represent the information being processed. The brain, operating with volleys of pulses, would be a digital computer only if each pulse were correlated with some symbol in an information-processing sequence; if, however, the *rate* at which pulses are transmitted turns out to be the minimum unit in an account of the relevant activity of the nervous system—as von Neumann seems to hold—then the brain would be operating as an analogue device.[4]*

Once this conceptual confusion has been cleared up, von Neumann can be understood as suggesting that the brain functions exclusively like an analogue computer, and subsequent work has tended to confirm this hypothesis. Even for those unfamiliar with the technical details of the following report, the conclusion is clear:

In the higher invertebrates we encounter for the first time phenomena such as the graded synaptic potential, which before any post-synaptic impulse has arisen can algebraically add the several incoming presynaptic barrages in a complex way. These incoming barrages are of a different value depending upon the pathway and a standing bias. Indeed, so much can be done by means of this graded and nonlinear local phenomenon prior to the initiation of any post-synaptic impulse that we can no more think of the typical synapse in integrative systems as being a digital device exclusively as was commonly assumed a few years ago, but rather as being a complex analog device. . . .[5]

The latest suggestion from Jerome Lettvin of M.I.T. is that the diameter of the axon may play a crucial role in processing information by acting as a filter.[6] An individual neuron fires at a certain frequency. The diameter of its various axon branches would act as low pass filters at different cutoff frequencies. Output from a given cell would then produce different frequencies at different terminals. The filter characteristics of the axon would vary with its diameter which in turn might be a function of the recency of signals passing down that axon, or even, perhaps, of the activation of immediately environing axons. If such time factors and field interactions play a crucial role, there is no reason to hope that the information processing on the neurophysiological level can be described in a digital formalism or, indeed, in any formalism at all.

In 1966, Walter Rosenblith of M.I.T., one of the pioneers in the use of computers in neuropsychology, summed up the situation:

We no longer hold the earlier widespread belief that the so-called all-or-none law from nerve impulses makes it legitimate to think of relays as adequate models for neurons. In addition, we have become increasingly impressed with the interactions that take place among neurons: in some instances a sequence of nerve impulses may reflect the activities of literally thousands of neurons in a finely graded manner. In a system whose numerous elements interact so strongly with each other, the functioning of the system is not necessarily best understood by proceeding on a neuron-by-neuron basis as if each had an independent personality. . . . Detailed comparisons of the organization of computer systems and brains would prove equally frustrating and inconclusive.[7]

Thus the view that the brain as a general-purpose symbol-manipulating device operates like a digital computer is an empirical hypothesis which has had its day. No arguments as to the possibility of artificial intelligence can be drawn from current empirical evidence concerning the brain. In fact, the *difference* between the "strongly interactive" nature of brain organization and the noninteractive character of machine organization suggests that insofar as arguments from biology are relevant, the evidence is against the possibility of using digital computers to produce intelligence.

4

The Psychological Assumption

Whether the *brain* operates like a digital computer is a strictly empirical question to be settled by neurophysiology. The computer model simply fails to square with the facts. No such simple answer can be given to the related but quite different question: whether the *mind* functions like a digital computer, that is, whether one is justified in using a computer model in psychology. The issue here is much harder to define. The brain is clearly a physical object which uses physical processes to transform energy from the physical world. But if psychology is to differ from biology, the psychologist must be able to describe some level of functioning other than the physical-chemical reactions in the brain.

The theory we shall criticize claims that there is such a level—the information-processing level—and that on this level the mind uses computer processes such as comparing, classifying, searching lists, and so forth, to produce intelligent behavior. This mental level, unlike the physical level, has to be introduced as a possible level of discourse. The issues involved in this discussion will, therefore, be philosophical rather than empirical. We shall see that the assumption of an information-processing level is by no means so self-evident as the cognitive simulators seem to think; that there are good reasons to doubt that there is any information processing going on, and therefore reason to doubt the validity of the claim that the mind functions like a digital computer.

In 1957 Simon predicted that within ten years psychological theories would take the form of computer programs, and he set out to fulfill this prediction by writing a series of programs which were meant to simulate human cognition by simulating the conscious and unconscious steps a person goes through to arrive at a specific cognitive performance. And we have seen that despite the general inadequacy of such programs, admitted even by enthusiasts such as Minsky, all those involved in the general area of artificial intelligence (Minsky included) share the assumption that human beings, when behaving intelligently, *are* following heuristic rules similar to those which would be necessary to enable a digital computer to produce the same behavior.

Moreover, despite meager results, Simon's prediction has nonetheless been partially fulfilled. There has been a general swing from behaviorism to mentalism in psychology. Many influential psychologists and philosophers of psychology have jumped on Simon's bandwagon and begun to pose their problems in terms of computer analogies. Ulric Neisser assumes that "the task of a psychologist trying to understand human cognition is analogous to that of a man trying to discover how a computer has been programmed."[1] And George Miller of Harvard now speaks of "recent developments in our understanding of man viewed as a system for processing information."[2]

Usually no argument is given for this new dogma that man is an information-processing system functioning like a heuristically programmed digital computer. It seems rather to be an unquestioned axiom underlying otherwise careful and critical analysis. There is no doubt some temptation to suppose that since the brain is a physical thing and can be metaphorically described as "processing information," there must be an information-processing level, a sort of flow chart of its operations, in which its information-processing activity can be described. But we have seen in Chapter 3 that just because the brain is physical and processes information is no reason for biologists to suppose that it functions like a digital computer. The same holds for the psychological level. Although psychologists describe that function called the mind as "processing information," this does not mean that it actually processes information in the modern technical sense, nor that it functions like a digital computer, that is, that it has a program.

"Information processing" is ambiguous. If this term simply means that the mind takes account of meaningful data and transforms them into other meaningful data, this is certainly incontrovertible. But the cybernetic theory of information, introduced in 1948 by Claude Shannon, has nothing to do with meaning in this ordinary sense. It is a nonsemantic, mathematical theory of the capacity of communication channels to transmit data. A bit (binary digit) of information tells the receiver which of two equally probable alternatives has been chosen.

In his classic paper "The Mathematical Theory of Communication" Shannon was perfectly clear that his theory, worked out for telephone engineering, carefully excludes as irrelevant the meaning of what is being transmitted.

The fundamental problem of communication is that of reproducing at one point either exactly or approximately a message selected at another point. Frequently the messages have *meaning;* that is they refer to or are correlated according to some system with certain physical or conceptual entities. These semantic aspects of communication are irrelevant to the engineering problem.[3]

Warren Weaver in explaining the significance of Shannon's paper is even more emphatic:

The word *information,* in this theory, is used in a special sense that must not be confused with its ordinary usage. In particular, *information* must not be confused with meaning.

In fact, two messages, one of which is heavily loaded with meaning and the other of which is pure nonsense, can be exactly equivalent, from the present viewpoint, as regards information. It is this, undoubtedly, that Shannon means when he says that "the semantic aspects of communication are irrelevant to the engineering aspects."[4]

When illegitimately transformed into a theory of meaning, in spite of Shannon's warning, information theory and its vocabulary have already built in the computer-influenced assumption that experience can be analyzed into isolable, atomic, alternative choices. As a theory of meaning this assumption is by no means obvious. Gestalt psychologists, for example, claim (as we have seen in Part I and shall argue in detail in Part

III) that thinking and perception involve global processes which cannot be understood in terms of a sequence or even a parallel set of discrete operations.[5]* Just as the brain seems to be, at least in part, an analogue computer, so the mind may well arrive at its thoughts and perceptions by responding to "fields," "force," "configurations," and so on, as, in fact, we seem to do insofar as our thinking is open to phenomenological description.[6]

It is precisely the role of the programmer to make the transition from statements which are meaningful (contain information in the ordinary sense) to the strings of meaningless discrete bits (information in the technical sense) with which a computer operates. The ambition of artificial intelligence is to program the computer to do this translating job itself. But it is by no means obvious that the human translator can be dispensed with.

Much of the literature of Cognitive Simulation gains its plausibility by shifting between the ordinary use of the term "information" and the special technical sense the term has recently acquired. Philosophical clarity demands that we do not foreclose the basic question whether human intelligence presupposes rulelike operations on discrete elements before we begin our analysis. Thus we must be careful to speak and think of "information processing" in quotation marks when referring to human beings.

Moreover, even if the mind did process information in Shannon's sense of the term, and thus function like a digital computer, there is no reason to suppose that it need do so according to a program. If the brain were a network of randomly connected neurons, there might be no flow chart, no series of rule-governed steps on the information-processing level, which would describe its activity.

Both these confusions—the step from ordinary meaning to the technical sense of information and from computer to heuristically programmed digital computer—are involved in the fallacy of moving from the fact that the brain in some sense transforms its inputs to the conclusion that the brain or mind performs some sequence of discrete operations. This fallacy is exhibited in the baldest form in a recent paper by Jerry Fodor. It is instructive to follow his argument.

Fodor begins with generally accepted facts about the central nervous system:

> If the story about the causal determination of depth estimates by texture gradients is true and if the central nervous system is the kind of organ most sensitive people now think it is, then some of the things the central nervous system *does*, some of the physical transactions that take place in the central nervous system when we make estimates of depth, must satisfy such descriptions as 'monitoring texture gradients', 'processing information about texture gradients', 'computing derivatives of texture gradients', etc.[7]

He thus arrives at the view that "every operation of the nervous system is identical with some sequence of elementary operations."[8]

Disregarding the question-begging use of "processing information" in this account, we can still object that computing the first derivative of a texture gradient is the sort of operation very likely to be performed by some sort of analogue device. There is, therefore, no reason at all to conclude from the fact that the nervous system responds to differences in texture gradients that "every operation of the nervous system is identical with some sequence of elementary operations. . . ." There is, indeed, not the slightest justification for the claim that "for each type of behavior in the repertoire of that organism, a putative answer to the question, How does one produce behavior of that type? takes the form of a set of specific instructions for producing the behavior by performing a set of machine operations."[9]

The argument gains its plausibility from the fact that if a psychologist were to take the first derivative of a texture gradient, he would compute it using a formalism (differential calculus) which can be manipulated in a series of discrete operations on a digital computer. But to say that the brain is necessarily going through a series of operations when it takes the texture gradient is as absurd as to say that the planets are necessarily solving differential equations when they stay in their orbits around the sun, or that a slide rule (an analogue computer) goes through the same steps when computing a square root as does a digital computer when using the binary system to compute the same number.

Consider an ion solution which might be capable of taking a texture gradient or of simulating some other perceptual process by reaching equilibrium. Does the solution, in reaching equilibrium, go through the series of discrete steps a digital computer would follow in solving the equations which describe this process? In that case, the solution is solving in moments a problem which it would take a machine centuries to solve—if the machine could solve it at all. Is the solution an ultrarapid computer, or has it got some supposedly clever heuristic like the chess master, which simplifies the problem? Obviously, neither. The fact that we can describe the process of reaching equilibrium in terms of equations and then break up these equations into discrete elements in order to solve them on a computer does not show that equilibrium is actually reached in discrete steps. *Likewise, we need not conclude from the fact that all continuous physicochemical processes involved in human "information processing" can in principle be formalized and calculated out discretely, that any discrete processes are actually taking place.*

Moreover, even if one could write such a computer program for simulating the physicochemical processes in the brain, it would be no help to psychology.

If simulation is taken in its weakest possible sense, a device is simulated by any program which realizes the same input/output function (within the range of interest). Whether achievable for the brain or not, this clearly lacks what is necessary for a psychological theory, namely an account of how the mind actually "works." For psychological *explanation,* a *representation,* somehow stronger than a mere *simulation,* is required. As Fodor notes:

We can say that a machine is *strongly* equivalent to an organism in some respect when it is weakly equivalent in that same respect *and* the processes upon which the behavior of the machine is contingent are of the same type as the processes upon which the behavior of the organism are contingent.[10]

That is, equivalence in the psychological respect demands machine processes, *of the psychological type.*[11]* Psychological operations must be the sort which human beings at least sometimes consciously perform when processing information—for example, searching, sorting, and storing— and not physicochemical processes in the organism. Thus a chess player's report as he zeroed in on his Rook, "And now my brain reaches the following chemical equilibrium, described by the following array of differential equations," would describe physiological processes no doubt correlated with "information processing," but not that "information processing" itself.

Fodor is not clear whether his argument is supposed to be *a priori* or empirical, that is, whether or not he thinks it follows logically or merely contingently from the claim that the brain is taking account of the texture gradient that it is performing a sequence of elementary operations. The fact that he chooses this example, which is one of the least plausible cases in which one would want to argue that the brain or the mind is performing any elementary operations at all, suggests that he thinks there is some kind of necessary connection between taking a texture gradient, computing, and performing a sequence of operations. When this argument is shown to be a series of confusions, however, the advocates of the psychological assumption can always shift ground and claim that theirs is not an *a priori* argument but an empirical conclusion based on their experiments.

Fodor took this tack in defending his paper at the meeting of the American Philosophical Association at which it was delivered, while Miller et al. justify their work strictly on the basis of what they take to be the success of CS.

A Plan is, for an organism, essentially the same as a program for a computer. . . . Newell, Shaw, and Simon have explicitly and systematically used the hierarchical structure of lists in their development of "information-processing languages" that are used to program high-speed digital computers to simulate human thought processes.

Their success in this direction—which the present authors find most impressive and encouraging—argues strongly for the hypothesis that a hierarchical structure is the basic form of organization of human problem-solving.[12]

We have seen in Part I that Newell, Shaw, and Simon's results are far from impressive. What then is this encouraging empirical evidence? We must now look at the way Newell, Shaw, and Simon's work is evaluated.

I. Empirical Evidence for the Psychological Assumption: Critique of the Scientific Methodology of Cognitive Simulation

The empirical justification of the psychological assumption poses a question of scientific methodology—the problem of the evaluation of evidence. Gross similarities of behavior between computers and people do not justify the psychological asumption, nor does the present inability to demonstrate these similarities in detail alone justify its rejection. A test of the psychological assumption requires a detailed comparison of the *steps* involved in human and machine information processing. As we have seen (Chapter 1, Sec. II), Newell, Shaw, and Simon conscientiously note the similarities and differences between human protocols and machine traces recorded during the solution of the same problem. We must now turn to their evaluation of the evidence thus obtained.

Newell and Simon conclude that their work

provide[s] a general framework for understanding problem-solving behavior . . . and finally reveals with great clarity that free behavior of a reasonably intelligent human can be understood as the product of a complex but finite and determinate set of laws.[13]

This is a strangely unscientific conclusion to draw, for Newell and Simon acknowledge that their specific theories—like any scientific theories—must stand or fall on the basis of their *generality,* that is, the *range of phenomena* which can be explained by the programs.[14] Yet their program is nongeneral in at least three ways. The available evidence has necessarily been restricted to those most favorable cases where the subject can to some extent articulate his information-processing protocols (game playing and the solution of simple problems) to the exclusion of pattern recognition and the acquisition and use of natural language. Moreover, even in these restricted areas the machine trace can only match the performance of one individual, and only after *ad hoc* adjustments. And finally, even the match is only partial. Newell and Simon note that their program "provides a complete explanation of the subject's task behavior with five exceptions of varying degrees of seriousness."[15]

In the light of these restrictions it is puzzling how Newell and Simon can claim a "general framework," and in the light of the exceptions it is hard to see how they can claim to have any kind of scientific understanding at all. There seems to be some confusion here concerning the universality of scientific laws or theories. In general, scientific *laws* do not admit of exceptions, yet here the exceptions are honestly noted—as if the frank recognition of these exceptions mitigates their importance; as if Galileo might, for example, have presented the law of falling bodies as holding for all but five objects which were found to fall at a different rate. Not that a scientific conjecture must necessarily be discarded in the face of a few exceptions; there are scientifically sanctioned ways of dealing with such difficulties. One can, to begin with, hold on to the generalization as a working hypothesis and wait to announce a scientific law until the exceptions are cleared up. A working hypothesis need not explain *all* the data. When, however, the scientist claims to present a *theory*, let alone a "general framework for understanding," he must deal with these exceptions either by subsuming them under the theory (as in the appeal to friction to explain deviations from the laws of motion), or by suggesting where to look for an explanation, or at least by showing how, according to the theory, one would expect such difficulties. Newell and Simon take none of these lines.

They might argue that there is no cause for concern, that there are exceptions to even the best theories. In his study of scientific revolutions, Thomas Kuhn notes the persistence of anomalies in all normal science.

There are always some discrepancies. . . . Even the most stubborn ones usually respond at last to normal practice. Very often scientists are willing to wait, particularly if there are many problems available in other parts of the field. We have already noted, for example, that for sixty years after Newton's original computation, the predicted motion of the moon's perigee remained only half of that observed.[16]

But this cannot be a source of comfort for Newell and Simon. Such tolerance of anomalies assumes that there already is an ongoing science, an "accepted paradigm" which "must seem better than its competitors.''[17] This supposes that the theory works perfectly in at least some clearly defined area. But Newell and Simon's cognitive theory is not only not general. It does not work even in a carefully selected special case. It is just where we would have to find a perfect match in order to establish a paradigm that we find the exceptions. Thus Newell and Simon's work, even though it offers some surprising approximations, does not establish a functioning science which would justify a claim to have found general laws even in the face of anomalies.

In discussing the Newtonian anomaly above, Kuhn goes on to point out that "Europe's best mathematical physicists continued to wrestle unsuccessfully with the well-known discrepancy. . . ."[18] The absence of this sort of concern further distinguishes Newell and Simon's work from normal scientific practice. After noting their exceptions, no one in CS— least of all Newell and Simon—seems interested in trying to account for them. Rather all go on to formulate, in some new area, further *ad hoc* rough generalizations.

There is one other acceptable way of dealing with exceptions. If one knew, on *independent grounds,* that mental processes *must* be the product of a rule-governed sequence of discrete operations, then exceptions could be dealt with as accidental difficulties in the experimental technique, or challenging cases still to be subsumed under the law. Only then would those involved in the field have a right to call each program which simulated intelligent behavior—no matter how approximately—an achievement and to consider all setbacks nothing but challenges for sharper heuristic hunting and further programming ingenuity. The problem, then, is how to justify independently the assumption that all human "information processing" proceeds by discrete steps. Otherwise the exceptions, along with the narrow range of application of the programs and the lack of progress during the last ten years, would tend to disconfirm rather than confirm this hypothesis. The "justification" seems to have two stages.

In the early literature, instead of attempting to justify this important and questionable digital-assumption, Newell and Simon present it as a postulate, a working hypothesis which directs their investigation. "We postulate that the subject's behavior is governed by a program organized from a set of elementary information processes."[19] This postulate, which alone might seem rather arbitrary, is in turn sanctioned by the basic methodological principle of parsimony. According to Newell, Shaw, and Simon, this principle enjoins us to assume *tentatively* the most simple hypothesis, in this case that all information processing resembles that sort of processing which can be programmed on a digital computer. We can suppose, for example, that in chess, when our subject is zeroing in, he is unconsciously counting out. In general, whenever the machine trace shows steps which the subject did not report, the principle of parsimony justifies picking a simple working hypothesis as a guide to experimentation and assuming that the subject unconsciously went through these steps. But of course further investigation must *support* the working hypothesis; otherwise, it must eventually be discarded.

The divergence of the protocols from the machine trace, as well as the difficulties raised by planning, indicate that things are not so simple as our craving for parsimony leads us to hope. In the light of these difficulties, it would be natural to revise the working hypothesis, just as scientists had to give up Newtonian Mechanics when it failed to account for certain observations; but at this point, research in Cognitive Simulation deviates from acceptable scientific procedures. In summarizing their work in CS, Newell and Simon conclude:

There is a growing body of evidence that the elementary information processes used by the human brain in thinking are highly similar to a subset of the elementary information processes that are incorporated in the instruction codes of the present-day computers.[20]

What is this growing body of evidence? Have the gaps in the protocols been filled and the exceptions explained? Not at all. The growing body of evidence seems to be the very programs whose lack of universality would cast doubt on the whole project but for the independent assumption of the information-processing hypothesis. Given the exceptions, the psychological assumption would have to already have been taken as independently justified, for the specific programs to be presented as established theories; yet now the assumption is recognized as an hypothesis whose sole confirmation rests on the success of the specific programs. An hypothesis based on a methodological principle is often confirmed later by the facts. What is unusual and inadmissible is that, in this case, the hypothesis *produces* the evidence by which it is later confirmed.

No independent, empirical evidence exists for the psychological assumption. In fact, the same empirical evidence presented for the assumption that the mind functions like a digital computer tends, when considered without making this assumption, to show that the assumption is empirically untenable.

This particular form of methodological confusion is restricted to those working in Cognitive Simulation, but even workers in Artificial Intelligence share this belief in the soundness of heuristic programs, this tendency to think of all difficulties as accidental, and this refusal to consider any setbacks as disconfirming evidence. Concluding from the small area in which search procedures are partially successful, workers of both schools find it perfectly clear that the unknown and troublesome areas are of exactly the same sort. Thus, all workers proceed as if the credit of the psychological assumption were assured, even if all do not—like those in Cognitive Simulation—attempt to underwrite the credit with a loan for which it served as collateral. For workers in the field, the psychological assumption seems not to be an empirical hypothesis that can be supported or disconfirmed, but some sort of philosophical axiom whose truth is assured *a priori*.

II. *A Priori* Arguments for the Psychological Assumption

A clue to the *a priori* character of this axiom can be gained from another look at the way Miller et al. introduce their computer model. The same page which concludes that Simon's success argues strongly for their position opens with a statement of their aims:

Any *complete description of behavior* should be adequate to serve as *a set of instructions,* that is, it should have the characteristics of a plan that could guide the action described.[21]

Miller et al. assume that our very notion of explanation or complete description *requires* that behavior be described in terms of a set of instructions, that is, a sequence of determinate responses to determinate situations. No wonder psychologists such as Newell, Neisser, and Miller find work in Cognitive Simulation encouraging. In their view, if psychology is to be possible at all, an explanation *must* be expressible as a computer program. This is not an empirical observation but follows from their definition of explanation. Divergences from the protocol and failures can be ignored. No matter how ambiguous the empirical results in Cognitive Simulation, they *must* be a first step toward a more adequate theory.

This definition of explanation clearly needs further investigation: Does it make sense? Even if it does, can one prejudge the results in psychology by insisting theories must be computer programs because otherwise psychology isn't possible? Perhaps, psychology as understood by the cognitive simulationists is a dead end.

To begin with it is by no means clear what the pronouncement that a complete description must take the form of a set of instructions means. Consider the behavior involved in selecting, on command, a red square from a multicolored array of geometrical figures. A *complete* description of that behavior according to Miller et al. would be a set of instructions, a plan to follow in carrying out this task. What instructions could one give a person about to undertake this action? Perhaps some very general rules such as listen to the instructions, look toward the objects, consider the shapes, make your selection. But what about the detailed instructions for identifying a square rather than a circle? One might say: "Count the sides; if there are four, it is a square." And what about the instructions for identifying a side? "Take random points and see if they fall on a line which is the shortest distance between the end points," and so on. And how does one find these points? After all, there are no points in the field of experience when I am confronting a display of geometrical figures. Perhaps here the instructions run out and one just says: "But you unconsciously see points and unconsciously count." But do you? And why do the instructions stop here and not earlier or later? And if all this does not seem strange enough, what instructions do you give someone for distinguishing red from blue? At this point it is no longer clear why or how a complete description in psychology should take the form of a set of instructions.

Still such a claim is the heir to a venerable tradition. Kant explicitly analyzed all experience, even perception, in terms of rules, and the notion that knowledge involves a set of explicit instructions is even older. In fact, we have seen that the conviction that a complete description involving an analysis into instructions must be possible, because only such an analysis enables us to *understand* what is going on, goes back to the beginning of philosophy, that is, to the time when our concepts of understanding and reason were first formulated. Plato, who formulated this analysis of understanding in the *Euthyphro,* goes on to ask in the *Meno* whether the rules required to make behavior intelligible to the philosopher are necessarily followed by the person who exhibits the behavior. That is, are the rules only necessary if the philosopher is to *understand* what is going on, or are these rules necessarily followed by the person insofar as he is able to behave intelligently? Since Plato generally thought of most skills as just pragmatic puttering, he no doubt held that rules were not involved in understanding (or producing) skilled behavior. But in the case of theorem proving or of moral action, Plato thought that although people acted without necessarily being aware of any rules, their action did have a rational structure which could be explicated by the philosopher, and he asks whether the mathematician and the moral agent are implicitly following this program when behaving intelligently.

This is a decisive issue for the history of our concepts of understanding and explanation. Plato leaves no doubt about his view: any action which is in fact sensible, i.e., nonarbitrary, has a rational structure which can be expressed in terms of some theory and any person taking such action will be following, at least implicitly, this very theory taken as a set of rules. For Plato, these instructions are already in the mind, preprogrammed in a previous life, and can be made explicit by asking the subjects the appropriate questions.[22] Thus, for Plato, a theory of human behavior which allows us to *understand what* a certain segment of that behavior accomplishes is also an *explanation* of *how* that behavior is produced. Given this notion of understanding and this identification of understanding and explanation, one is bound to arrive at the cognitive simulationists with their assumption that it is self-evident that a complete description of behavior is a precise set of instructions for a digital computer, and that these rules can actually be used to program computers to *produce* the behavior in question.

We have already traced the history of this assumption that thinking is calculating.[23] We have seen that its *attraction* harks back to the Platonic realization that moral life would be more bearable and knowledge more definitive if it were true. Its *plausibility,* however, rests only on a confusion between the mechanistic assumptions underlying the success of modern physical science and a correlative formalistic assumption underlying what would be a science of human behavior if such existed.

On one level, this *a priori* assumption makes sense. Man is an object. The success of modern physical science has assured us that a *complete description* of the behavior of a physical object can be expressed in precise laws, which in turn can serve as instructions to a computer which can then, at least in principle, simulate this behavior. This leads to the idea of a neurophysiological description of human behavior in terms of inputs of energy, physical-chemical transactions in the brain, and outputs in terms of motions of the physical body, all, in principle, simulatable on a digital machine.

This level of description makes sense, at least at first approximation, and since the time of Descartes has been part of the idea of a total physical description of all the objects in the universe. The brain is clearly an energy-transforming organ. It detects incoming signals; for example, it detects changes in light intensity correlated with changes in texture gradient. Unfortunately for psychologists, however, this physical description, excluding as it does all psychological terms, is in no way a *psychological* explanation. On this level one would not be justified in speaking of human agents, the mind, intentions, perceptions, memories, or even of colors or sounds, as psychologists want to do. Energy is being received and transformed and that is the whole story.

There is, of course, another level—let us call it phenomenological—

on which it does make sense to talk of human agents, acting, perceiving objects, and so forth. On this level what one sees are tables, chairs, and other people, what one hears are sounds and sometimes words and sentences, and what one performs are meaningful actions in a context already charged with meaning. But this level of description is no more satisfactory to a psychologist than the physiological level, since here there is no awareness of following instructions or rules; there is no place for a psychological *explanation* of the sort the cognitive simulationist demands. Faced with this conceptual squeeze, psychologists have always tried to find a third level on which they can do their work, a level which is *psychological* and yet offers an *explanation* of behavior.

If psychology is to be a science of human behavior, it must study man as an object. But not as a physical object, moving in response to inputs of physical energy, since that is the task of physics and neurophysiology. The alternative is to try to study human behavior as the response of some other sort of object to some other sort of input. Just what this other sort of object and input are is never made clear, but whatever they are, if there is to be an *explanation,* man must be treated as some device responding to discrete elements, according to laws. These laws can be modeled on causal laws describing how *fixed propensities* in the organism interact with inputs from the environment to produce complex forms of behavior. The device, then, is a reflex machine, and the laws are the laws of association. This gives us the empiricist psychology of David Hume with its modern descendant, S–R psychology. Or the object can be treated as an information-processing device and the laws can be understood on the Kantian model, as *reasons,* which are *rules in the mind* applied by the mind to the input. In psychology this school was called idealist, intellectualist, or mentalist, and is now called "cognitive psychology."

Until the advent of the computer the empiricist school had the edge because the intellectualist view never succeeded in treating man as a calculable object. There was always a subject, a "transcendental ego," applying the rules, which simply postponed a scientific theory of behavior by installing a little man (homunculus) in the mind to guide its actions. Computers, however, offer the irresistible attraction of operating according to rules without appeal to a transcendental ego or homunculus. Moreover, computer programs provide a model for the analysis of behavior such as speaking a natural language which seems to be too complex to be accounted for in terms of S–R psychology. In short, there is now a device which can serve as a model for the mentalist view, and it is inevitable that regardless of the validity of the arguments or the persuasiveness of the empirical evidence, psychologists dissatisfied with behaviorism will clutch at this high-powered straw.

A computer is a physical object, but to describe its operation, one does not describe the vibrations of the electrons in its transistors, but rather the levels of organization of its on/off flip/flops. If psychological concepts can be given an interpretation in terms of the higher levels of organization of these rule-governed flip/flops, then psychology will have found a language in which to explain human behavior.

The rewards are so tempting that the basic question, whether this third level between physics and phenomenology is a coherent level of discourse or not, is not even posed. But there are signs of trouble. The language of books such as those by Miller et al., Neisser, and Fodor is literally incoherent. On almost every page one finds sentences such as the following:

When an *organism executes* a Plan *he* proceeds step by step, completing one part and then moving to the next.[24]*

Here all three levels exist in unstable and ungrammatical suspension. "When an *organism* [biological] *executes* [machine analogy borrowed from human agent] a Plan *he* [the human agent] . . ." Or, one can have it the other way around and instead of the organism being personified, one can find the mind mechanized. Fodor speaks of "mental processing,"[25] or "mental operations,"[26] as if it were clear what such a form of words could possibly mean.

This new form of gibberish would merely be bizarre if it did not reveal more serious underlying conceptual confusions. These are implicit in the work of Miller et al. but become clear in the works of Neisser and Fodor, who, of all the writers in this area, make the greatest effort to articulate their philosophical presuppositions. The confusion can best be brought to light by bearing firmly in mind the neurophysiological and phenomenological levels of description and then trying to locate the psychological level somewhere between these two.

In trying to make a place for the information-processing level Neisser tells us:

There is certainly a real world of trees and people and cars and even books. . . . However, we have no immediate access to the world nor to any of its properties.[27]

This is certainly true insofar as man is regarded as a physical object.[28]* As Neisser puts it, ". . . the sensory input is not the page itself; it is a pattern of light rays. . . ."[29] So far so good, but then, Neisser goes on to bring the physical and the phenomenological levels together: "Suitably focussed by the lens . . . the rays fall on the sensitive retina, where they can initiate the neural processes that *eventually lead to seeing and reading and remembering.*"[30] Here, however, things are by no means obvious. There are two senses of "lead to." Light waves falling on the retina *eventually lead to* physical and chemical processes in the brain, but in this sequential sense, the light rays and neural processes can never eventually lead to seeing.[31]* Seeing is not a chemical process; thus it is not a final step in a series of such processes. If, on the other hand, "lead to" means "necessary and sufficient condition for," then, either seeing is the whole chain or something totally different from the chain or any link of it. In either case it is no longer clear why Neisser says we have no immediate access to the perceptual world.

Once the neural and phenomenological levels have thus been illegitimately amalgamated into one series, which stands between the person and the world, a new vocabulary is required. This no-man's-land is described in terms of "sensory input" and its "transformations."

As used here, the term "cognition" refers to all the processes by which the *sensory input* is *transformed,* reduced, elaborated, stored, recovered, and used. . . . Such terms as sensation, perception, imagery, retention, recall, problem-solving, and thinking, among many others, refer to hypothetical stages or aspects of cognition.[32]

Once a "sensory input" which differs from the world we normally see has been introduced, it seems necessary that our perception be "developed from," or a "transformation of" this "stimulus input."[33]* But what this transformation means depends on the totally ambiguous notion of "stimulus input." If the input is energy, then it is only necessary that it be transformed into other energy—the processes in the brain are surely physical from beginning to end. Matter-energy can be transformed, reduced, elaborated, stored, recovered, and used, but it will never be anything but matter-energy. If, however, the stimulus is some sort of primitive *perception,* as Neisser later seems to suggest—"a second stimulus will have some effect on how the first brief one is perceived"[34]—then we have to know more about what this new percept is. Philosophers have ceased to believe in sense data, and if Neisser has some notion of a primitive percept, it cannot be introduced without a great deal of argument and evidence. Phenomenologically we directly perceive physical objects. We are aware of neither sense data nor light rays. If Neisser wants to shift his notion of input from physical to perceptual, it is up to him to explain what sort of perception he has in mind, and what evidence he has that such a percept, which is neither a pattern of light rays nor a perspectival view of a physical object, exists.

"Information" is the concept which is supposed to rescue us from this confusion. Neisser says *"Information* is what is transformed, and the structured pattern of its transformation is what we want to understand."[35] But as long as the notion of "stimulus input" is ambiguous, it remains unclear what information is and how it is supposed to be related to the "stimulus input," be it energy or direct perception.

Finally, in a dazzling display of conceptual confusion, these two interdependent and ambiguous notions, "stimulus input" and "information," are combined in the "central assertion" of the book:

The central assertion is that seeing, hearing, and remembering are all acts of *construction,* which may make more or less use of stimulus information [*sic*] depending on circumstances. The constructive processes are assumed to have two stages of which the first is fast, crude, wholistic, and parallel, while the second is deliberate, attentive, detailed, and sequential.[36]

The ambiguity of "stimulus information" and the subsequent incoherence of the conceptual framework underlying this approach and its consequences can best be seen by following a specific example. Let us take Neisser's analysis of the perception of a page.

> If we see moving objects as unified things, it must be because perception results from an integrative process over time. The same process is surely responsible for the construction of visual objects from the successive "snapshots" taken by the moving eye.[37]

The question to be asked here is: What are these snapshots? Are they "patterns of energy" or are they momentary pictures of a page? If they are patterns of energy they are in no sense perceived, and are integrated not by the subject (the perceiver) but by the brain as a physical object. On the other hand, on the phenomenological level, we do not have to integrate distinct snapshots of the page at all. The page is steadily seen, and the notion that it is seen as a series of "snapshots" or "inputs" is an abstraction from this continuously presented page. Of course, this steadily seen page is correlated with some "processing," but not the processing of rudimentary perceptual objects, or "snapshots"—which could only give rise to the question of how these elementary perceptual objects were themselves "constructed"—but the processing of some fluctuating pattern of energy bombarding the eye.[38]*

This conceptual confusion, which results from trying to define a level of discourse between the physiological and the phenomenological, is even more pronounced in Fodor's work, because he tries even harder to be clear on just these points. In discussing the perception of visual and acoustic patterns Fodor notes that "the concept you have of a face, or a tune, or a shape . . . includes a representation of the formal structure of each of these domains and the act of recognition involves the application of such information to the integration of current sensory inputs."[39]

One wonders again what "sensory input" means here. If the "sensory input" is already a face, or a tune, or a shape, then the job is already done. On the other hand, if the "sensory input" is the physical energy reaching the sense organ, then it is impossible to understand what Fodor means by the "application" of a "concept" or of "information" to the integration of such inputs, since what would integrate such physical energy would surely be further energy transformations.

Of course, if we begged the question and assumed that the brain is a digital computer, then sense could be made of the notion that a concept is a formal structure for organizing data. In that case the "sensory input" would be neither a percept nor a pattern of energy, but a series of bits, and the concept would be a set of instructions for relating these bits to other bits already received, and classifying the result. This would amount to an hypothesis that human behavior can be understood on the model of a digital computer. It would require a theory of just what these bits are and would then have to be evaluated on the basis of empirical evidence.

But for Fodor, as for Miller et al., the notion of "sensory input" and of a concept as a rule for organizing this input seems to need no justification but rather to be contained in the very notion of a psychological explanation.

Insofar as it seeks to account for behavior, a psychological theory may be thought of as a function that maps an infinite set of possible inputs to an organism onto an infinite set of possible outputs.[40]

As a conceptual analysis of the relation of perception and behavior, which is supposed to be accepted independently of empirical assumptions about the brain, such an account is incomprehensible.

As with Neisser, this incoherence can best be seen in a specific case. Fodor takes up the problem of how "we have learned to hear as similar" —as one melody—"what may be physically quite different sequences of tones."[41] Here the question-begging nature of the analysis is clear: Are these sequences of tones physical or phenomenal? Are they patterns of sound waves or percepts? The talk of their physical difference suggests the former. And indeed on the level of physical energy it is no doubt true that inputs of energy of various frequencies are correlated with the same perceptual experience. The energy transformations involved will presumably someday be discovered by neurophysiologists. But such *physical* sequences of tones cannot be "heard"—we do not hear frequencies; we hear sounds—and thus *a fortiori* these frequencies cannot be "heard as similar." If, on the other hand, we try to understand the input as sequences of *phenomenal* tones, which it would make sense to "hear as similar," then we are on the level of perception, and unfortunately for Fodor the problem of how we hear these sequences of tones as similar vanishes; for in order to pose the problem in the first place we have already assumed that the phenomenal tone sequences are heard as similar. On the phenomenal level we hear them as similar because they sound similar.

To put it another way, Fodor speaks of "which note in particular (i.e., which absolute values of key, duration, intensity, stress, pitch, amplitude, etc.) we expect after hearing the first few notes of a performance of Lilliburlero. . . ."[42] But we do not "expect" any "absolute values" at all. We expect notes *in a melody.* The absolute values pose a problem for the neurophysiologist with his oscilloscope, or for someone hearing the notes in isolation, not for the perceiver.

If we did perceive and expect these "absolute values," we would indeed need the "elaborate conceptualism" defended by Fodor, in order to recognize the same melody in various sequences:

It is unclear how to account for the ability to recognize identity of type despite gross variations among tokens unless we assume that the concepts employed in recognition are of formidable abstractness. But then it is unclear how the *application* of such concepts . . . is to be explained, unless one assumes psychological mechanisms whose operations must be complicated in the extreme.[43]

Here the confusion shows up in the use of "token" and "type." What are these tokens? The perceived phenomenal sound sequence (the melody) cannot be an abstraction (a type) of which the physical energy inputs are instantiations (tokens). The percept and the physical energy are equally concrete and are totally different sorts of phenomena. No amount of complication can bridge the gap between shifting energy inputs and the perception of an enduring sound. One is not an instantiation of the other. But neither can the tokens be taken to be the phenomenal sequence of isolated absolute tones (as a sense data theorist would have it). In listening to a melody absolute tones are not perceived, so under this interpretation there would be no tokens at all.

Even if one assumes that Fodor has in mind the physical model, which could be computerized, this kind of pattern recognition could conceivably be accomplished by a neural net or by an analogue device, if it could be accomplished at all. There is no reason to suppose that it is accomplished by a heuristic program (a set of abstract concepts), let alone that such a program is a conceptual necessity.

Yet Fodor never questions the assumption that there is an information-processing level on which energy transformation can be discussed in terms of a sequence of specific operations. His only question is: How can we tell that we and the machine have the same program, that is, perform the same operations? Thus, for example, after asking how one could know whether one had a successful machine simulation, Fodor replies: ". . . we need only accept the convention that we individuate forms of behavior by reference not solely to the observable gestures output by an organism but also to *the sequence of mental operations that underlie those gestures.*"[44]

Or even more baldly:

strong equivalence requires that the operations that underlie the production of machine behavior be of the same type as the operations that underlie the production of organic behavior.[45]

It should now be clear that Fodor's argument depends on two sorts of assumptions: First, like Miller et al. and Neisser, he introduces the ambiguous notion of "input" to allow a level of description on which it seems to make sense to analyze perception as if man were a computer receiving some sort of data called "stimulus information." This amounts to the assumption that besides energy processing, "data processing is involved in perception."[46]

Fodor then makes two further assumptions of a second sort, of which he seems to be unaware: (1) that this data processing takes place as if on a digital computer, that is, consists of discrete operations, and (2) that this digital computer operates serially according to something like a heuristic program, so that one can speak of a sequence of such operations. Fodor's defense of his "elaborate conceptualism," of his notion that perception requires complicated mental operations, seems to turn on thus dogmatically introducing information processing and then simply overlooking all alternative forms of computers and even alternative forms of digital data processing. This blindness to alternatives can be seen in the conclusion of Fodor's discussion of such phenomena as the recognition of melodies:

Characteristically such phenomena have to do with "constancies"—that is, cases in which normal perception involves radical and uniform departure from the informational content of the physical input. It has been recognized since Helmholtz that such cases provide the best argument for *unconscious mental operations for there appears to be no alternative to invoking such operations if we are to explain the disparity between input and percept.*[47]

Fodor's whole discussion of the logic of computer simulation is vitiated by his unquestioned reliance on these questionable assumptions. The ease with which his nonarguments pass for conceptual analysis reveals the grip of the Platonic tradition, and the need to believe in the information-processing level if psychology is to be a science.

Of course, the use of the computer as a model is legitimate as long as it is recognized as an hypothesis. But in the writing of Miller et al., Neisser, and Fodor, as we have seen, this hypothesis is treated as an *a priori* truth, as if it were the result of a conceptual analysis of behavior.

Occasionally one glimpses an empirical basis for this assumption: Fodor's argument for the legitimacy of a computer program as a psychological theory ultimately rests on the hypothetical supposition "that we have a machine that satisfies whatever experimental tests we can devise for correspondences between its repertoire and that of some organism."[48] However, this covertly empirical character of the argument is implicitly denied since the whole discussion is couched in terms of "sequences of mental operations," as if it were already certain that such a machine could exist.

Only if such a machine existed, and only if it did indeed operate in sequences of steps, would one be justified in using the notions connected with heuristically programmed digital computers to suggest and interpret experiments in psychology. But to decide whether such an intelligent machine can exist, and therefore whether such a conceptual framework is legitimate, one must first try to program such a machine, or evaluate the programs already tried. To use computer language as a *self-evident* and *unquestionable* way of formulating the conceptional framework in terms of which experiments are undertaken and understood without valid *a priori* arguments or an empirical existence-proof of the possibility of such a machine, can only lead to confusion.

Conclusion

So we again find ourselves moving in a vicious circle. We saw at the end of Section I of this chapter that the empirical results, riddled with unexplained exceptions, and unable to simulate higher-order processes such as zeroing in and essential/inessential discrimination, are only promising if viewed in terms of an *a priori* assumption that the mind must work like a heuristically programmed digital computer. But now we have seen that the only legitimate argument for the assumption that the mind functions like a computer turns on the actual or possible existence of such an intelligent machine.

The answer to the question whether man can make such a machine must rest on the evidence of work being done. And on the basis of actual achievements and current stagnation, the most plausible answer seems to be, No. It is impossible to process an indifferent "input" without distinguishing between relevant and irrelevant, significant and insignificant data. We have seen how Newell, Shaw, and Simon have been able to avoid this problem only by predigesting the data, and how Miller et al. have been able to avoid it only by mistakenly supposing that Newell, Shaw, and Simon had a program which performed this original selection. But if there is no promising empirical evidence, the whole self-supporting argument tumbles down like a house of cards.

The only alternative way to cope with selectivity would be analogue processing, corresponding to the selectivity of our sense organs. But then all processing would no longer be digital, and one would have reason to wonder whether this analogue processing was only peripheral. All of which would cast doubt on the "sequence of operations" and reopen the whole discussion. These difficulties suggest that, although man is surely a physical object processing physical inputs according to the laws of physics and chemistry, man's behavior may not be explainable in terms of an information-processing mechanism processing inputs which represent features of the world. Nothing from physics or experience suggests that man's actions can be so explained, since on the physical level we are confronted with continuously changing patterns of energy, and on the phenomenological level with objects in an already organized field of experience.

An analysis of this field of experience would provide an alternative area of study for psychology. But before we turn to this alternative theory in Part III, we must follow up two other assumptions, which, even if work in CS cannot be defended, seem to lend plausibility to work in AI.

5

The Epistemological Assumption

It should now be evident that it is extremely difficult to define what the mental level of functioning is, and that whatever the mind is, it is by no means obvious that it functions like a digital computer. This makes practically unintelligible the claims of those working in Cognitive Simulation that the mind can be understood as processing information according to heuristic rules. The computer model turns out not to be helpful in explaining what people actually do when they think and perceive, and, conversely, the fact that people do think and perceive can provide no grounds for optimism for those trying to reproduce human performance with digital computers.

But this still leaves open another ground for optimism: although human performance might not be *explainable* by supposing that people are actually following heuristic rules in a sequence of unconscious operations, intelligent behavior may still be *formalizable* in terms of such rules and thus reproduced by machine.[1]* This is the epistemological assumption.

Consider the planets. They are not solving differential equations as they swing around the sun. They are not *following* any rules at all; but their behavior is nonetheless lawful, and to understand their behavior we find a formalism—in this case differential equations—which expresses their behavior as motion *according to* a rule. Or, to take another example:

A man riding a bicycle may be keeping his balance just by shifting his weight to compensate for his tendency to fall. The intelligible content of what he is doing, however, might be expressed according to the rule: wind along a series of curves, the curvature of which is inversely proportional to the square of the velocity.[2]* The bicycle rider is certainly not following this rule consciously, and there is no reason to suppose he is following it unconsciously. Yet this formalization enables us to express or understand his *competence,* that is, what he can accomplish. It is, however, in no way an *explanation* of his *performance.* It tells us what it *is* to ride a bicycle successfully, but nothing of what is going on in his brain or in his mind when he performs the task.

There is thus a subtle but important difference between the psychological and the epistemological assumptions. Both assume the Platonic notion of understanding as formalization, but those who make the psychological assumption (those in CS) suppose that the rules used in the formalization of behavior are *the very same rules* which produce the behavior, while those who make the epistemological assumption (those in AI) only affirm that all nonarbitrary behavior can be formalized according to some rules, and that these rules, whatever they are, can then be used by a computer to reproduce the behavior.

The epistemological assumption is weaker and thus less vulnerable than the psychological assumption. But it is vulnerable nonetheless. Those who fall back on the epistemological assumption have realized that their formalism, as a theory of competence, need not be a theory of *human* performance, but they have not freed themselves sufficiently from Plato to see that a theory of competence may not be adequate as a theory of *machine* performance either. Thus, the epistemological assumption involves two claims: (a) that all nonarbitrary behavior can be formalized, and (b) that the formalism can be used to reproduce the behavior in question. In this chapter we shall criticize claim (a) by showing that it is an unjustified generalization from physical science, and claim (b) by trying to show that a theory of competence cannot be a theory of performance: that unlike the technological application of the laws of physics to produce physical phenomena, a timeless, contextless theory of competence *cannot* be used to reproduce the moment-to-moment involved behavior required for human performance; that indeed there cannot be a *theory* of human performance. If this argument is convincing, the epistemological assumption, in the form in which it seems to support AI, turns out to be untenable, and, correctly understood, argues against the possibility of AI, rather than guaranteeing its success.

Claim (a), that all nonarbitrary behavior can be formalized, is not an axiom. It rather expresses a certain conception of understanding which is deeply rooted in our culture but may nonetheless turn out to be mistaken. We must now turn to the empirical arguments which can be given in support of such a hypothesis. It should also be clear by now that no empirical arguments from the success of AI are acceptable, since it is precisely the interpretation, and, above all, the possibility of significant extension of the meager results such as Bobrow's which is in question.

Since two areas of successful formalization—physics and linguistics— seem to support the epistemological assumption, we shall have to study both these areas. In physics we indeed find a formalism which describes behavior (for example, the planets circling the sun), but we shall see that this sort of formalism can be of no help to those working in AI. In linguistics we shall find, on the other hand, a formalism which is relevant to work in AI, and which argues for the assumption that all nonarbitrary behavior can be formalized, but we will find that this formalism which expresses the *competence* of the speaker—that is, what he is able to accomplish—cannot enable one to use a computer to reproduce his *performance*—that is, his accomplishment.

I. A Mistaken Argument from the Success of Physics

Minsky's optimism—that is, his conviction that all nonarbitrary behavior can be formalized and the resulting formalism used by a digital computer to reproduce that behavior—is a pure case of the epistemological assumption. It is this belief which allows Minsky to assert with confidence that "there is no reason to suppose that machines have any limitations not shared by man."[3] We must now examine the arguments supporting this claim, but first we must be clear what the formalist means by machine.

A digital computer is a machine which operates according to the sort of criteria Plato once assumed could be used to understand any orderly behavior. This machine, as defined by Minsky, who bases his definition on that of Turing, is a "rule-obeying mechanism." As Turing puts it: "The . . . computer is supposed to be following fixed rules. . . . It is the duty of the control to see that these instructions are obeyed correctly and in the right order. The control is so constructed that this necessarily happens."[4] So the machine in question is a restricted but very fundamental sort of mechanism. It operates on determinate, unambiguous bits of data, according to strict rules which apply unequivocally to these data. The claim is made that this sort of machine—a Turing machine—which expresses the essence of a digital computer can, in principle, do anything that human beings can do—that it has, in principle, only those limitations shared by man.

Minsky considers the antiformalist counterclaim that "perhaps there are processes . . . which simply *cannot* be described in any formal language, but which can nevertheless be carried out, e.g., by minds."[5] Rather than answer this objection directly, he refers to Turing's "brilliant" article which, he asserts, contains arguments that "amount . . . to a satisfactory refutation of many such objections."[6] Turing does, indeed, take up this sort of objection. He states it as follows: "It is not possible to produce a set of rules purporting to describe what a man should do in every conceivable set of circumstances."[7] This is presumably Turing's generalization of Wittgenstein's argument that it is impossible to supply normative rules which prescribe in advance the correct use of a word in all situations. Turing's "refutation" is to make a distinction between "rules of conduct" and "laws of behavior" and then to assert that "we cannot so easily convince ourselves of the absence of complete laws of behavior as of complete rules of conduct."[8]

Now as an answer to the Wittgensteinian claim, this is well taken. Turing is in effect arguing that although we cannot formulate the normative rules for the correct application of a particular predicate, this does not show that we cannot formulate the rules which describe how, *in fact*, a particular individual applies such a predicate. In other words, while Turing is ready to admit that it may in principle be impossible to provide a set of rules describing what a person *should* do in every circumstance, he holds there is no reason to doubt that one could in principle discover a set of rules describing what he *would* do. But why does this supposition seem so self-evident that the burden of proof is on those who call it into question? Why should we have to "convince ourselves of the *absence* of complete laws of behavior" rather than of their presence? Here we are face to face again with the epistemological assumption. It is important to try to root out what lends this assumption its implied *a priori* plausibility.

To begin with, "laws of behavior" is ambiguous. In one sense human behavior is certainly lawful, if lawful simply means orderly. But the assumption that the laws in question are the sort that could be embodied in a computer program or some equivalent formalism is a different and much stronger claim, in need of further justification.

The idea that any description of behavior can be formalized in a way appropriate to computer programming leads workers in the field of artificial intelligence to overlook this question. It is assumed that, in principle at least, human behavior can be represented by a set of independent propositions describing the inputs to the organism, correlated with a set of propositions describing its outputs. The clearest statement of this assumption can be found in James Culbertson's move from the assertion that one could build a robot using only flip/flops to the claim that in theory at least it could therefore reproduce all human behavior.

Using suitable receptors and effectors we can connect them together via central cells. *If we could get enough central cells and if they were small enough and if each cell had enough endbulbs and if we could put enough bulbs at each synapse and if we had time enough to assemble them,* then we could construct robots to satisfy *any* given input-output specification, i.e., we could construct robots that would behave in any way we desired under any environmental circumstances. There would be no difficulty in constructing a robot with behavioral properties just like John Jones or Henry Smith or in constructing a robot with any desired behavioral improvements over Jones and Smith.[9]

Or put more baldly:

Since [these complete robots] can, in principle, satisfy any given input-output specifications, they can do any prescribed things under any prescribed circumstances—ingeniously solve problems, compose symphonies, create works of art and literature and engineering, and pursue any goals.[10]

But as we have seen in Chapter 4, it is not clear in the case of human beings what these inputs and outputs are supposed to be.[11]* Culbertson's assumption that the brain can be understood as correlating isolated bits of data rests on the assumption that the neurons act as on/off switches. Since, as we have seen in Chapter 3, this is probably not the case, there is no reason to suppose, and several reasons to doubt, that human inputs and outputs can be isolated and their correlation formalized. Culbertson's assumption is an assumption and nothing more, and so in no way justifies his conclusions.

The committed formalist, however, has one more move. He can exploit the ambiguity of the notion of "laws of behavior," and take behavior to mean not meaningful human actions, but simply the physical movements of the human organism. Then, since human bodies are part of the physical world and, as we have seen, objects in the physical world have been shown to obey laws which can be expressed in a formalism manipulable on a digital computer, the formalist can still claim that there must be laws of human behavior of the sort required by his formalism. To be more specific, if the nervous system obeys the laws of physics and chemistry, which we have every reason to suppose it does, then even if it is not a digital computer, and even if there is no input-output function directly describing the behavior of the human being, we still ought to be able to reproduce the behavior of the nervous system with some physical device which might, for example, take the form of a new sort of "analogue computer" using ion solutions whose electrical properties change with various local saturations. Then, as we pointed out in Chapter 4, knowing the composition of the solutions in this device would enable us at least in principle to write the physicochemical equations describing such wet components and to solve these equations on a dry digital computer.

Thus, given enough memory and time, any computer—even such a special sort of analogue computer—could be simulated on a digital machine. In general, by accepting the fundamental assumptions that the nervous system is part of the physical world and that all physical processes can be described in a mathematical formalism which can in turn be manipulated by a digital computer, one can arrive at the strong claim that the behavior which results from human "information processing," whether directly formalizable or not, can always be indirectly reproduced on a digital machine.

This claim may well account for the formalist's smugness, but what in fact is justified by the fundamental truth that every form of "information processing" (even those which *in practice* can only be carried out on an "analogue computer") must *in principle* be simulable on a digital computer? We have seen it does not prove the mentalist claim that, even when a human being is unaware of using discrete operations in processing information, he must nonetheless be unconsciously following a set of instructions. Does it justify the epistemological assumption that all nonarbitrary behavior can be formalized?

One must delimit what can count as information processing in a computer. A digital computer solving the equations describing an analogue information-processing device and thus simulating its *function* is not thereby simulating its "information processing." It is not processing the information which is processed by the simulated analogue, but *entirely different information* concerning the physical or chemical properties of the analogue. Thus the strong claim that *every form of information* can be processed by a digital computer is misleading. One can only show that for any given type of information a digital computer can in principle be programmed to simulate a device which can process that information.

Thus understood as motion—as the input and output of physical signals—human behavior is presumably completely lawful in the sense the formalists require. But this in no way supports the formalist assumption as it appears in Minsky and Turing. For when Minsky and Turing claim that man is a Turing machine, they cannot mean that a man is a physical system. Otherwise it would be appropriate to say that planes or boats are Turing machines. Their behavior, too, can be described by mathematically formulable laws—relating their intake and output of energy—and can at least in principle be reproduced to any degree of accuracy on a digital computer. No, when Minsky or Turing claims that man can be understood as a Turing machine, they must mean that a digital computer can reproduce human behavior, not by solving physical equations but by *processing data representing facts about the world using logical operations* that can be reduced to matching, classifying, and Boolean operations. As Minsky puts it:

Mental processes resemble . . . the kinds of processes found in computer programs: arbitrary symbol associations, treelike storage schemes, conditional transfers, and the like.[12]

Workers in AI are claiming that there is such a *mental level* of symbolic descriptions which can be described in a digital formalism. All AI research is dedicated to using logical operations to manipulate data *representing the world,* not to solving physical equations describing physical objects. Considerations from physics show only that inputs of energy, and the neurological activity involved in transforming them, can in principle be described and manipulated in digital form.

No one has tried, or hopes to try, to use the laws of physics to calculate in detail the motion of human bodies. Indeed, this may well be physically impossible, for H. J. Bremermann has shown that:

No data processing system whether artificial or living can process more than (2×10^{47}) bits per second per gram of its mass.[13]

Bremermann goes on to draw the following conclusions:

There are $\pi \times 10^7$ seconds in a year. The age of the earth is about 10^9 years, its mass less than 6×10^{27} grams. Hence even a computer of the size of the earth could not process more than 10^{93} bits during a time equal to the age of the earth. [Not to mention the fact, one might add, that the bigger the computer the more the speed of light would be a factor in slowing down its operation.] . . . Theorem proving and problem solving . . . lead to exponentially growing problem trees. If our conjecture is true then it seems that the difficulties that are currently encountered in the field of pattern recognition and theorem proving will not be resolved by sheer speed of data processing by some future super-computers.[14]

If these calculations are correct, there is a special kind of impossibility involved in any attempt to simulate the brain as a physical system. *The enormous calculations necessary may be precluded by the very laws of physics and information theory such calculations presuppose.*

Yet workers in the field of AI from Turing to Minsky seem to take refuge in this confusion between physical laws and information-processing rules to convince themselves that there is reason to suppose that human behavior can be formalized; that the burden of proof is on those who claim that "there are processes . . . which simply cannot be described in a formal language but which can nevertheless be carried out, e.g., by minds."[15] Once we have set straight the equivocation between physical laws and information-processing rules, what argument remains that human behavior, at what AI workers have called "the information processing level," can be described in terms of strict rules?

II. A Mistaken Argument from the Success of Modern Linguistics

If no argument based on the success of physics is relevant to the success of AI, because AI is concerned with formalizing human behavior not physical motion, the only hope is to turn to areas of the behavioral sciences themselves. Galileo was able to found modern physics by abstracting from many of the properties and relations of Aristotelian physics and finding that the mathematical relations which remained were sufficient to describe the motion of objects. What would be needed to justify the formalists' optimism would be a Galileo of the mind who, by making the right abstractions, could find a formalism which would be sufficient to describe human behavior.

John McCarthy expresses this longing for a rapprochement between physics and the behavioral sciences:

Although formalized theories have been devised to express the most important fields of mathematics and some progress has been made in formalizing certain empirical sciences, there is at present no formal theory in which one can express the kind of means-ends analysis used in ordinary life. . . . Our approach to the artificial-intelligence problem requires a formal theory.[16]

Recently such a breakthrough has occurred. Chomsky and the transformational linguists have found that by abstracting from human *performance*—the use of particular sentences on particular occasions—they can formalize what remains, that is, the human ability to recognize grammatically well-formed sentences and to reject ill-formed ones. That is, they can provide a formal theory of much of linguistic *competence*.[17]* This success is a major source of encouragement for those in AI who are committed to the view that human behavior can be formalized without reduction to the physical level, for such success tends to confirm at least the first half of the epistemological hypothesis. A segment of orderly behavior which at first seems nonrulelike turns out to be describable in terms of complex rules, rules of the sort which can be processed directly by a digital computer (directly—that is, without passing by way of a physical description of the motions of the vocal cords of a speaker or the physiochemical processes taking place in his brain).

But such a formalization only provides justification for half the epistemological hypothesis. Linguistic competence is not what AI workers wish to formalize. If machines are to communicate in natural language, their programs must not only incorporate the rules of grammar; they must also contain rules of linguistic performance. In other words, what was omitted in order to be able to formalize syntactic theory—the fact that people are able to *use* their language—is just what must also be formalized.

The question whether the epistemological hypothesis is justified thus comes down to the test case: is there reason to suppose that there can be a formal theory of what linguists call pragmatics? There are two reasons to believe that such a generalization of syntactic theory is impossible: (1) An argument of principle (to which we shall turn in the next chapter): for there to be a formal theory of pragmatics, one would have to have a theory of all human knowledge; but this may well be impossible. (2) A descriptive objection (to which we shall now turn): not all linguistic behavior is rulelike. We recognize some linguistic expressions as odd —as breaking the rules —and yet we are able to understand them.

There are cases in which a native speaker recognizes that a certain linguistic usage is odd and yet is able to understand it—for example, the phrase "The idea is in the pen" is clear in a situation in which we are discussing promising authors; but a machine at this point, with rules for what size physical objects can be in pig pens, playpens, and fountain pens, would not be able to go on. Since an idea is not a physical object, the machine could only deny that it could be in the pen or at best make an arbitrary stab at interpretation. The listener's understanding, on the other hand, is far from arbitrary. Knowing what he does about the shadow which often falls between human projects and their execution, as well as what one uses to write books, he gets the point, and the speaker will often agree on the basis of the listener's response that the listener has understood. Does it follow, then, that in understanding or using the odd utterance, the human speakers were acting according to a rule—in this case a rule for how to modify the meaning of "in"? It certainly does not seem so to the speakers who have just recognized the utterance as "odd."

This case takes us to the heart of a fundamental difficulty facing the simulators. Programmed behavior is either arbitrary or strictly rulelike. Therefore, in confronting a new usage a machine must either treat it as a clear case falling under the rules, or take a blind stab. A native speaker feels he has a third alternative. He can recognize the usage as odd, not falling under the rules, and yet he can make sense of it—give it a meaning in the context of human life in an apparently nonrulelike and yet nonarbitrary way.

Outright misuse of language demonstrates an even more extreme form of this ability. People often understand each other even when one of the speakers makes a grammatical or semantic mistake. The utterance may not only be outside the rules but actually proscribed by them, and yet such violations often go unnoticed, so easily are they understood.

Human beings confronted with these odd cases and outright errors adapt as they go along and then may reflect on the revisions they have made. A machine has either to fail first and then, when given the correct answer, revise its rules to take account of this new usage, or it would have to have all the rules—even the rules for how to break the rules and still be understood—built into it beforehand. To adopt the first approach, failing first and revising later, would be to admit that in principle, not just in practice, machines must always trail behind men—that they could not be humanly intelligent. To assume, on the other hand, that the rules covering all cases must be explicitly built in or learned—since this is the only way a digital computer could simulate the human ability to cope with odd uses—runs counter to logic and experience.

Logically, it is hard to see how one could formulate the rules for how one could intelligibly break the rules; for, no matter what metarules are formulated, it seems intuitively obvious that the native speaker could break them too and count on the context to get his meaning across to another speaker. Thus no matter what order of metarules one chooses, it seems there will be a higher order of tacit understanding about how to break those rules and still be understood.

Phenomenologically, or empirically, the postulation of a set of unconscious metarules of which we are not aware leads to other difficulties. Just as in chess the acceptance of the digital model led to the assumption that the chess player must be using unconscious heuristics, even when the player reported that he was zeroing in on patterns of strength and weakness, the assumption of the pre-existence of rules for disambiguation introduces a process of which we have no experiential evidence, and fails to take seriously our sense of the oddness of certain uses.

And here, as in the case of chess, this flouting of phenomenological evidence leads to a teleological puzzle: Why, if every understandable use of language is covered by rule, should some of these uses appear odd to us? So odd, indeed, that we cannot supply any rule to explain our interpretation. Why, if we have such a hierarchy of rules and lightning-fast capacity for using them on the unconscious level, should we be left consciously perplexed in certain cases and find them peculiar *even after* we have understood them?

These considerations suggest that, although a general theory of syntax and semantic competence can be scientific—because it is a timeless formalism which makes no claim to formalize the understanding of language in specific situations, serious problems arise when one demands a comparable formalism for linguistic *use.*

These difficulties do not disturb those linguists who, like scientists, carefully limit themselves to linguistic competence, that is, the general principles which apply to all cases, and exclude as extralinguistic our ability to deal with utterances in pragmatic contexts. As Kierkegaard points out in his *Concluding Unscientific Postscript,* the laws of science are universal and timeless, treating all experience as if it could as well be in the past.[18] AI workers, however, want their machines to interact with people in present real-life situations in which objects have special local significance. But computers are not involved in a situation. Every bit of data always has the same value. True, computers are not what Kant would call "transcendentally stupid"; they can apply a rule to a specific case if the specific case is already unambiguously described in terms of general features mentioned in the rule. They can thus simulate one kind of theoretical understanding. But machines lack practical intelligence. They are "existentially" stupid in that they cannot cope with specific situations. Thus they cannot accept ambiguity and the breaking of rules until the rules for dealing with the deviations have been so completely specified that the ambiguity has disappeared. To overcome this disability, AI workers would have to develop an a-temporal, nonlocal, theory of ongoing, situated, human activity.

The originality, the importance, and the curse of work in machine communication in a natural language is that the machine must use its formalism to cope with real-life situations *as they occur.* It must deal with phenomena which belong to the situational world of human beings as if these phenomena belonged to the objective formal universe of science. The believer in machine understanding and use of natural language who is encouraged by the success of linguistics is not laboring under a misconception about the way consciousness functions, but rather under a misconception about the relation between theoretical and practical understanding. He supposes that one can understand the practical world of an involved active individual in the same terms one can understand the objective universe of science. In short, he claims, as Leibniz first claimed, that one can have a theory of practice.

But such an applied theory could not be the same as the technological application of a physical theory, which it seems to parallel. When one uses the laws of physics to guide missiles, for example, the present performance of the missile is an instantiation of timeless, universal laws which make no reference to the situation except in terms of such laws. But in linguistics, as we have seen, speakers using the language take for granted common situational assumptions and goals. Thus the general laws of competence cannot be directly applied to simulate behavior. To get from the linguistic formalism to specific performance, one has to take into account the speaker's understanding of his situation. If there could be an autonomous theory of performance, it would have to be an entirely new kind of theory, a theory for a local context which described this context entirely in universal yet nonphysical terms. Neither physics nor linguistics offers any precedent for such a theory, nor any comforting assurance that such a theory can be found.

Conclusion

But to refute the epistemological assumption that there must be a theory of practical activity—in the case of language, to deny that the rules governing the *use* of actual utterances can in principle be completely formalized—it is not sufficient to point out that thus far no adequate language translation system has been developed, or that our language is used in flexible and apparently nonrulelike ways. The formalizer can offer the Platonic retort that our failure to formalize our ability to use language shows only that we have not fully understood this behavior; we have not yet found the rules for completely formalizing pragmatics.[19]*

This defense might at first seem to be similar to the heuristic programmer's assurance that he will someday find the heuristics which will enable a machine to play chess, even if he has not yet found them. But there is an important difference. The heuristic programmer's confidence is based on an unfounded psychological assumption concerning the way the mind processes information, whereas the formalist's claim is based on a correct understanding of the nature of scientific explanation. To the extent that we have not specified our behavior in terms of unique and precisely defined reactions to precisely defined objects in universally defined situations, we have not understood that behavior in the only sense of "understanding" appropriate to science.

To answer this *a priori* claim of the theoretical understanding one cannot counter with a phenomenological description. One must show that the theoretical claim is untenable on its own terms: that the skill which enables a native speaker to speak *cannot* be completely formalized; that the epistemological assumption is not only implausible but leads to contradictions.

Wittgenstein was perhaps the first philosopher since Pascal to note: "In general we don't *use* language according to strict rules—it hasn't been taught us by means of strict rules either."[20] But Wittgenstein did not base his argument against the claim that language was a calculus solely on a phenomenological description of the nonrulelike use of language. His strongest argument is a dialectical one, based on a regress of rules. He assumes, like the intellectualist philosophers he is criticizing, that all nonarbitrary behavior must be rulelike, and then reduces this assumption to absurdity by asking for the rules which we use in applying the rules, and so forth.

Here it is no longer a question of always being able to break the rules and still be understood. After all, we only *feel* we can go on breaking the rules indefinitely. We might be mistaken. It is a question of whether a complete understanding of behavior in terms of rules is intelligible. Wittgenstein is arguing, as Aristotle argued against Plato, that there must always be a place for interpretation. And this is not, as Turing seemed to think, merely a question of whether there are rules governing what we *should* do, which can legitimately be ignored. It is a question of whether there can be rules even describing what speakers *in fact* do. To have a complete theory of what speakers are able to do, one must not only have grammatical and semantic rules but further rules which would enable a person or a machine to recognize the context in which the rules must be applied. Thus there must be rules for recognizing the situation, the intentions of the speakers, and so forth. But if the theory then requires further rules in order to explain how these rules are applied, as the pure intellectualist viewpoint would suggest, we are in an infinite regress. Since we do manage to use language, this regress cannot be a problem for human beings. If AI is to be possible, it must also not be a problem for machines.

Both Wittgenstein and the computer theorists must agree that there is some level at which rules are simply applied and one no longer needs rules to guide their application. Wittgenstein and the AI theorists differ fundamentally, however, on how to describe this stopping point. For Wittgenstein there is no absolute stopping point; we just fill in as many rules as are necessary for the practical demands of the situation. At some level, depending on what we are trying to do, the interpretation of the rule is simply evident and the regress stops.[21]*

For the computer people the regress also stops with an interpretation which is self-evident, but this interpretation has nothing to do with the demands of the situation. It cannot, for the computer is not in a situation. It generates no local context. The computer theorist's solution is to build the machine to respond to ultimate bits of context-free, completely determinate data which require no further interpretation in order to be understood. Once the data are in the machine, all processing must be rulelike, but in reading in the data there is a direct response to determinate features of the machine's environment as, for example, holes in cards or the mosaic of a TV camera, so on this ultimate level the machine does not need rules for applying its rules. Just as the feeding behavior of the baby herring gull is triggered by a red spot and the frog's eye automatically signals the presence of a moving black spot, so human behavior, if it is to be completely understood and computerized, must be understood as if triggered by specific features of the environment.

As a theory of human psychology (CS) this is surely not a plausible hypothesis. Our sense of oddness of deviant linguistic uses, as well as our feeling that there is nothing in the environment to which we have an inevitable and invariable response, argue against this view. Moreover, as a theory of our "practical competence" (no matter how we actually produce our behavior), this hypothesis is no more attractive. The general adaptability of our language, which enables us to modify meanings and invent analogies, as well as the general flexibility of human and even higher animal behavior, are incomprehensible on this view. Still, these objections are all based on appearances. They are plausible, but not necessarily convincing to those committed to the epistemological assumption.

A full refutation of the epistemological assumption would require an argument that the world *cannot* be analyzed in terms of context-free data. Then, since the assumption that there are basic unambiguous elements is the only way to save the epistemological assumption from the regress of rules, the formalist, caught between the impossibility of always having rules for the application of rules and the impossibility of finding ultimate unambiguous data, would have to abandon the epistemological assumption altogether.

This assumption that the world can be exhaustively analyzed in terms of context-free data or atomic facts is the deepest assumption underlying work in AI and the whole philosophical tradition. We shall call it the ontological assumption, and now turn to analyzing its attraction and its difficulties.

6

The Ontological Assumption

Up to now we have been seeking in vain the arguments and evidence that the mind processes information in a sequence of discrete steps like a heuristically programmed digital computer, or that human behavior can be formalized in these terms. We have seen that there are four types of human "information processing" (fringe consciousness, ambiguity tolerance, essential/inessential discrimination, and perspicuous grouping), which have resisted formalization in terms of heuristic rules. And we have seen that the biological, psychological, and epistemological assumptions which allow workers to view these difficulties as temporary are totally unjustified and may well be untenable. Now we turn to an even more fundamental difficulty facing those who hope to use digital computers to produce artificial intelligence: the data with which the computer must operate if it is to perceive, speak, and in general behave intelligently, must be discrete, explicit, and determinate; otherwise, it will not be the sort of information which can be given to the computer so as to be processed by rule. Yet there is no reason to suppose that such data about the human world are available to the computer and several reasons to suggest that no such data exist.

The ontological assumption that everything essential to intelligent behavior must in principle be understandable in terms of a set of determinate independent elements allows AI researchers to overlook this problem. We shall soon see that this assumption lies at the basis of all thinking in AI, and that it can seem so self-evident that it is never made explicit or questioned. As in the case of the epistemological assumption, we shall see that this conviction concerning the indubitability of what in fact is only an hypothesis reflects two thousand years of philosophical tradition reinforced by a misinterpretation of the success of the physical sciences. Once this hypothesis is made explicit and called into question, it turns out that no arguments have been brought forward in its defense and that, when used as the basis for a theory of practice such as AI, the ontological assumption leads to profound conceptual difficulties.

In his introduction to *Semantic Information Processing,* Minsky warns against

the dreadfully misleading set of concepts that people get when they are told (with the best intentions) that computers are nothing but assemblies of flip-flops; that their programs are really nothing but sequences of operations upon binary numbers, and so on.[1]

He tries to combat this discouraging way of looking at digital computers:

While this is one useful viewpoint, it is equally correct to say that the computer is nothing but an assembly of symbol-association and process-controlling elements and that programs are nothing but networks of interlocking goal-formulating and means-ends evaluation processes. This latter attitude is actually much healthier because it reduces one's egotistical tendency to assume total comprehension of all the possible future implications.[2]

But Minsky sees only half the difficulty arising from his restriction that the computer must operate on determinate, independent elements. It is true that programmers formulate higher-order rules for the operation of a computer so that the fact that there are flip/flops never appears in the flow chart, that is, on the information-processing level.[3]* (On this level, as we have seen in the preceding two chapters, trouble arises because there must always be explicit rules, not because these rules must ultimately be a sequence of operations on binary numbers.) The information-processing model, however, restricts the kind of information the machine can be given. We have seen that Newell quite frankly described GPS—a program whose information-processing level is correctly described in terms of interlocking goals and means-ends—as "a program for accepting a task environment defined in terms of discrete objects."⁴ It is these discrete objects which are organized into the data structure which makes up the computer's representation of the world. Every program for a digital computer must receive its data in this discrete form.

This raises a special problem, or, more exactly, it *creates* a problem by determining the way all questions concerning giving information to computers must be raised. Stated in a neutral way the problem is this: as we have seen, in order to understand an utterance, structure a problem, or recognize a pattern, a computer must select and interpret its data in terms of a context. But how are we to impart this context itself to the computer? The sharpest statement of this problem—still in neutral terms —occurs in Eden's evaluation of work in handwriting recognition:

> . . . when [a human being] reads a letter written in a difficult script . . . he can reconstruct it with the help of his knowledge of the grammar of the language, the meaning of the text he has been able to read, the character of the subject matter, and, perhaps, the state of mind of the writer. *There is now, alas, no hint of how to embody such knowledge of the world and its ways in the computer.*⁵

Here Eden wisely takes no stand on what we know when we have "knowledge of the world and its ways." The information-processing model, however, along with the ontological assumption, dictates an answer to this question which is no longer neutral, but rather embodies the computer's requirements. When one asks what this knowledge of the world is, the answer comes back that it must be a great mass of discrete facts.

Thus at the end of his introduction to *Semantic Information Processing*, when Minsky finally asks "what is the magnitude of the mass of knowledge required for a humanoid intelligence?"⁶ he has already prejudged the question and unhesitatingly answers in terms of numbers of facts:

> If we discount specialized knowledge and ask instead about the common-everyday structures—that which a person needs to have ordinary common sense—we will find first a collection of indispensable categories, each rather complex: geo-

metrical and mechanical properties of things and of space; uses and properties of a few thousand objects; hundreds of "facts" about hundreds of people, thousands of facts about tens of people, tens of facts about thousands of people; hundreds of facts about hundreds of organizations. As one tries to classify all his knowledge, the categories grow rapidly at first, but after a while one encounters more and more difficulty. My impression, for what it's worth, is that one can find fewer than ten areas each with more than ten thousand "links." One can't find a hundred things that he knows a thousand things about. Or a thousand things each with a full hundred new links. I therefore feel that a machine will quite critically need to acquire the order of a hundred thousand elements of knowledge in order to behave with reasonable sensibility in ordinary situations. A million, if properly organized, should be enough for a very great intelligence. If my argument does not convince you, multiply the figures by ten.[7]

Granting for the moment that all human knowledge can be analyzed as a list of objects and of facts about each, Minsky's analysis raises the problem of how such a large mass of facts is to be stored and accessed. How could one structure these data—a hundred thousand discrete elements—so that one could find the information required in a reasonable amount of time? When one assumes that our knowledge of the world is knowledge of millions of discrete facts, the problem of artificial intelligence becomes the problem of storing and accessing a large data base. Minsky sees that this presents grave difficulties:

. . . As everyone knows, it is hard to find a knowledge-classifying system that works well for many different kinds of problems: it requires immense effort to build a plausible thesaurus that works even within one field. Furthermore, any particular retrieval structure is liable to entail commitments making it difficult to incorporate concepts that appear after the original structure is assembled. One is tempted to say: "It would be folly to base our intelligent machine upon some particular elaborate, thesaurus-like classification of knowledge, some *ad hoc* synopticon. Surely that is no road to 'general intelligence.' "[8]

And, indeed, little progress has been made toward solving the large data base problem. But, in spite of his own excellent objections, Minsky characteristically concludes:

But we had better be cautious about this caution itself, for it exposes us to a far more deadly temptation: to seek a fountain of pure intelligence. I see no reason to believe that intelligence can exist apart from a highly organized body of knowledge, models, and processes. The habit of our culture has always been to suppose that intelligence resides in some separated crystalline element, call it *consciousness, apprehension, insight, gestalt,* or what you will but this is merely to confound naming the problem with solving it. The problem-solving abilities of a highly intelligent person lies partly in his superior heuristics for managing his knowledge-structure and partly in the structure itself; these are probably somewhat inseparable. In any case, there is no reason to suppose that you can be intelligent except through the use of an adequate, particular, knowledge or model structure.[9]

But this is no argument for optimism. True, people manage to be intelligent, but without the ontological assumption this would be no consolation to workers in AI. It is by no means obvious that in order to be intelligent human beings have somehow solved or needed to solve the large data base problem. The problem may itself be an artifact created by the fact that AI workers must operate with discrete elements. Human knowledge does not seem to be analyzable as an explicit description as Minsky would like to believe. A mistake, a collision, an embarrassing situation, etc., do not seem on the face of it to be objects or facts about objects. Even a chair is not understandable in terms of any set of facts or "elements of knowledge." To recognize an object as a chair, for example, means to understand its relation to other objects and to human beings. This involves a whole context of human activity of which the shape of our body, the institution of furniture, the inevitability of fatigue, constitute only a small part. And these factors in turn are no more isolable than is the chair. They all may get *their* meaning in the context of human activity of which they form a part (see Chapter 8).

In general, we have an implicit understanding of the human situation which provides the context in which we encounter specific facts and make them explicit. There is no reason, only an ontological commitment, which makes us suppose that all the facts we can make explicit about our situation are already unconsciously explicit in a "model structure," or that we could ever make our situation completely explicit even if we tried.[10]*

Why does this assumption seem self-evident to Minsky? Why is he so unaware of the alternative that he takes the view that intelligence involves a "particular, knowledge or model structure," a great systematic array of facts, as an axiom rather than as an hypothesis? Ironically, Minsky supposes that in announcing this axiom he is combating the tradition. "The habit of our culture has always been to suppose that intelligence resides in some separated crystalline element, call it consciousness, apprehension, insight, gestalt. . . ." In fact, by supposing that the alternatives are either a well-structured body of facts, or some disembodied way of dealing with the facts, Minsky is so traditional that he can't even see the fundamental assumption that he shares with the whole of the philosophical tradition. In assuming that what is given are facts at all, Minsky is simply echoing a view which has been developing since Plato and has now become so ingrained as to *seem* self-evident.

As we have seen, the goal of the philosophical tradition embedded in our culture is to eliminate uncertainty: moral, intellectual, and practical. Indeed, the demand that knowledge be expressed in terms of rules or definitions which can be applied without the risk of interpretation is already present in Plato, as is the belief in simple elements to which the rules apply.[11]* With Leibniz, the connection between the traditional idea of knowledge and the Minsky-like view that the world *must* be analyzable into discrete elements becomes explicit. According to Leibniz, in understanding we analyze concepts into more simple elements. In order to avoid a regress of simpler and simpler elements, then, there must be ultimate simples in terms of which all complex concepts can be understood. Moreover, if concepts are to apply to the world, there must be simples to which these elements correspond. Leibniz envisaged "a kind of alphabet of human thoughts"[12] whose "characters must show, when they are used in demonstrations, some kind of connection, grouping and order which are also found in the objects."[13] The empiricist tradition, too, is dominated by the idea of discrete elements of knowledge. For Hume, all experience is made up of impressions: isolable, determinate, atoms of experience. Intellectualist and empiricist schools converge in Russell's logical atomism, and the idea reaches its fullest expression in Wittgenstein's *Tractatus,* where the world is defined in terms of a set of atomic facts which can be expressed in logically independent propositions. This is the purest formulation of the ontological assumption, and the necessary precondition of all work in AI as long as researchers continue to suppose that the world must be represented as a structured set of descriptions which are themselves built up from primitives. Thus both philosophy and technology, in their appeal to primitives continue to posit what Plato sought: a world in which the possibility of clarity, certainty, and control is guaranteed; a world of data structures, decision theory, and automation.

No sooner had this certainty finally been made fully explicit, however, than philosophers began to call it into question. Continental phenomenologists recognized it as the outcome of the philosophical tradition and tried to show its limitations. Merleau-Ponty calls the assumption that all that exists can be treated as determinate objects, the *préjugé du monde,* "presumption of commonsense."[14] Heidegger calls it *rechnende Denken,*[15] "calculating thought," and views it as the goal of philosophy, inevitably culminating in technology. Thus, for Heidegger, technology, with its insistence on the "thoroughgoing calculability of objects,"[16]* is the inevitable culmination of metaphysics, the exclusive concern with beings (objects) and the concomitant exclusion of Being (very roughly our sense of the human situation which determines what is to count as an object). In England, Wittgenstein less prophetically and more analytically recognized the impossibility of carrying through the ontological analysis proposed in his *Tractatus* and became his own severest critic.[17]*

In Part III, we shall have occasion to follow at length the Merleau-Pontyian, Wittgensteinian, and Heideggerian critique of the traditional ontological assumption, and the alternative view they propose. We have already seen enough, however, to suggest that we do not experience the world as a set of facts in our everyday activities, nor is it self-evident that it is possible to carry through such an analysis.

But if the ontological assumption does not square with our experience, why does it have such power? Even if what gave impetus to the philosophical tradition was the demand that things be clear and simple so that we can understand and control them, if things are not so simple why persist in this optimism? What lends plausibility to this dream? As we have already seen in another connection, the myth is fostered by the success of modern physics. Here, at least to a first approximation, the ontological assumption works. It was only after Galileo was able to treat motion in terms of isolable objects moving under the influence of computable, determinate forces that Hobbes was encouraged to announce that all thinking was the addition of parcels. It has proved profitable to think of the *physical universe* as a set of independent interacting elements. The ontological assumption that the human world too can be treated in terms of a set of elements gains plausibility when one fails to distinguish between world and universe, or what comes to the same thing, between the human situation and the state of a physical system.

In Minsky's work this confusion remains implicit; in the work of his former colleague, John McCarthy, now directing AI research at Stanford, it becomes the very cornerstone of the argument. In his paper "Programs with Common Sense," included in the Minsky volume, McCarthy proposes an "advice taker"—a program for "solving problems by manipulating sentences in formal languages," the behavior of which "will be improvable merely by making statements to it, telling it about its symbolic environment and what is wanted from it."[18] McCarthy sees clearly that "the first requirement for the advice taker is a formal system in which facts about situation, goals, and actions can be expressed."[19] This leads immediately to the basic problem: how can one describe the situation in a formal system? McCarthy, however, does not see this as a serious problem because he assumes without question that a situation is a physical state:

One of the basic entities in our theory is the *situation*. Intuitively, a situation is the complete state of affairs at some instant in time. The laws of motion of a system determine all future situations from a given situation. Thus, a situation corresponds to the notion of a point in phase space.[20]

But the same type of situation can reoccur, involving different objects, different people, and *a fortiori* different physical states. Moreover, the same physical organization of matter can be seen as many different situations, depending on the goals and intentions of the various human beings involved. Thus, although at any given moment the universe is in only one physical state, there may be as many situations as there are people. When McCarthy says "there is only one situation corresponding to a given value of time,"[21] he has clearly confused situation with physical state of the universe. More specifically, he has confused *token* states and *types* of states. A situation token *can* be identical with a physical state token (specified by a point in phase space). But a *type* of situation cannot be identical to a *type* of physical state.

A concrete example will help to pinpoint this confusion. A situation which McCarthy discusses at length is "being at home." " 'At (I, home) (s)'means I am at home in situation s."[22] McCarthy seems to assume that this is the same thing as being in my house, that is, that it is a physical state. But I can be at home and be in the backyard, that is, not physically in my house at all. I can also be physically in my house and not be at home; for example, if I own the house but have not yet moved my furniture in. Being at home is a human situation, not in any simple correspondence with the physical state of a human body in a house. Not to mention the fact that it is a necessary if not sufficient condition for being at home in the sense in question that I own or rent the house, and owning or renting a house is a complicated institutional set of relations not reducible to any set of physical states. Even a physical description of a certain pattern of ink deposited on certain pieces of paper in a specific temporal sequence would not constitute a necessary and sufficient condition for a transfer of ownership. Writing one's name is not always signing, and watching is not always witnessing.

It is easy to see why McCarthy would like to treat the situation as if it were a physical state. The evolution of a physical state can, indeed, be formalized in differential equations and reproduced on a digital computer. Situations, however, pose formidable problems for those who would like to translate them into a formal system. Such a formalization may well be impossible in principle, as can best be seen by returning to the problem of machine translation.

We have seen in Part I that automatic language translation has failed because natural language turns out to be much more ambiguous than was supposed. In narrowing down this semantic and syntactic ambiguity the native speaker may appeal to specific information about the world. Bar-Hillel makes this point in an argument which according to him "amounts to an almost full-fledged demonstration of the unattainability of fully automatic high quality translation, not only in the near future but altogether."[23] The argument is sufficiently important at this point to merit quoting at some length.

I shall show that there exist extremely simple sentences in English—and the same holds, I am sure, for any other natural language—which, within certain linguistic contexts, would be uniquely (up to plain synonymy) and unambiguously translated into any other language by anyone with a sufficient knowledge of the two languages involved, though I know of no program that would enable a machine to come up with this unique rendering unless by a completely arbitrary and *ad hoc* procedure whose futility would show itself in the next example.

A sentence of this kind is the following:

The box was in the pen.

The linguistic context from which this sentence is taken is, say, the following:

Little John was looking for his toy box. Finally he found it. The box was in the pen. John was very happy.

Assume, for simplicity's sake, that *pen* in English has only the following two meanings: (1) a certain writing utensil, (2) an enclosure where small children can play. I now claim that no existing or imaginable program will enable an electronic computer to determine that the word *pen* in the given sentence within the given context has the second of the above meanings, whereas every reader with a sufficient knowledge of English will do this "automatically."

What makes an intelligent human reader grasp this meaning so unhesitatingly is, in addition to all the other features that have been discussed by MT workers . . . , his *knowledge* that the relative sizes of pens, in the sense of writing implements, toy boxes, and pens, in the sense of playpens, are such that when someone writes under ordinary circumstances and in something like the given context, "The box was in the pen," he almost certainly refers to a playpen and most certainly not to a writing pen.[24]*

And, as Bar-Hillel goes on to argue, the suggestion, such as Minsky's, that a computer used in translating be supplied with a universal encyclopedia is "utterly chimerical." "The number of facts we human beings know is, in a certain very pregnant sense, infinite."[25]

Bar-Hillel's point is well taken; his example, however, based on a particular physical fact, is unfortunate; it tempts AI workers such as Minsky to propose a solution in terms of a model of the facts of physics:

". . . it would be a good idea to build into the semantic model enough common-sense geometrical physics to make it unlikely that the box is in the fountain-pen. . . ."[26]*

There is a second kind of disambiguation, however, which gets us to the very heart of the difficulty. In disambiguating, one may appeal to a sense of the situation as in the following example from Katz and Fodor:

An ambiguous sentence such as "He follows Marx" occurring in a setting in which it is clear that the speaker is remarking about intellectual history cannot bear the reading "he dogs the footsteps of Groucho."[27]

Katz and Fodor discuss this sort of difficulty in their article "The Structure of a Semantic Theory":

Since a complete theory of setting selection must represent as part of the setting of an utterance any and every feature of the world which speakers need in order to determine the preferred reading of that utterance, and since . . . practically any item of information about the world is essential to some disambiguations, two conclusions follow. First, such a theory cannot in principle distinguish between the speaker's knowledge of his language and his knowledge of the world. . . . Second, since there is no serious possibility of systematizing all the knowledge about the world that speakers share . . . [such a theory] is not a serious model for linguistics.[28]

Katz and Fodor continue:

None of these considerations is intended to rule out the possibility that, by placing relatively strong limitations on the information about the world that a theory can represent in the characterization of a setting, a *limited* theory of selection by sociophysical setting can be constructed. What these considerations do show is that a *complete* theory of this kind is not a possibility.[29]

Thus Bar-Hillel claims we must appeal to specific *facts,* such as the size of pens and boxes; Katz and Fodor assume we must appeal to the *sociophysical setting.* The appeal to context, would, moreover, seem to be more fundamental than the appeal to facts, for the context determines the *significance* of the facts. Thus in spite of our *general* knowledge about the relative size of pens and boxes, we might interpret "The box is in the pen," when whispered in a James Bond movie, as meaning just the opposite of what it means at home or on the farm. And, conversely, when no specifically odd context is specified, we assume a "normal" context and assign to the facts about relative size a "normal" significance. Minsky's physical model hides but does not obviate the need for this implicit appeal to the situation.

The important difference between disambiguation by facts and disambiguation by appeal to the situation is not noted by Minsky, Bar-Hillel, or Fodor and Katz, presumably because they each assume that the setting is itself identified by features which are facts, and functions like a fact in disambiguation. We shall see, however, that disregarding the difference between fact and situation leads to an equivocation in both Bar-Hillel and Fodor-Katz as to whether mechanical translation is impractical or impossible.

In Bar-Hillel's "demonstration" that since disambiguation depends on the use of facts, and the number of facts is "in a certain very pregnant sense infinite," fully automatic high-quality mechanical translation is unattainable; it is unclear what is being claimed. If "unattainable" means that in terms of present computers, and programs in operation or envisaged, no such massive storage and retrieval of information can be carried out, then the point is well made, and is sufficient to cast serious doubt on claims that mechanical translation has been achieved or can be achieved in the foreseeable future. But if "unattainable" means theoretically impossible—which the appeal to infinity seems to imply—then Bar-Hillel is claiming too much. A machine would not have to store an infinite number of facts, for, as Minsky sees, from a large number of facts and rules for concatenating them, such as the laws of physics, it could produce further ones indefinitely. True, no present program would enable a machine to sort through such an endless amount of data. At present there exist no machine and no program capable of storing even a very large body of data so as to gain access to the relevant information in manageable time. Still, there is work being done on what are called "associative memories" and ingenious tricks used in programming, such as hash coding, which may in the distant future provide the means of storing and accessing vast bodies of information. Then if all that was needed was facts, the necessary information might be stored in such a way that in any given case only a finite number of relevant facts need be considered.

As long as Katz and Fodor, like Bar-Hillel, accept the ontological assumption and speak of the setting in terms of "items of information," their argument is as equivocal as his. They have no right to pass from the claim that there is "no serious possibility" of systematizing the knowledge necessary for disambiguation, which seems to be a statement about our technological capabilities, to the claim that a complete theory of selection by sociophysical setting is "not a possibility." If a program for handling all knowledge is ever developed, and in their world there is no theoretical reason why it should not be, it will be such a theory.

Only if one rejects the ontological assumption that the world can be analyzed as a set of facts—items of information—can one legitimately move beyond practical impossibility. We have already seen examples which suggest that the situation might be of a radically different order and fulfill a totally different function than any concatenation of facts. In the "Marx" example, the situation (academic) determines how to disambiguate "Marx" (Karl) and furthermore tells us which facts are relevant to disambiguate "follows," as ideological or chronological. (When was the follower born, what are his political views, etc.?) In the box-pen example the size of the box and pen are clearly relevant since we are speaking of physical objects being "in" other physical objects; but here the situation, be it agricultural, domestic, or conspiratorial, determines the *significance* of the facts involved. Thus it is our sense of the situation which enables us to select from the potential infinity of facts the immediately relevant ones, and once these relevant facts are found, enables us to estimate their significance. This suggests that unless there are some facts whose relevance and significance are invariant in all situations—and no one has come up with such facts—we will have to give the computer a way of recognizing situations; otherwise, it will not be able to disambiguate and thus it will be, in principle, unable to understand utterances in a natural language.

Among workers in AI, only Joseph Weizenbaum seems to be aware of these problems. In his work on a program which would allow people to converse with a computer in a natural language, Weizenbaum has had to face the importance of the situation, and realizes that it cannot be treated simply as a set of facts. His remarks on the importance of global context are worth quoting at length:

No understanding is possible in the absence of an established global context. To be sure, strangers do meet, converse, and immediately understand one another. But they operate in a shared culture—provided partially by the very language they speak—and, under any but the most trivial circumstances, engage in a kind of hunting behavior which has as its object the creation of a contextual framework.[30]

In real conversation global context assigns meaning to what is being said in only the most general way. The conversation proceeds by establishing subcontexts, sub-subcontexts within these, and so on.[31]

Weizenbaum sees difficulties in all this but no problems of principle.

I call attention to the contextual matter . . . to underline the thesis that, while a computer program that "understands" natural language in the most general sense is for the present beyond our means, the granting of even a quite broad contextual framework allows us to construct practical language recognition procedures.[32]

Thus, Weizenbaum proposes to program a nest of contexts in terms of a "contextual tree": "beginning with the topmost or initial node, a new node representing a subcontext is generated, and from this one a new node still, and so on to many levels."[33] He clearly supposes these contexts can themselves ultimately be treated as sets of facts: "the analogue of a conversation tree is what the social psychologist Abelson calls a *belief structure*,"[34] that is, an organized collection of facts concerning a person's knowledge, emotional attitudes, goals, and so forth.

Evidently, an understanding of the crucial role of the situation does not by itself constitute a sufficient argument for abandoning AI. The traditional ontologist, reincarnated in Weizenbaum and every AI researcher, can grant that facts used in conversation are selected and interpreted in terms of the global context and simply conclude that we need only first pick out and program the features which identify this broader situation. But Weizenbaum's observations contain the elements of an objection in principle to the development of humanly intelligent machines. To see this we must first show that Weizenbaum's way of analyzing the problem—separating the meaning of the context from the meaning of the words used in the context—is not accidental but is dictated by the nature of a digital machine. In our everyday experience we do not find ourselves making such a separation. We seem to understand the situation in terms of the meaning of the words as much as we understand the meaning in terms of the situation. For a computer, however, this reciprocal determination must be broken down into a series of separate operations. Since Weizenbaum sees that we cannot determine the sense of the words until we know the meaning of the context, he correctly concludes, from a programmer's point of view, that we must first specify the context and then use this fixed context to determine the meaning of the elements in it.

Moreover, Weizenbaum's analysis suggests that the computerized understanding of a natural language requires that the contexts be organized as a nested hierarchy. To understand why Weizenbaum finds it necessary to use a hierarchy of contexts and work down from the top node, we must return to the general problem of situation recognition. If computers must utilize the situation or context in order to disambiguate, and in general to understand utterances in a natural language, the programmer must be able to program into the machine, which is not involved in a situation, a way of recognizing a context and using it. But the same two problems which arose in disambiguation and necessitated appeal to the situation in the first place arise again on the level of context recognition and force us to envisage working down from the broadest context: (1) If in disambiguation the number of possibly relevant facts is in some sense infinite so that selection criteria must be applied before interpretation can begin, the number of facts that might be relevant to recognizing a context is infinite too. How is the computer to consider all the features such as how many people are present, the temperature, the pressure, the day of the week, and so forth, any one of which might be a defining feature of some context? (2) Even if the program provides rules for determining relevant facts, these facts would be ambiguous, that is, capable of defining several different contexts, until they were interpreted.

Evidently, a broader context will have to be used to determine which of the infinity of features is relevant, and how each is to be understood.

But if, in turn, the program must enable the machine to identify the broader context in terms of *its* relevant features—and this is the only way a computer which operates in terms of discrete elements could proceed —the programmer must either claim that some features are intrinsically relevant and have a fixed meaning regardless of context—a possibility already excluded in the original appeal to context—or the programmer will be faced with an infinite regress of contexts. There seems to be only one way out: rather than work up the tree to ever broader contexts the computer must work down from an ultimate context—what Weizenbaum calls our shared culture.

Fortunately, there does seem to be something like an ultimate context, but, as we shall see, this proves to be as unprogrammable as the regress it was introduced to avoid. We have seen that in order to identify which facts are relevant for recognizing an academic or a conspiratorial situation, and to interpret these facts, one must appeal to a broader context. Thus it is only in the broader context of social intercourse that we see we must normally take into account what people are wearing and what they are doing, but not how many insects there are in the room or the cloud formations at noon or a minute later. Also only this broader context enables us to determine whether these facts will have their normal significance.

Moreover, even the facts necessary to recognize social intercourse can only be singled out because social intercourse is a subcase of human activity, which also includes working alone or studying a primitive tribe. And finally, human activity itself is only a subclass of some even broader situation—call it the human life-world—which would have to include even those situations where no human beings were directly involved. But what facts would be relevant to recognizing this broadest situation? Or does it make sense to speak of "recognizing" the life-world at all? It seems we simply take for granted this ultimate situation in being people. As Wittgenstein puts it:

What has to be accepted, the given, is—so one could say—*forms of life.*[35]

Well then, why not make explicit the significant features of the human form of life from within it? Indeed, this deus ex machina solution has been the implicit goal of philosophers for two thousand years, and it should be no surprise that nothing short of a formalization of the human form of life could give us artificial intelligence (which is not to say that this is what gives us normal intelligence). But how are we to proceed? Everything we experience in some way, immediate or remote, reflects our human concerns. Without some *particular* interest, without some *particular* inquiry to help us select and interpret, we are back confronting the infinity of meaningless facts we were trying to avoid.

It seems that given the artificial intelligence worker's conception of reason as calculation on facts, and his admission that which facts are relevant and significant is not just given but is context determined, his attempt to produce intelligent behavior leads to an antinomy. On the one hand, we have the thesis: there must always be a broader context; otherwise, we have no way to distinguish relevant from irrelevant facts. On the other hand, we have the antithesis: there must be an ultimate context, which requires no interpretation; otherwise, there will be an infinite regress of contexts, and we can never begin our formalization.

Human beings seem to embody a third possibility which would offer a way out of this dilemma. Instead of a hierarchy of contexts, the present situation is recognized as a continuation or modification of the previous one. Thus we carry over from the immediate past a set of anticipations based on what was relevant and important a moment ago. This carryover gives us certain predispositions as to what is worth noticing.

Programming this alternative, however, far from solving the problem of context recognition merely transforms a hierarchical regress into a temporal one. How does the situation which human beings carry along get started? To the programmer this becomes the question: how can we originally select from the infinity of facts those relevant to the human form of life so as to determine a context we can sequentially update? Here the answer seems to be: human beings are simply wired genetically as babies to respond to certain features of the environment such as nipples and smiles which are crucially important for survival. Programming these initial reflexes and letting the computer learn might be a way out of the context recognition problem; but it is important to note two reservations: no present work in artificial intelligence is devoted to this approach.[36]* In fact, artificial intelligence as it is now defined by Feigenbaum, Simon, Minsky, Weizenbaum, and others seems to be the attempt to produce fully formed adult intelligence, the way Athena sprang full grown from the head of Zeus. Moreover, it is by no means clear that the above proposal avoids the original dilemma. It leaves unexplained how the child develops from fixed responses elicited by fixed features of the environment, to the determination of meaning in terms of context which even AI workers agree characterizes the adult.

Once the child can determine meanings in terms of the situation, the past situation can indeed be updated to arrive at the present one, but the original transition from fixed response to flexible response in terms of the meaning of the situation remains as obscure as before. Either the transition must be understood as an ongoing modification of the previous situation, and we have assumed what was to be explained, or the so-called global context must be recognized in terms of fixed context-free features, and we have ignored the problem rather than solved it. Either the child or machine is able to select relevant facts, assign a normal significance to all relevant facts, and also to override this normal significance in an open-ended way—and then no set of fixed features, not even the infant's, can be taken as having a fixed significance in terms of which to begin this process; or fixed features are all that is needed, but then we have to reject as illusory the very flexibility we were trying to explain. There seems to be no way to get into a situation and no way to recognize one from the outside.

We nonetheless observe that generality and flexibility are developed gradually through learning, but now the whole problem is hidden in this learning process. The child seems at each moment to be either developing more complex fixed responses, or to have always already interpreted specific facts in terms of the overall context and to be gaining a more structured sense of the situation. If we reject the analysis in terms of fixed responses as inadequate because inapplicable to the adult, we are back facing a temporal version of the original antinomy. Either there must be a first context which a machine would not be able to recognize for want of a previous context in terms of which to single out its relevant features, or there will be a temporal regress of contexts extending infinitely into the past and the machine will not be able to begin the recognition process.

As Kant noted, the resolution of an antinomy requires giving up the assumption that the two alternatives considered are the only possible ones. They are, indeed, the only alternatives open to someone trying to construct *artificial* reason.[37]* There *must be* another alternative, however, since language is used and understood. There must be some way of avoiding the self-contradictory regress of contexts, or the incomprehensible notion of recognizing an ultimate context, as the only way of giving significance to independent, neutral facts. The only way out seems to be to deny the separation of fact and situation, which we saw Weizenbaum was led to assume because of the serial procedure forced on him by the digital computer. If, as all agree, we are unable to eliminate the situation in favor of facts whose relevance and significance are fixed regardless of context, then the only alternative way of denying the separation of fact and situation is to give up the independence of the facts and understand them as a product of the situation. This would amount to arguing that only in terms of situationally determined relevance are there any facts at all. It also amounts to avoiding the problem of how to recognize the situation from outside by arguing that for an intelligence to have any facts to interpret, it must already be in a situation.

Part III will show how this latter alternative is possible and how it is related to the rest of human life. Only then will it become clear why the fixed-feature alternative is empirically untenable, and also why the human form of life cannot be programmed.

Conclusion

In surveying the four assumptions underlying the optimistic interpretation of results in AI we have observed a recurrent pattern: In each case the assumption was taken to be self-evident—an axiom seldom articulated and never called into question. In fact, the assumption turned out to be only one alternative hypothesis, and a questionable one at that. The biological assumption that the brain must function like a digital computer no longer fits the evidence. The others lead to conceptual difficulties.

The psychological assumption that the mind must obey a heuristic program cannot be defended on empirical grounds, and *a priori* arguments in its defense fail to introduce a coherent level of discourse between the physical and the phenomenological. This does not show that the task set for Cognitive Simulation is hopeless. However, this lack of defense of the psychological axiom does eliminate the only argument which suggested any particular reason for hope. If it could have been argued that information processing *must* proceed by heuristic rules, Cognitive Simulation would have had the promising task of finding these rules. Without the defense provided by this axiom, however, all difficulties besetting Cognitive Simulation research during the past ten years take on new significance; there is no reason to deny the growing body of evidence that human and mechanical information processing proceed in entirely different ways.

Researchers in AI (taking over from CS as Minsky has taken over from Simon) have written programs which allow the digital machine to *approximate,* by means of logical operations, the result which human beings seem to achieve by avoiding rather than resolving the difficulties inherent in formalization. But formalization of restricted contexts is an *ad hoc* "solution" which leaves untouched the problem of how to formalize the totality of human knowledge presupposed in intelligent behavior. This fundamental difficulty is hidden by the epistemological and ontological assumptions that all human behavior must be analyzable in terms of rules relating atomic facts.

But the conceptual difficulties introduced by these assumptions are even more serious than those introduced by the psychological one. The inevitable appeal to these assumptions as a final basis for a theory of practice leads to a regress of more and more specific rules for applying rules or of more and more general contexts for recognizing contexts. In the face of these contradictions, it seems reasonable to claim that, on the information processing level, as opposed to the level of the laws of physics, we cannot analyze human behavior in terms of rule-governed manipulation of a set of elements. And since we have seen no argument brought forward by the AI theorists for the assumption that human behavior *must be* reproducible by a digital computer operating with strict rules on determinate bits, we would seem to have good philosophical grounds for rejecting this assumption.

If we do abandon all four assumptions, then the empirical data available to date would take on different significance. It no longer seems obvious that one can introduce search heuristics which enable the speed and accuracy of computers to bludgeon through in those areas where human beings use more elegant techniques. Lacking any *a priori* basis for confidence, we can only turn to the empirical results obtained thus far. That brute force can succeed to some extent is demonstrated by the early work in the field. The present difficulties in game playing, language translation, problem solving, and pattern recognition, however, indicate a limit to our ability to substitute one kind of "information processing" for another. Only experimentation can determine the extent to which newer and faster machines, better programming languages, and cleverer heuristics can continue to push back the frontier. Nonetheless, the dramatic slowdown in the fields we have considered and the general failure to fulfill earlier predictions suggest the boundary may be near. Without the four assumptions to fall back on, current stagnation should be grounds for pessimism.

This, of course, has profound implications for our philosophical tradition. If the persistent difficulties which have plagued all areas of artificial intelligence are reinterpreted as failures, these failures must be interpreted as empirical evidence against the psychological, epistemological, and ontological assumptions. In Heideggerian terms this is to say that if Western Metaphysics reaches its culmination in Cybernetics, the recent difficulties in artificial intelligence, rather than reflecting technological limitations, may reveal the limitations of technology.

PART III

ALTERNATIVES TO THE

TRADITIONAL ASSUMPTIONS

Introduction

The psychological, epistemological, and ontological assumptions have this in common: they assume that man must be a *device* which calculates according to rules on data which take the form of atomic facts. Such a view is the tidal wave produced by the confluence of two powerful streams: first, the Platonic reduction of all reasoning to explicit rules and the world to atomic facts to which alone such rules could be applied without the risks of interpretation; second, the invention of the digital computer, a general-purpose information-processing device, which calculates according to explicit rules and takes in data in terms of atomic elements logically independent of one another. In some other culture, the digital computer would most likely have seemed an unpromising model for the creation of artificial reason, but in our tradition the computer seems to be the very paradigm of logical intelligence, merely awaiting the proper program to accede to man's essential attribute of rationality.

The impetus gained by the mutual reinforcement of two thousand years of tradition and its product, the most powerful device ever invented by man, is simply too great to be arrested, deflected, or even fully understood. The most that can be hoped is that we become aware that the direction this impetus has taken, while unavoidable, is not the only possible direction; that the assumptions underlying the conviction that artificial reason is possible are assumptions, not axioms—in short, that there may be an alternative way of understanding human reason which explains both why the computer paradigm is irresistible and why it must fail.

Such an alternative view has many hurdles to overcome. The greatest of these is that it cannot be presented as an alternative scientific explanation. We have seen that what counts as "a complete description" or an explanation is determined by the very tradition to which we are seeking an alternative. We will not have *understood* an ability, such as the human mastery of a natural language, until we have found a theory, a formal system of rules, for describing this competence. We will not have understood behavior, such as the *use* of language, until we can specify that behavior in terms of unique and precisely definable reactions to precisely defined objects in universally defined situations. Thus, Western thought has already committed itself to what would count as an explanation of human behavior. It must be a theory of practice, which treats man as a device, an object responding to the influence of other objects, according to universal laws or rules.

But it is just this sort of theory, which, after two thousand years of refinement, has become sufficiently problematic to be rejected by philosophers both in the Anglo-American tradition and on the Continent. It is just this theory which has run up against a stone wall in research in artificial intelligence. It is not some specific explanation, then, that has failed, but the whole conceptual framework which assumes that an explanation of human behavior can and must take the Platonic form, successful in physical explanation; that situations can be treated like physical states; that the human world can be treated like the physical universe. If this whole approach has failed, then in proposing an alternative account we shall have to propose a different *sort* of explanation, a different sort of answer to the question "How does man produce intelligent behavior?" or even a different sort of question, for the notion of "producing" behavior instead of simply exhibiting it is already colored by the tradition. For a product must be produced in some way; and if it isn't produced in some definite way, the only alternative seems to be that it is produced magically.

There is a kind of answer to this question which is not committed beforehand to finding the precise rulelike relations between precisely defined objects. It takes the form of a phenomenological description of the behavior involved. It, too, can give us understanding if it is able to find the general characteristics of such behavior: what, if any one thing, is involved in seeing a table or a house, or, more generally, in perception, problem solving, using a language, and so forth. Such an account can even be called an explanation if it goes further and tries to find the fundamental features of human activity which serve as the necessary and sufficient conditions for all forms of human behavior.

Such an explanation owes a debt to Aristotle's method, although not to his arguments or descriptions. Whereas Plato sought rulelike criteria, Aristotle tried to describe the general structure of perception and judgment. But, as his notion that action is based on a practical syllogism shows, Aristotle still thought of man as a calculable and calculating sort of object—a reckoning animal—so that his actual descriptions are one step in the tradition which finally separated the rationality from the animality and tried to simulate the reckoning all by itself.

It is only recently, now that the full implications of the attempt to treat man merely as an object or device have become apparent, that philosophers have begun to work out a new view. The pioneers were Heidegger and Wittgenstein. Since then many others, notably Maurice Merleau-Ponty and Michael Polanyi have, each on his own, applied, consolidated, and refined similar insights; and young thinkers such as Charles Taylor and Samuel Todes are continuing their research. In trying to lay out the alternative view that emerges when we confront the three basic assumptions of the tradition with a phenomenological description of the structure of human behavior, I shall be drawing on the work of all these men.

I am fully aware that this "account" is vaguer and less experimental than that of either the behaviorists or intellectualists which it is meant to supplant.[1]* But one must not become so fascinated with the formalizable aspects of a subject that one forgets the significant questions which originally gave rise to the research, nor should one be so eager for experimental results that one continues to use old techniques just because they work, when they have ceased to lead to new insights. Chomsky is one of the few in the behavioral sciences who see this danger.

Without wishing to exalt the cult of gentlemanly amateurism, one must nevertheless recognize that the classical issues have a liveliness and significance that may be lacking in an area of investigation that is determined by the applicability of certain tools and methods, rather than by problems that are of intrinsic interest in themselves.

The moral is not to abandon useful tools; rather, it is, first, that one should maintain enough perspective to be able to detect the arrival of that inevitable day when the research that can be conducted with these tools is no longer important; and, second, that one should value ideas and insights that are to the point, though perhaps premature and vague and not productive of research at a particular stage of technique and understanding.[2]

Taking this suggestion to heart, we shall explore three areas necessarily neglected in CS and AI but which seem to underlie all intelligent behavior: the role of the body in organizing and unifying our experience of objects, the role of the situation in providing a background against which behavior can be orderly without being rulelike, and finally the role of human purposes and needs in organizing the situation so that objects are recognized as relevant and accessible.

The Role of the Body in Intelligent Behavior

Adherents of the psychological and epistemological assumptions that human behavior must be formalizable in terms of a heuristic program for a digital computer are forced to develop a theory of intelligent behavior which makes no appeal to the fact that a man has a body, since at this stage at least the computer clearly hasn't one. In thinking that the body can be dispensed with, these thinkers again follow the tradition, which from Plato to Descartes has thought of the body as getting in the way of intelligence and reason, rather than being in any way indispensable for it. If the body turns out to be indispensable for intelligent behavior, then we shall have to ask whether the body can be simulated on a heuristically programmed digital computer. If not, then the project of artificial intelligence is doomed from the start. These are the questions to which we must now turn.

Descartes, the first to conceive the possibility of robots, was also the first to suggest the essential inadequacy of a finite state machine. He remarks in the *Discourses:*

Although such machines could do many things as well as, or perhaps even better than men, they would infallibly fail in certain others. . . . For while reason is a universal instrument which can be used in all sorts of situations, the organs of a machine have to be arranged in a particular way for each particular action. From this it follows that it is morally [i.e., practically] impossible that there should be enough different devices in a machine to make it behave in all the occurrences of life as our reason makes us behave.[1]

Thus, although not aware of the difference between a situation and a physical state, Descartes already saw that the mind can cope with an indefinite number of situations, whereas a machine has only a limited set of states and so will eventually reveal itself by its failure to respond appropriately. This intrinsic limitation of mechanism, Descartes claims, shows the necessity of presupposing an *immaterial soul.*

This is an interesting argument, and some version of it may indeed be valid, but it gets its plausibility from the assumption that a robot can be in only a relatively small number of states. When in a modern computer the number of possible states is of the order of $10^{10^{10}}$, it is not clear just how much Descartes' objection proves. Such a machine could at least in principle respond to what would appear to be an indefinite number of situations. It would thus, on Descartes' view, be indistinguishable from a human being, destroying his argument that intelligent behavior is possible only if the mechanism behaving is somehow attached to a non-material soul. But one can raise a new objection, in some ways the exact opposite of Descartes'. A brain in a bottle or a digital computer might still not be able to respond to new sorts of situations because our ability to be in a situation might depend, not just on the flexibility of our nervous system, but rather on our ability to engage in practical activity. After some attempts to program such a machine, it might become apparent that what distinguishes persons from machines, no matter how cleverly constructed, is not a detached, universal, immaterial soul but an involved, situated, material body.

Indeed, it is just the bodily side of intelligent behavior which has caused the most trouble for artificial intelligence. Simon, who has been only slightly daunted by the failures of the last ten years, now feels that "machines will be capable, within *twenty* years, of doing any work that a man can do,"[2] but he admits: "Automation of a flexible central nervous system will be feasible long before automation of a comparatively flexible sensory, manipulative, or locomotive system."[3] But what if the work of the central nervous system depends on the locomotive system, or to put it phenomenologically, what if the "higher," determinate, logical, and detached forms of intelligence are necessarily derived from and guided by global and involved "lower" forms? Then Simon's optimism, based on the three assumptions underlying artificial intelligence and traditional philosophy, would be unjustified.

The intractability of the "lower" functions has already produced a certain irony. Computer technology has been most successful in simulating the so-called higher rational functions—those which were once supposed to be uniquely human. Computers can deal brilliantly with ideal languages and abstract logical relations. It turns out that it is the sort of intelligence which we share with animals, such as pattern recognition (along with the use of language, which may indeed be uniquely human) that has resisted machine simulation.

Let us reconsider the holism we have already noted in two related areas where AI has not fulfilled early expectations: chess playing and pattern recognition. Thus far I have tried to account for these failures by arguing that the task in question cannot be formalized, and by isolating the nonformal form of "information processing" necessarily involved. Now I shall try to show that the nonformalizable form of "information processing" in quesion is possible only for embodied beings.

To make this clear we shall first have to consider human pattern recognition in more detail. With the aid of concepts borrowed from phenomenology, I shall try to show how pattern recognition requires a certain sort of indeterminate, global anticipation. This set or anticipation is characteristic of our body as a "machine" of nerves and muscles whose function can be studied by the anatomist, and also of our body as experienced by us, as our power to move and manipulate objects in the world. I shall argue that a body in both these senses cannot be reproduced by a heuristically programmed digital computer—even one on wheels which can operate manipulators, and that, therefore, by virtue of being embodied, we can perform tasks beyond the capacities of any heuristically programmed robot.

We have seen that the restricted applicability of pattern recognition programs suggests that human pattern recognition proceeds in some other way than searching through lists of traits. Indeed, phenomenologists and Gestalt psychologists have pointed out that our recognition of ordinary spatial or temporal objects does not seem to operate by checking off a list of isolable, neutral, specific characteristics at all. For example, in recognizing a melody, the notes get their values by being perceived as part of the melody, rather than the melody's being recognized in terms of independently identified notes. Likewise, in the perception of objects there are no neutral traits. The same hazy layer which I would see as dust if I thought I was confronting a wax apple might appear as moisture if I thought I was seeing one that was fresh. The significance of the details and indeed their very look is determined by my perception of the whole.

The recognition of spoken language offers the most striking demonstration of this global character of our experience. From time to time brash predictions such as Rosenblatt's have been made about mechanical secretaries into which (or at whom) one could speak, and whose programs would analyze the sounds into words and type out the results. In fact, no one knows how to begin to make such a versatile device, and further progress is unlikely, for current work has shown that the same physical constellation of sound waves is heard as quite different phonemes, depending on the expected meaning.

Oettinger has given considerable attention to the problem. His analysis of speech recognition work is worth reproducing in detail, both because this pattern recognition problem is important in itself and because this work exhibits the early success and subsequent failure to generalize which we have come to recognize as typical of artificial intelligence research.

There was considerable initial success in building apparatus that would eke out a sequence of discrete phonemes out of the continuous speech waveform. While phonemic analysis has been dominant in that area, numerous other approaches to this decoding problem have also been followed. All have shared this initial degree of success and yet all, so far, have proved to be incapable of significant expansion beyond the recognition of the speech of a very few distinct individuals and the recognition of a very few distinct sound patterns whether they be phonemes or words or whatever. All is well as long as you are willing to have a fairly restricted universe of speakers, or sounds, or of both.

Within these limitations you can play some very good tricks. There are now lots of machines, some experimental, some not so experimental, that will recognize somewhere between 20 and 100 distinct sound patterns, some of them quite elaborate. Usually the trick is something like identifying a number of features, treating these as if they were coordinates in some hyperspace, then passing planes that cordon off, if you will, different blocks of this space. If your speech event falls somewhere within one of these blocks you say that it must have been that sound and you recognize it.

This game was fairly successful in the range of twenty to a hundred or so distinct things, but after that, these blocks become so small and clustered so close together that you no longer can achieve any reliable sort of separation. Everything goes to pot.[4]

This leads Oettinger to a very phenomenological observation:

Perhaps . . . in perception as well as in conscious scholarly analysis, the phoneme comes after the fact, namely . . . it is constructed, if at all, as a *consequence* of perception not as a step in the process of perception itself.[5]

This would mean that the total meaning of a sentence (or a melody or a perceptual object) determines the value to be assigned to the individual elements.

Oettinger goes on reluctantly to draw this conclusion:

This drives me to the unpopular and possibly unfruitful notion that maybe there is some kind of Gestalt perception going on, that here you are listening to me, and somehow the meaning of what I'm saying comes through to you all of a piece. And it is only a posteriori, and if you really give a damn, that you stop and say, "Now, here was a sentence and the words in it were of such and such type, and maybe here was a noun and here was a vowel and that vowel was this phoneme and the sentence is declarative, etc."[6]

Phenomenologists, not committed to breaking down the pattern so that it can be recognized by a digital computer, while less appalled, are no less fascinated by the gestalt character of perception. Indeed, it has been systematically studied in their account of perceptual horizons. Two forms of awareness are involved. First there is the basic figure-ground phenomenon, necessary for there to be any perception at all: whatever is prominent in our experience and engages our attention appears on a background which remains more or less indeterminate. This background, which need never have been made determinate, affects the appearance of what is determinate by letting it appear as a unified, bounded figure. In Rubin's famous "Peter-Paul Goblet" (Figure 4), "the contour which divides figure from ground 'belongs' to the figure only and changes its shape radically if a figure-ground reversal occurs."[7] Thus the figure has specific determinate characteristics, while the background can be characterized only as that-which-is-not-the figure.

Figure 4

This indeterminacy plays a crucial role in human perception. Merleau-Ponty points out that most of what we experience must remain in the background so that something can be perceived in the foreground.

When Gestalt theory informs us that a figure on a background is the simplest sense-datum available to us, we reply that this is not a contingent characterization of factual perception, which leaves us free, in an ideal analysis, to bring in the notion of impression. It is the very definition of the phenomenon of perception. . . . The perceptual 'something' is always in the middle of something else; it always forms part of a 'field.'[8]

It is this ground, or outer horizon as Edmund Husserl, the founder of phenomenology, called it, which in our chess example remains indeterminate and yet provides the context of the specific counting out, so that one always has a sense of the relevance of the specific move under consideration to the rest of the game. Similarly, our sense of the overall context may organize and direct our perception of the details when we understand a sentence. For a computer, which must take up every bit of information explicitly or not at all, there could be no outer horizon. Any information to be taken into account would have to be as determinate as the figure. This leads to the unwieldy calculations which we have seen in chess programs and which Oettinger deplores in language programs.

This outer horizon, then, describes how background "information" about a conversation or a particular game is ignored without being excluded. It does not, however, describe the way the background provides information which contributes to the player zeroing in on one area of the chess board rather than another, or how our anticipation of a sentence's meaning determines our understanding of its elements as they fall into place. To understand this, we must consider a second kind of perceptual indeterminacy investigated by Husserl and Gestalt psychologists: what Husserl calls the inner horizon. The something-more-than-the-figure is, in this case, not as indeterminate as the outer horizon. When we perceive an object we are aware that it has more aspects than we are at the moment considering. Moreover, once we have experienced these further aspects, they will be experienced as copresent, as covered up by what is directly presented. Thus, in ordinary situations, we say we perceive the whole object, even its hidden aspects, because the concealed aspects directly affect our perception. We perceive a house, for example, as more than a façade—as having some sort of back—some inner horizon. We respond to this whole object first and then, as we get to know the object better, fill in the details as to inside and back. A machine with no equivalent of an inner horizon would have to process this information in the reverse order: from details to the whole. Given any aspect of an object, the machine would either pick it up on its receptors or it would not. All additional information about other aspects of the object would have to be explicitly stored in memory—in Minsky's sort of model—or counted out again when it was needed. This lack of horizons is the essential difference between an image in a movie or on a TV screen and the same scene as experienced by a human being.

When, in a film, the camera is trained on an object and moves nearer to it to give a close-up view, we can *remember* that we are being shown the ash tray or an actor's hand, we do not actually identify it. This is because the scene has no horizons.[9]

In chess and in recognizing sentences, we find the same phenomenon playing a crucial role. Our sense of the whole situation, outer horizon, and our past experience with the specific object or pattern in question, inner horizon, give us a sense of the whole and guide us in filling in the details.[10]*

This process can best be noticed when it is breaking down. If you reach for a glass of water and get milk by mistake, on taking a sip your first reaction is total disorientation. You don't taste water, but you don't taste milk either. You have a mouthful that approaches what Husserl would call pure sensuous matter or hyletic data, and naturally you want to spit it out. Or, if you find the right global meaning fast enough, you may recover in time to recognize the milk for what it is. Its other characteristics, whether it is fresh or sour, buttermilk or skimmed milk, will then fall into place.

One might well wonder how one knows enough to try "milk" rather than, say, "gasoline." Doesn't one need some neutral features to begin this process of recognition? The perceiver's apparent clairvoyance seems so paradoxical that one is tempted to embrace the computer model in spite of its difficulties. But the process seems less mysterious when we bear in mind that each new meaning is given in an outer horizon which is already organized, in this case a meal, on the basis of which we already have certain expectations. It is also important that we sometimes *do* give the wrong meaning; in these cases the data coming in make no sense at all, and we have to try a new *total* hypothesis.

A computer, which must operate on completely determinate data according to strictly defined rules, could at best be programmed to try out a series of hypotheses to see which best fit the fixed data. But this is far from the flexible interaction of underdetermined data and underdetermined expectations which seems to be characteristic of human pattern recognition.

As one might expect, the computer people, again with the support of the philosophical tradition, and the success of physics, have rarely faced this problem. Philosophers have thought of man as a contemplative mind passively receiving data about the world and then ordering the elements. Physics has made this conception plausible on the level of the brain as a physical object. The brain does passively receive energy from the physical world and process it in terms of its present state which is a function of past energy received. If one accepts the passive view of mind and fails to distinguish the physical-processing level from the "information-processing" level, it seems self-evident that the mind, like the computer, simply receives bits of determinate data. In his introduction to the *Scientific American* issue on computers, McCarthy naïvely confuses brain and mind, energy and information, so that the passivity of the computer appears to be a self-evident model for human "information processing."

The human brain also accepts inputs of information, combines it with information stored somehow within, and returns outputs of information to its environment.[11]

Neisser is much more subtle. He too underestimates the problems posed by the role of anticipation, but his work in psychology has at least led him to see the need for "wholistic operations which form the units to which attention may then be directed,"[12] and he tries to fit this fact into his overall commitment to a digital computer model. The result is a confusion between what "global or wholistic" means in a gestalt analysis and what it would have to mean in a computer program, which is sufficiently revealing to be worth following in detail.

A general characterization of the gestalt, or global, phenomenon is: the interpretation of a part depends on the whole in which it is embedded. But this is too general. Such a definition allows Minsky, for example, to miss the whole problem. In his *Scientific American* article he speaks of Evans' analogy-solving program as being able to "recognize a 'global' aspect of the situation."[13] This turns out to mean that, on the basis of calculations made on certain local features of a figure, the program segments two superimposed figures in one way rather than another. There is nothing here to surprise or interest those concerned with the way the gestalt, or global, configuration functions in our experience.

To see the difference between the holistic processes which interest Neisser and what Minsky calls global recognition, one needs a sharper characterization of the gestalt phenomenon. Neisser gives such a characterization in terms of a temporal gestalt, a rhythm (a favorite example of the Gestaltists):

The parts (individual beats) get their meaning (relative position) from the whole, even though that whole does not exist at any moment of time. It exists, as one might say, in the subject's mind, as an intent, . . . a Gestalt. . . .[14]

The crucial feature of this gestalt interpretation, that *what counts as a part is defined in terms of the whole,* is missing in Minsky's example, as it must be, since, as we have seen, for a digital computer, each complex whole must be constructed by the logical combination of *independently defined* elements. In Minsky's example, the elements already have a precise significance (or rather two possible precise significances), and it is simply a question of deciding which interpretation is appropriate in terms of a decision based on other determinate local features of the figure.

Neisser's description of the "mind's intent," the anticipations which segment the individual beats, on the other hand, brings us to the center of the problem. The question is how the partially determinate anticipations, involved in game playing, pattern recognition, and intelligent behavior in general, can be simulated on a heuristically programmed digital computer so that the computer does not have to passively receive meaningless data but has anticipations of relevant information. Specifically for Neisser, the problem is how to reconcile his gestaltist analysis with a computer model of human performance.

Neisser thinks he has a way. In discussing linguistic performance as an example of the gestalt effect, Neisser thinks of the rules of grammar as the wholes into which the words fit as parts.

The rules are *structural.* That is, they do not dictate what particular words are to be used, but rather how they are to be related to each other and to the sentence as a whole.[15]

But this will not work. In the case of the rhythm, the whole *determined what counted as* an element — there is no such thing as a syncopated beat, for example, existing all by itself—but for Neisser, in the case of language, the words already have a determinate set of possible meanings; the grammar simply provides a rule for selecting a meaning and combining it with others. The elements in this case are completely determinate and can be defined independently of the rules. It is, therefore, misleading when Neisser concludes:

A sentence is more than the sum of its parts. This is not an unfamiliar slogan. Long ago, the Gestalt psychologists used it to describe the wholistic aspects of visual perception.[16]

This confusion is already latent in Neisser's description of the anticipation involved in hearing a rhythm in the example quoted above. The description concludes: "[The anticipation] exists . . . in the subject's mind as an intent, a gestalt, *a plan, a description of a response that can be executed without further consideration.*"[17] This slide from gestalt anticipation to preset plan is an obfuscation necessitated by the computer model: A gestalt defines what counts as the elements it organizes; a plan or a rule simply organizes independently defined elements. Moreover, just as the elements (the beats) cannot be defined independently of the gestalt, the gestalt (the rhythm) is nothing but the organization of the elements. A plan, on the other hand, can be stated as a rule or program, independently of the elements. Clearly his computer model of a formal program defined and stored separately from the independently defined bits of data which it organizes leads Neisser to betray his own gestaltist illustration. This difference is neglected in all CS models, yet it is the essence of the gestaltist insight, and accounts for the flexibility of human pattern recognition compared to that of machines.

Thus far computer programs have been unable to approach this interdependence of parts and whole. Neisser himself never sees this problem, but he unwittingly casts some new light on the important differences between mechanist and gestaltist models of psychological processes when he contrasts the digital model of neural processes postulated by the transformational linguists with the analogue model of the brain espoused by the early Gestalt psychologists.

[The Gestaltists] were "nativists," believing that the perceptual processes were determined by necessary and innate principles rather than by learning. The proper figural organization. . . . was due to processes in the brain, which followed unvarying (and wholistic) laws of physics and chemistry. . . . The perceived world always took the "best," the "structurally simplest" form, because of the equilibrium principle that transcends any possible effects of learning or practice.[18]

Such an analogue model of brain function, in which information is integrated by equilibrium forces rather than on/off switches, was necessary if the Gestalt psychologists were to account for the role of global anticipations in structuring experience. They had been led to break with the rationalist tradition running from Descartes to Kant, which conceived of the mind as bringing independently defined innate principles (Descartes) or rules (Kant) to bear on otherwise unstructured experience. This rationalist conception (with the addition of minimal bits of determinate experience) lends itself perfectly to a computer model, but the Gestaltists saw that their principles of organization—like the equilibrium patterns formed by charged particles on curved surfaces—could not be separated from the elements they organized. Thus, even if the digital model of the brain had existed at the time, the Gestaltists would have rejected it.[19]*

Neisser does not see this. He supposes that the digital model of built-in rules, which the linguists have been led to propose, is an improvement on the analogue model proposed by the Gestaltists. Neisser's praise of the linguists' "improvement," ignoring as it does the difficulties in artificial intelligence, the latest developments in neurophysiology, and the reason the Gestaltists proposed an analogue model in the first place can only be a non sequitur:

The Gestalt psychologists were never able to provide any satisfactory description or analysis of the structures involved in perception. The few attempts to specify "fields of force" in vision, or "ionic equilibria" in the brain, were ad hoc and ended in failure. In linguistics, by contrast, the study of "syntactic structures" has a long history.[20]

How the long history of syntactic structures is supposed to show that the linguists have a better model of neural processes than the Gestaltists is totally unclear. It seems to mean that at least the rules the linguists are looking for would be, if they were found, the sort of rules one could process with a digital computer which we already understand, whereas the gestaltist equilibrium principles could only be simulated on a brain-like analogue computer, which no one at present knows how to design.

This is no doubt true, but it reminds one of the story of the drunk who lost a key in the dark but looked for it under a street lamp because the light was better. It would indeed be nice to have a programmable model in linguistics, and in psychology in general, but the fact remains that modern linguists have no more detailed account of what goes on in the brain than did the Gestaltists, and, moreover, as a theory of competence, not performance, modern linguistics is not even trying to provide answers to the problem of how we produce intelligent behavior. Worse, in this case, the street lamp is not even lit. We have seen that when digital computers have been used to try to simulate linguistic *performance,* they have had remarkably little success.

The upshot of Neisser's comparison of gestalt and linguistic models of the brain, in opposition to his intent, is to call attention to a difference in brain model which exactly parallels the difference in the conception of the holistic processes, which he also overlooks. The sort of gestalt process illustrated in Neisser's example of the rhythm which gives meaning to and is made up of its beats suggests that however the brain integrates stimuli, it does not do it like a digital computer applying independently defined heuristic rules to independently defined bits of data.

Among computer experts only Donald MacKay has seen this point. He concludes:

It may well be that only a special-purpose 'analogue' mechanism could meet all detailed needs. . . . We on the circuit side had better be very cautious before we insist that the kind of information processing that a brain does can be replicated in a realizable circuit. Some kind of 'wet' engineering may turn out to be inevitable.[21]

If, in the light of the phenomenological and neurophysiological evidence, we accept the view that the nervous system is some sort of analogue computer operating with equilibrium fields, we must still be on guard against transferring to psychology this model of the nervous system, conceived as a brain in a bottle receiving energy from the world and sending out responses. The human perceiver must be understood in different terms than his nervous system. To have an alternative account of intelligent behavior we must describe the general and fundamental features of human activity. In the absence of a workable digital computer model, and leaving to the neurophysiologist the question of how the brain integrates incoming physical stimuli, we must again ask, How do human beings use an underdetermined, wholistic expectation to organize their experience?

Husserl has no further account beyond the assertion that we do: that "transcendental consciousness" has the *"wunderbar"* capacity for giving meanings and thus making possible the perception, recognition, and exploration of enduring objects. Like the Gestaltists, he thinks of these meanings as partially indeterminate wholes, not as explicit programs or rules. But even Husserl is not free from the traditional intellectualist view, and thus he too is vulnerable to the criticism directed at Neisser. Husserl, like Descartes and Kant, thinks of form as separable from content, of the global anticipation as separable from its sensuous feeling. Thus, his noema, or perceptual anticipation, is like a rule or program in one crucial way: it exists in the mind or transcendental consciousness independently of its application to the experience it structures.

Merleau-Ponty tries to correct Husserl's account on this point and at the same time develop a general description which supports the Gestaltists. He argues that it is the body which confers the meanings discovered by Husserl. After all, it is our body which captures a rhythm. We have a body-set to respond to the sound pattern. This body-set is not a rule in the mind which can be formulated or entertained apart from the actual activity of anticipating the beats.

Generally, in acquiring a skill—in learning to drive, dance, or pronounce a foreign language, for example—at first we must slowly, awkwardly, and consciously follow the rules. But then there comes a moment when we finally can perform automatically. At this point we do not seem to be simply dropping these same rigid rules into unconsciousness; rather we seem to have picked up the muscular gestalt which gives our behavior a new flexibility and smoothness. The same holds for acquiring the skill of perception. To take one of Merleau-Ponty's examples: to learn to feel silk, one must learn to move or be prepared to move one's hand in a certain way and to have certain expectations. Before we acquire the appropriate skill, we experience only confused sensations.

It is easiest to become aware of the body's role in taste, hearing, and touch, but seeing, too, is a skill that has to be learned. Focusing, getting the right perspective, picking out certain details, all involve coordinated actions and anticipations. As Piaget remarks, "Perceptual constancy seems to be the product of genuine actions, which consist of actual or potential movements of the glance or of the organs concerned. . . ."[22]

These bodily skills enable us not only to recognize objects in each single sense modality, but by virtue of the felt equivalence of our exploratory skills we can see and touch the same object. A computer to do the same thing would have to be programmed to make a specific list of the characteristics of a visually analyzed object and compare that list to an explicit list of traits recorded by moving tactical receptors over that same object. This means that there would have to be an internal model of each object in each sense modality, and that the recognition of an object seen and felt must pass through the analysis of that object in terms of common features.

My body enables me to by-pass this formal analysis. A skill, unlike a fixed response or set of responses can be brought to bear in an indefinite number of ways. When the percipient acquires a skill, he

does not weld together individual movements and individual stimuli but acquires the power to respond with a certain type of solution to situations of a certain general form. The situations may differ widely from place to place, and the response movements may be entrusted sometimes to one operative organ, sometimes to another, both situations and responses in the various cases having in common not so much a partial identity of elements as a shared significance.[23]

Thus I can recognize the resistance of a rough surface with my hands, with my feet, or even with my gaze. My body is thus what Merleau-Ponty calls a "synergistic system,"[24] "a ready-made system of equivalents and transpositions from one sense to another."[25]

Any object presented to one sense calls upon itself the concordant operation of all the others. I see a surface colour because I have a visual field, and because the arrangement of the field leads my gaze to that surface—I perceive a thing because I have a field of existence and because each phenomenon, on its appearance, attracts towards that field the whole of my body as a system of perceptual powers.[26]

A human perceiver, like a machine, needs feedback to find out if he has successfully recognized an object. But here too there is an important difference in the feedback involved. A machine can, at best, make a specific set of hypotheses and then find out if they have been confirmed or refuted by the data. The body can constantly modify its expectations in terms of a more flexible criterion: as embodied, we need not check for specific characteristics or a specific range of characteristics, but simply for whether, on the basis of our expectations, we are coping with the object. Coping need not be defined by any specific set of traits but rather by an ongoing mastery which Merleau-Ponty calls *maximum grasp*. What counts as maximum grasp varies with the goal of the agent and the resources of the situation. Thus it cannot be expressed in situation-free, purpose-free terms.

To conclude: Pattern recognition is relatively easy for digital computers if there are a few specific traits which define the pattern, but complex pattern recognition has proved intractable using these methods. Transcendental phenomenologists such as Husserl have pointed out that human beings recognize complex patterns by projecting a somewhat indeterminate whole which is progressively filled in by anticipated experiences. Existential phenomenologists such as Merleau-Ponty have related this ability to our active, organically interconnected body, set to respond to its environment in terms of a continual sense of its own functioning and goals.

Since it turns out that pattern recognition is a bodily skill basic to all intelligent behavior, the question of whether artificial intelligence is possible boils down to the question of whether there can be an artificial embodied agent. The question is philosophically interesting only if we restrict ourselves to asking if one can make such a robot by using a digital computer. (I assume there is no reason why, in principle, one could not construct an artificial embodied agent if one used components sufficiently like those which make up a human being.)

A project to build such a *digitally* controlled robot is currently under way at M.I.T., and it is philosophically interesting to consider its program and its underlying assumptions. The project director, Minsky again, is modestly trying to make only a mechanical shoulder, arm, and hand, coordinated with a TV eye, but he proposes to make it use tools to construct things. The first simple task was to program a simplified robot arm to pick up blocks. This has indeed been accomplished and represents the early success one has learned to expect in the field. The problem which remains is, as usual, that of generalizing the present successful techniques. To bring a simple arm over to pick up a block requires locating the block in objective space, locating the arm in the same space, and then bringing the two together. This is already quite a feat. A mathematical description of the way an arm moves in objective space runs into surprising discontinuities. There are points which are contiguous in objective space which are far apart in reaching space. For example, to scratch our back we do not simply extend the position we use for scratching our ear. Living in our bodies we have built up a motor space, in which we sense these objectively contiguous points as far apart. We automatically reach for them in very different ways, and do not feel we have gone through the mathematics necessary to work out the optimal path for each specific case. For the programmer, however, who has to program the computer to calculate the movements of the mechanical arm in objective space, these discontinuities have so far proved an insurmountable obstacle. The more flexible the arm—the more degrees of freedom it has—the more difficult and time consuming such calculations become. Rumor has it that an elaborate arm with six degrees of freedom, built by Minsky by 1965, has still not even been programmed to move, let alone pick up blocks or use tools. If one adds to this the fact that, in the case of any skill which takes place in real time (such as playing Ping-Pong), all calculations must be completed in real time (before the ball arrives), the outlook is not very promising. As Feigenbaum notes in his report on the current state of robot work:

Both the MIT and Stanford University groups have worked on programs for controlling a variety of arm-hand manipulators, from the very simple to the very complex, from the anthropomorphic variety to the very non-anthropomorphic. None of the more esoteric manipulators seems to have worked out very well, though there is no published documentation of successes, failures, and reasons.[27]

In the light of these difficulties, what encourages researchers to devote their research facilities to such a project? Simply the conviction that since we are, as Minsky ingenuously puts it, "meat machines" and are able to play Ping-Pong, there is no reason in principle or in practice why a metal machine cannot do likewise. But before jumping to such a conclusion, the robot makers ought first to examine their underlying assumption that no essential difference exists between meat machines and metal machines, between being embodied and controlling movable manipulators. How do human beings play Ping-Pong, or to make the matter simpler, how do human beings use tools?

Heidegger, Merleau-Ponty, and Michael Polanyi have each devoted a great deal of thought to this question. Each discusses the important way that our experience of a tool we are using differs from our experience of an object. A blind man who runs his hand along the cane he uses to grope his way will be aware of its objective position and its characteristics such as weight, hardness, smoothness, and so forth. When he is using it, however, he is not aware of its position in physical space, its features, nor of the varying pressure in the palm of his hand. Rather, the stick has become, like his body, a transparent access to the objects he touches with it. As Polanyi puts it:

While we rely on a tool or a probe, these are not handled as external objects . . . they remain on our side . . . forming part of ourselves, the operating persons. We pour ourselves out into them and assimilate them as parts of our existence. We accept them existentially by dwelling in them.[28]

In this way we are able to bring the probe into contact with an object in physical space without needing to be aware of the physical location of the probe. Merleau-Ponty notes that:

The whole operation takes place in the domain of the phenomenal; it does not run through the objective world, and only the spectator, who lends his objective representation of the living body to the active subject, can believe that . . . the hand moves in objective space.[29]

But Merleau-Ponty admits that this ability seems "magical" from the point of view of science, so we should not be surprised to find that rather than have no explanation of what people are able to do, the computer scientist embraces the assumption that people are unconsciously running with incredible speed through the enormous calculation which would be involved in programming a computer to perform a similar task. However implausible, this view gains persuasiveness from the absence of an alternative account.

To make embodiment an acceptable alternative we will have to show how one could perform physical tasks without in any way appealing to the principles of physics or geometry. Consider the act of randomly waving my hand in the air. I am not trying to place my objective hand at an objective point in space. To perform this waving I need not take into account geometry, since I am not attempting any specific achievement. Now suppose that, in this random thrashing about, I happen to touch something, and that this satisfies a need to cope with things. (More about need in Chapter 9.) I can then repeat *whatever I did*—this time *in order to* touch something—without appealing to the laws necessary to describe my movement as a physical motion. I now have a way of bringing two objects together in objective space without appealing to any principle except: "Do that again." This is presumably the way skills are built up. The important thing about skills is that, although *science* requires that the skilled performance be *described* according to rules, these rules need in no way be *involved* in producing the performance.

Human beings are further capable of remembering, refining, and reorganizing these somewhat indeterminate motor schemata. Piaget has amassed an enormous amount of evidence tracing the development of these motor skills, which he calls operations, and has come to a Gestaltist conclusion:

The specific nature of operations . . . depends on the fact that they never exist in a discontinuous state. . . . A single operation could not be an operation because the peculiarity of operations is that they form systems. Here we may well protest vigorously against logical atomism . . . a grievous hindrance to the psychology of thought.[30]*

This same analysis helps dissipate the mistaken assumptions underlying early optimism about language translation. If human beings had to apply semantic and syntactic rules and to store and access an infinity of facts in order to understand a language, they would have as much trouble as machines. The native speaker, however, is not aware of having generated multiple semantic ambiguities which he then resolved by appeal to facts any more than he is aware of having picked out complex patterns by their traits or of having gone through the calculations necessary to describe the way he brings his hand to a certain point in objective space. Perhaps language, too, is a skill acquired by innately guided thrashing around and is used in an nonrulelike way. Many skills such as our repertoire of ways to sit in and get up from a wide variety of chairs allow an indefinite number of orderly variations without being generated by strict rules.

Such a view is not behavioristic. Our ability to use language in a situation and in general the wholistic way the functional meaning organizes and structures the components of skilled acts cannot be accounted for in terms of the arbitrary association of neutral determinate elements any more than it can be analyzed in terms of their combination according to rules.

If language is understood as a motor skill, we would then assimilate language and dwell in it the way we assimilate an instrument. As Polanyi puts it,

To use language in speech, reading and writing, is to extend our bodily equipment and become intelligent human beings. We may say that when we learn to use language, or a probe, or a tool, and thus make ourselves aware of these things as we are of our body, we *interiorise* these things and *make ourselves dwell in them.*[31]*

Again, because we are embodied, the rules necessary to give an objective analysis of our competence need in no way be involved in our performance.

The AI researcher and the transcendental phenomenologist share the assumption that there is only one way to deal with information: it must be made an object for a disembodied processor. For the transcendental phenomenologist this assumption makes the organization of our intelligent behavior unintelligible. For the AI researcher it seems to justify the assumption that intelligent behavior can be produced by passively receiving data and then running through the calculations necessary to describe the objective competence. But, as we have seen, being embodied creates a second possibility. The body contributes three functions not present, and not as yet conceived in digital computer programs: (1) the inner horizon, that is, the partially indeterminate, predelineated anticipation of partially indeterminate data (this does not mean the anticipation of some completely determinate alternatives, or the anticipation of completely unspecified alternatives, which would be the only possible digital implementation); (2) the global character of this anticipation which determines the meaning of the details it assimilates and is determined by them; (3) the transferability of this anticipation from one sense modality and one organ of action to another. All these are included in the general human ability to acquire bodily skills. Thanks to this fundamental ability an embodied agent can dwell in the world in such a way as to avoid the infinite task of formalizing everything.

This embodied sort of "information processing," in which the meaning of the whole is prior to the elements, would seem to be at work in the sort of complex pattern recognition such as speech recognition with which we began our discussion. Indeed, sensory motor skills underlie perception whose basic figure/ground structure seems to underlie all "higher" rational functions; even logic and mathematics have an horizontal character. In all these cases individual features get their significance in terms of an underdetermined anticipation of the whole.

If these global forms of pattern recognition are not open to the digital computer, which, lacking a body, cannot respond as a whole, but must build up its recognition starting with determinate details, then Oettinger is justified in concluding his speech recognition paper on a pessimistic note: "If indeed we have an ability to use a global context without recourse to formalization . . . then our optimistic discrete enumerative approach is doomed. . . ."[32]

8

The Situation: Orderly Behavior Without Recourse to Rules

   In discussing problem solving and language translation we have come up against the threat of a regress of rules for determining relevance and significance. Likewise, in starting a learning process, something must be known before any rules can be taught or applied. In each case we have found that if there are no facts with fixed significance, only an appeal to the context can bring this regress to a halt. We must now turn directly to a description of the situation or context in order to give a fuller account of the unique way human beings are "in-the-world," and the special function this world serves in making orderly but nonrulelike behavior possible.

   To focus on this question it helps to bear in mind the opposing position. In discussing the epistemological assumption (Chapter 5) we saw that our philosophical tradition has come to assume that whatever is orderly can be formalized in terms of rules. This view has reached its most striking and dogmatic culmination in the conviction of AI workers that every form of intelligent behavior can be formalized. Minsky has even developed this dogma into a ridiculous but revealing theory of human free will. He is convinced that all regularities are rule governed. He therefore theorizes that our behavior is either completely arbitrary or it is regular and completely determined by rules. As he puts it:

". . . whenever a regularity is observed [in our behavior], its representation is transferred to the deterministic rule region."[1] Otherwise our behavior is completely arbitrary and free. The possibility that our behavior might be regular but not rule governed never even enters his mind.

We shall now try to show not only that human behavior can be regular without being governed by formalizable rules, but, further, that it has to be, because a total system of rules whose application to all possible eventualities is determined in advance makes no sense.

In our earlier discussion of problem solving we restricted ourselves to formal problems in which the subject had to manipulate unambiguous symbols according to a given set of rules, and to other context-free problems such as analogy intelligence tests. But if CS is to provide a psychological theory—and if AI programs are to count as intelligent— they must extend mechanical information processing to *all* areas of human activity, even those areas in which people confront and solve open-structured problems in the course of their everyday lives.[2]*

Open-structured problems, unlike games and tests, raise three sorts of difficulties: one must determine which facts are possibly relevant; which are actually relevant; and, among these, which are essential and which inessential. To begin with, in a given situation not all facts fall within the realm of possible relevancy. They do not even enter the situation. Thus, in the context of a game of chess, the weight of the pieces is irrelevant. It can never come into question, let alone be essential or inessential for deciding on a specific move. In general, deciding whether certain facts are relevant or irrelevant, essential or inessential, is not like taking blocks out of a pile and leaving others behind. What counts as essential depends on what counts as inessential and vice versa, and the distinction cannot be decided in advance, independently of some particular problem, or some particular stage of some particular game. Now, since facts are not relevant or irrelevant in a fixed way, but only in terms of human purposes, all facts are possibly relevant in some situation. Thus for example, if one is *manufacturing* chess sets, the weight is *possibly* relevant (although in most decisions involved in making and marketing chess sets, it will not be actually relevant, let alone essential). This situational character of relevance works both ways: In any particular situation an indefinite number of facts are possibly relevant and an indefinitely large number are irrelevant. Since a computer is not in a situation, however, it must treat *all* facts as possibly relevant at all times. This leaves AI workers with a dilemma: they are faced either with storing and accessing an infinity of facts, or with having to exclude some possibly relevant facts from the computer's range of calculations.

But even if one could restrict the universe for each particular problem to possibly relevant facts—and so far this can only be done by the programmer, not the program—the problem remains to determine what information is actually relevant. Even in a nonformal game like playing the horses—which is much more systematic than everyday open-structured problems—an unlimited, indefinitely large number of facts remain as possibly relevant. In placing a bet we can usually restrict ourselves to such facts as the horse's age, jockey, past performance, and competition. Perhaps, if restricted to these facts from the racing form, the machine could do fairly well, possibly better than an average handicapper; but there are always other factors such as whether the horse is allergic to goldenrod or whether the jockey has just had a fight with the owner, which *may* in some cases be decisive. Human handicappers are no more omniscient than machines, but they are capable of recognizing the relevance of such facts if they come across them. The artificial intelligence approach to this human ability would have to be to give the machine knowledge about veterinary medicine, how people behave when they fight their employers, and so forth. But then the problem arises of sorting through this vast storehouse of data. To which the answer is that all this information would be properly coded and tagged in the machine memory so that the machine would just have to do a scan for "horse-race betting" and get out the relevant material. But not all relevant material would, have been encoded with a reference to this particular use. As Charles Taylor has pointed out in an elaboration of this example:

The jockey might not be good to bet on today because his mother died yesterday. But when we store the information that people often do less than their best just after their near relations die, we can't be expected to tag a connection with betting on horses. This information can be relevant to an infinite set of contexts.

The machine might select on the basis of the key concepts it was worrying about, horses, jockeys, jockey Smith, etc. and pick out all facts about these. But this too would give an absurdly wide scatter. Via jockey, man and horse, one would find oneself pulling out all facts about centaurs. The only way the machine could zero in on the relevant facts would be to take this broad class, or some other selected on such a broad swoop basis, and test to see whether each one had causal relevance to the outcome of the race, taking it into account if it had, and forgetting it if it hadn't.[3]*

But if the machine were to examine explicitly each possibly relevant factor as a determinate bit of information in order to determine whether to consider or ignore it, it could never complete the calculations necessary to predict the outcome of a single race. If, on the other hand, the machine systematically excluded possibly relevant factors in order to complete its calculations, then it would sometimes be incapable of performing as well as an intelligent human to whom the same information was available.

Even the appeal to a random element will not help here, since in order to take up a sample of excluded possibilities at random so that no possibility is in principle excluded, the machine would have to be provided with an explicit list of all such other possibly relevant facts or a specific set of routines for exploring all classes of possibly relevant facts, so that no facts would be in principle inaccessible. This is just what could be done in a completely defined system such as chess, where a finite number of concepts determines totally and unequivocally the set of all possible combinations in the domain; but in the real world the list of such possibly relevant facts, or even classes of possibly relevant facts, would be indefinitely large ("infinite in a pregnant sense," to use Bar-Hillel's phrase). All the everyday problems—whether in language translation, problem solving, or pattern recognition—come back to these two basic problems: (1) how to restrict the class of possibly relevant facts while preserving generality, and (2) how to choose among possibly relevant facts those which are actually relevant.

Even Minsky implicitly admits that no one knows how to cope with the amount of data which must be processed if one simply tries to store all facts:

At each moment in the course of thinking about a problem, one is involved with a large collection of statements, definitions, associations, and so on, and a network of goals. One has to deal not only with facts about objects, relations between objects, and the like, but also facts about facts, classes of facts, relations between such classes, etc. The heuristic programs that, as we shall see, so neatly demonstrate principles when applied to small models will not work efficiently when applied to large ones. Problems like looping, branching, measuring progress, and generally keeping track of what is happening will come to require a disproportional part of the computation time.[4]

Whatever it is that enables human beings to zero in on the relevant facts without definitively excluding others which might become relevant is so hard to describe that it has only recently become a clearly focused problem for philosophers. It has to do with the way man is at home in his world, has it comfortably wrapped around him, so to speak. Human beings are somehow already situated in such a way that what they need in order to cope with things is distributed around them where they need it, not packed away like a trunk full of objects, or even carefully indexed in a filing cabinet. This system of relations which makes it possible to discover objects when they are needed is our home or our world. To put this less metaphorically it is helpful to return to Charles Taylor's extension of the horse-racing example.

Much of a human being's knowledge of situations and their possibilities is know-how, that is, it cannot be exhaustively unpacked into a set of specific instructions or factual statements, but is a general capacity to generate appropriate actions and therefore, if necessary, the "instructions" underlying them. Usually we think of this kind of indefinitely unpackable form of knowledge as bound up with the know-how which underlies our actions. But the same kind of knowledge underlies what we suffer, our "passions." Thus just as I have a general grasp on what it is to walk around, use my hands, drive a car, conduct a case in court (if I'm a lawyer), etc. So I have a general grasp on what it is to be threatened, to hear good news, to be jilted by my girl friend, to be made a fool of in public.

Now the human handicapper has this general grasp of certain common human actions and passions. He has the sense of the race as a perilous enterprise which needs all the will and effort of jockey (and horse) to win. But included in this sense is the capacity to imagine or recognize an indefinite number of ways in which this will and effort could miscarry or be countered by fortune. These are not stored somewhere as separate facts in the mind or brain, they are not "unpacked"; they are just generatable from the general grasp of the situation. Of course, the general grasp of different men may differ in scope and exactitude. If the handicapper has ever ridden horses, then he has a much firmer grasp on the activity; he can sense a lot more finely what may go wrong. But even the city-bred gangster has some general grasp of what it is to fight and strain hard to win.

But the artificial intelligence proponent may still want to protest that all this just represents an alternative method of "storage." Even if he admits that this method is not available to the machine, he might still ask how it solves the retrieval problem. How does the handicapper recognize just those odd factors which are relevant? The answer is that if we understand our grasp of the world as arising out of our dealing with it according to our different capacities, and our being touched by it according to our different concerns, then we can see that the problem of how a given concern or purpose comes to select the relevant features of our surroundings *doesn't arise. For being concerned in a certain way or having a certain purpose is not something separate from our awareness of our situation; it just is being aware of this situation in a certain light,* being aware of a situation with a certain structure. Thus being anxious for my own life because I have fallen among thugs is to sense the menace in that bulge in his pocket, to feel my vulnerability to his fist which might at any moment be swung at my face, and so on.[5]

The human world, then, is prestructured in terms of human purposes and concerns in such a way that what counts as an object or is significant about an object already is a function of, or embodies, that concern. This cannot be matched by a computer, which can deal only with universally defined, i.e., context-free, objects. In trying to simulate this field of concern, the programmer can only assign to the already determinate facts further determinate facts called values, which only complicates the retrieval problem for the machine.

In *Being and Time* Heidegger gives a description of the human world in which man is at home, on the model of a constellation of implements *(Zeuge),* each referring to each other, to the whole workshop and ultimately to human purposes and goals. The directional signal on a car serves as an example of a "fact" which gets its whole meaning from its pragmatic context:

The directional signal is an item of equipment which is ready-to-hand for the driver in his concern with driving, and not for him alone: those who are not travelling with him—and they in particular—also make use of it, either by giving way on the proper side or by stopping. This sign is ready-to-hand within-the-world in the whole equipment-context of vehicles and traffic regulations. It is equipment for indicating, and as equipment, it is constituted by reference or assignment.[6]

Wittgenstein too makes frequent references to human forms of life and concerns and to certain very general "facts of natural history" taken for granted in our use of language and in structuring our everyday activities —facts, incidentally, of a very special kind which would presumably elude the programmer trying to program all of human knowledge. As Wittgenstein says, "The aspects of things that are most important for us are hidden because of their simplicity and familiarity. (One is unable to notice something—because it is always before one's eyes.)"[7] Facts, moreover, which would be so pervasively connected with all other facts that even if they could be made explicit, they would be difficult if not impossible to classify. The basic insight dominates these discussions that the situation is organized from the start in terms of human needs and propensities which give the facts meaning, make the facts what they are, so that there is never a question of storing and sorting through an enormous list of *meaningless, isolated* data.

Samuel Todes[8]* has described in detail the field-structure of experience which is prior to the facts and implicitly determines their relevance and significance. He points out that the world is experienced as fields within fields. Bits or aspects of objects are not experienced as isolated facts but as nested in a series of contexts. And "in" has many different senses, none of them that of mere physical inclusion, which Minsky and McCarthy take as primary. Parts of objects are experienced as *in* objects which they *comprise,* objects are *in* places which they *fill,* a place is *situated in* a local environment, which itself is *in* the horizon of possible situations *in* a human world. Data, then, are far from brute; aspects of objects are not given as directly in the world but as characterizing objects in places in a local environment in space and time in the world.

We can and do zero in on significant content in the field of experience because this field is not neutral to us but is structured in terms of our interests and our capacity for getting at what is in it. Any object which we experience must appear in this field and therefore must appear in terms of our dominant interest at that moment, and as attainable by some variant of the activity which generated the field. Since we create the field in terms of our interests, only possibly relevant facts can appear.

Relevance is thus already built in. In the horse race case, racing fits into a nested context of activities, games, sports, contests. To see an activity as a horse race is to organize it in terms of the intention to win. To return to Taylor's account:

> The handicapper is concerned to pick a winner. As a human being he has a sense of what is involved in the enterprise of winning, and his being concerned means that he is aware of a horse, jockey, etc., in a way in which dangers are salient. Hence he notices when he reads in the obituary columns that Smith's mother died yesterday (Smith being the jockey, and one he knows to be very susceptible), and for once he bets against the form. The machine would pick out Smith's mother's death, as a fact about Smith, along with all the others, such as that Smith's second cousin has been elected dogcatcher in some other city, etc., but will then have to do a check on the probable consequences of these different facts before it decides to take them into account or not in placing the bet.[9]

Thus our present concerns and past know-how always already determines what will be ignored, what will remain on the outer horizon of experience as possibly relevant, and what will be immediately taken into account as essential.

Wittgenstein constantly suggests that the analysis of a situation into facts and rules (which is where the traditional philosopher and the computer expert think they must begin) is itself only meaningful in some context and for some purpose. Thus again the elements already reflect the goals and purposes for which they were carved out. When we try to find the ultimate context-free, purpose-free elements, as we must if we are going to find the ultimate bits to feed a machine—bits that will be relevant to all possible tasks because chosen for none—we are in effect trying to free the facts in our experience of just that pragmatic organization which makes it possible to use them flexibly in coping with everyday problems.

Not that a computer model is ever really purpose-free; even a model in terms of information storage must somehow reflect the context, but such an analysis of context in terms of facts and rules is rigid and restricting. To see this, let us grant that all the properties of objects (whatever that might mean) could be made explicit in a decision tree so that each node recorded whether the object has a certain situation-independent predicate or its converse. This sort of classification structure has been programmed by Edward Feigenbaum in his EPAM model.[10]* Such a discrimination net might, in principle, represent an exhaustive, explicit, apparently situation-free characterization of an object, or even of a situation, insofar as it was considered as an object. It thus seems to provide efficient information storage, while avoiding the field/object distinction. But something crucial is omitted in the description of such an information structure: the organization of the structure itself, which plays a crucial role in the informative storage. *The information in the tree is differently stored and differently accessible depending on the order in which the discriminations are made.* As William Wynn notes in a discussion of EPAM:

EPAM's Classification process is . . . too history-dependent and unadaptable, for the discrimination net can be grown only from the bottom down and cannot be reorganized from the top. Tests inserted in the net which later prove to be of little discriminatory power over a given stimulus set cannot be removed, nor can new tests be inserted in the upper portion of the net. Thus, once it is formed, EPAM's discrimination net is difficult to reorganize in the interest of greater retrieval efficiency. Any procedure that reorganizes the tests in the structure seriously impairs retrieval of many items held in the memory.[11]

So the order of discriminations is crucial. But in the physical world all predicates have the same priority. Only the programmer's sense of the situation determines the order in the decision tree. Through the programmer's judgment the distinction between the field and the objects in the field is introduced into the computerized model. The pragmatic context used by the programmer can indeed itself be characterized in a decision tree, but only in some order of discriminations which reflects a broader context. At each level information concerning this broader context is indeed embodied in the general structure of the tree, but at no particular node. At each level the situation is reflected in the pragmatic intuitions of the programmer governing the order of decisions; but this fixes the facts in one order based on a particular purpose, and inevitably introduces the lack of flexibility noted by Wynn.

If, on the other hand, in the name of flexibility all pragmatic ordering could be eliminated so that an unstructured list of purified facts could be assimilated by machine—facts about the sizes and shapes of objects in the physical world and even about their possible uses, as isolable functions—then all these facts would have to be explicitly included or excluded in each calculation, and the computer would be overwhelmed by their infinity.

This is not to deny that human beings *sometimes* take up isolated data and try to discover their significance by trying to fit them into a previously accumulated store of information. Sherlock Holmes and all detectives do this as a profession; everyone does it when he is in a very unfamiliar situation. But even in these cases there must be some more general context in which we are at home. A Martian might have to proceed in a very unfamiliar context if he were on earth, but if he shared *no* human purposes his task of sorting out the relevant from the irrelevant, essential from the inessential, would be as hopeless as that of the computer.

We all know also what it is to store and use data according to rules in some restricted context. We do this, for example, when we play a game such as bridge, although even here a good bridge player stores data in terms of purpose and strategies and takes liberties with the heuristic rules. We also sometimes play out alternatives in our imagination to predict what will happen in the real game before us. But it is just because we know what it is to have to orient ourselves in a world in which we are not at home; or to follow rulelike operations like the heuristics for bidding in bridge; and how to model in our imagination events which have not yet taken place, that we know that we are not aware of doing this most of the time. The claim that we are nonetheless carrying on such operations unconsciously is either an empirical claim, for which there is no evidence, or an *a priori* claim based on the very assumption we are here calling into question.

When we are at home in the world, the meaningful objects embedded in their context of references among which we live are not a model of the world stored in our mind or brain; *they are the world itself.* This may seem plausible for the public world of general purposes, traffic regulations, and so forth. But what about *my* experience, one may ask; my private set of facts, surely that is in my mind? This seems plausible only because one is still confusing this human world with some sort of physical universe. My personal plans and my memories are inscribed in the things around me just as are the public goals of men in general. My memories are stored in the familiar look of a chair or the threatening air of a street corner where I was once hurt. My plans and fears are already built into my experience of some objects as attractive and others as to be avoided. The "data" concerning social tasks and purposes which are built into the objects and spaces around me are overlaid with these personal "data" which are no less a part of my world. After all, personal threats and attractions are no more subjective than general human purposes.

Now we can see why, even if the nervous system must be understood as a physical object—a sort of analogue computer—whose energy exchange with the world must in principle be expressible as an input/output function, it begs the question and leads to confusion to suppose that on the information-processing level the human perceiver can be understood as an analogue computer having a precise I/O function reproducible on a digital machine. The whole I/O model makes no sense here. There is no reason to suppose that the human world can be analyzed into independent elements, and even if it could, one would not know whether to consider these elements the input or the output of the human mind.

If this idea is hard to accept, it is because this phenomenological account stands in opposition to our Cartesian tradition which thinks of the physical world as impinging on our mind which then organizes it according to its previous experience and innate ideas or rules. But even Descartes is not confused in the way contemporary psychologists and artificial intelligence researchers seem to be. He contends that the world which impinges on us is *a world of pure physical motions,* while the world "in the mind" is the world of objects, instruments, and so forth. Only the relation between these two worlds is unclear. Artificial intelligence theorists such as Minsky, however, have a cruder picture in which the world of implements does not even appear. As they see it, details of the everyday world—snapshots, as it were, of tables, chairs, etc.—are received by the mind. These fragments are then reassembled in terms of a model built of other facts the mind has stored up. The outer world, a mass of isolated facts, is interpreted in terms of the inner storehouse of other isolated, but well catalogued, facts—which somehow was built up from earlier experiences of this fragmented world—and the result is a further elaboration of this inner model. Nowhere do we find the familiar world of implements organized in terms of purposes.

Minsky has elaborated this computer-Cartesianism into an attempt at philosophy. He begins by giving a mechanized description of what is in fact the role of imagination:

If a creature can answer a question about a hypothetical experiment without actually performing it, then it has demonstrated some knowledge about the world. For, his [sic] answer to the question must be an encoded description of the behavior (inside the creature) of some submachine or "model" responding to an encoded description of the world situation described by the question.[12]

Minsky then, without explanation or justification, generalizes this dubious description of the proper function of imagination to all perception and knowledge:

Questions about things in the world are answered by making statements about the behavior of corresponding structures in one's model of the world.[13]

He is thus led to introduce a formalized copy of the external world; as if besides the objects which solicit our action, we need an encyclopedia in which we can look up where we are and what we are doing:

A man's model of the world has a distinctly bipartite structure: One part is concerned with matters of mechanical, geometrical, physical character, while the other is associated with things like goals, meanings, social matters, and the like.[14]

If all knowledge requires a model we, of course, need a model of ourselves:

When a man is asked a general question about his own nature, he will try to give a general description of his model of himself.[15]

And, of course, for this self-description to be complete we will need a description of our model of our model of ourselves, and so forth. Minsky thinks of this self-referential regress as the source of philosophical confusions concerning mind, body, free will, and so on. He does not realize that his insistence on models has introduced the regress and that this difficulty is proof of the philosophical incoherence of his assumption that nothing is ever known directly but only in terms of models.

In general the more one thinks about this picture the harder it is to understand. There seem to be two worlds, the outer data- and the inner data-structure, neither of which is ever experienced and neither of which is the physical universe or the world of implements we normally *do* experience. There seems to be no place for the physical universe or for our world of interrelated objects, but only for a library describing the universe and human world which, according to the theory, cannot exist.

To dismiss this theory as incoherent is not to deny that physical energy bombards our physical organism and that the result is our experience of the world. It is simply to assert that the physical processing of the physical energy is not a psychological process, and does not take place in terms of sorting and storing human-sized facts about tables and chairs. Rather, the human world is the result of this energy processing and the human world does not need another mechanical repetition of the same process in order to be perceived and understood.

This point is so simple and yet so hard to grasp for those brought up in the Cartesian tradition that it may be necessary to go over the ground once again, this time returning to a specific case of this confusion. As we have seen, Neisser begins his book *Cognitive Psychology* with an exposition of what he calls "the central problem of cognition."

There is certainly a real world of trees and people and cars and even books. . . . However, we have no direct, immediate access to the world, nor to any of its properties.[16]

Here, as we have noted in Chapter 4, the damage is already done. There is indeed a world to which we have no immediate access. We do not directly perceive the world of atoms and electromagnetic waves (if it even makes sense to speak of perceiving them)—but the world of cars and books is just the world we *do* directly experience. In Chapter 4 we saw that at this point, Neisser has recourse to an unjustified theory that we perceive "snapshots" or sense data. His further account only compounds the confusion:

Physically, this page is an array of small mounds of ink, lying in certain positions on the more highly reflective surface of the paper.[17]

But *physically*, what is there are atoms in motion, not paper and small mounds of ink. Paper and small mounds of ink are elements in the human world. Neisser, however, is trying to look at them in a special way, as if he were a savage, a Martian, or a computer, who didn't know what they were for. There is no reason to suppose that these strangely isolated objects are what men directly perceive (although one may perhaps approximate this experience in the very special detached attitude which comes over a cognitive psychologist sitting down to write a book). What we normally perceive is a printed page.

Again Neisser's middle-world, which is neither the world of physics nor the human world, turns out to be an artifact. No man has ever seen such an eerie world; and no physicist has any place for it in his system. Once we postulate it, however, it follows inevitably that the human world will somehow have to be reconstructed out of these fragments.

One-sided in their perspective, shifting radically several times each second, unique and novel at every moment, the proximal stimuli bear little resemblance to either the real object that gave rise to them or to the object of experience that the perceiver will construct as a result.[18]

But this whole construction process is superfluous. It is described in terms which make sense only if we think of man as a computer receiving isolated facts from a world in which it has no purposes; programmed to use them, plus a lot of other meaningless data it has accumulated or been given, to make some sort of sense (whatever that might mean) out of what is going on around it.

There is no reason to suppose that a normal human being has this problem, although some aphasics do. A normal person experiences the objects of the world as already interrelated and full of meaning. There is no justification for the assumption that we first experience isolated facts, or snapshots of facts, or momentary views of snapshots of isolated facts, and *then* give them significance. The analytical superfluousness of such a process is what contemporary philosophers such as Heidegger and Wittgenstein are trying to point out. To put this in terms of Neisser's discussion as nearly as sense will allow, we would have to say: "The human world *is* the brain's response to the physical world." Thus there is no point in saying it is "in the mind," and no point in inventing a third world—between the physical and the human world—which is an arbitrarily impoverished version of the world in which we live, out of which the human world has to be built up again.

Oettinger, alone among computer experts, has seen that in the world of perception and language, where the linguist and artificial intelligence worker begins his analysis, a global meaning is always already present.

What I want to suggest is not necessarily a novel suggestion; but it does seem to have been lost from sight, perhaps deservedly so, because, as I have pointed out, it doesn't tell one what to do next. What I suggest is that it almost seems as if the perception of meaning were primary and everything else a consequence of understanding meaning.[19]

But Oettinger does not seem to see that if one simply looks for some new sort of process, by which this global meaning is "produced," thereby reversing the current misunderstanding, one is bound to find what seems a mystery or a dead end.

When we try to turn this around and say, "Well now, here is this stream of sound coming at you or its equivalent on a printed page, and what is it that happens to your listening to me or in reading a printed page that enables you to react to the meaning of what I say?" we seem to hit a dead end at this point.[20]

What Oettinger too fails to understand is that there are *both* sound waves *and* there is meaningful discourse. The meaning is not *produced* from meaningless elements, be they marks or sounds. The stream of sounds is a problem for physics and neurophysiology, while on the level of meaningful discourse, the necessary energy processing has already taken place, and the *result* is a meaningful world for which no *new* theory of production is required nor can be consistently conceived.

To avoid inventing problems and mysteries we must leave the physical world to the physicists and neurophysiologists, and return to our description of the human world which we immediately perceive. The problem facing contemporary philosophers is to describe the context or situation in which human beings live, without importing prejudices from the history of philosophy or the current fascination with computer models. This brings us back to the problem of regularity and rules.

Our context-guided activity in terms of which we constantly modify the relevance and significance of particular objects and facts is quite regular, but the regularity need not and cannot be completely rule governed. As in the case of ambiguity tolerance, our activity is simply as rule governed as is necessary for the task at hand—the task itself, of course, being no more precise than the rules.

Wittgenstein, like Heidegger, sees the regulation of traffic as paradigmatic:

> The regulation of traffic in the streets permits and forbids certain actions on the part of drivers and pedestrians; but it does not attempt to guide the totality of their movements by prescription. And it would be senseless to talk of an 'ideal' ordering of traffic which would do that; in the first place we should have no idea what to imagine as this ideal. If someone wants to make traffic regulations stricter on some point or other, that does not mean that he wants to approximate to such an ideal.[21]

This contextual regularity, never completely rule governed, but always as orderly as necessary, is so pervasive that it is easily overlooked. Once, however, it has been focused on as the background of problem solving, language use, and other intelligent behavior, it no longer seems necessary to suppose that all ordered behavior is rule governed. The rule-model only seems inevitable if one abstracts himself from the human situation as philosophers have been trying to do for two thousand years, and as computer experts must, given the context-free character of information processing in digital machines.

9

The Situation as a Function of Human Needs

We are at home in the world and can find our way about in it because it is *our* world produced by us as the context of our pragmatic activity. So far we have been describing this world or situation and how it enables us to zero in on significant objects in it. We have also suggested that this field of experience is structured in terms of our tasks. These are linked to goals, and these in turn correspond to the social and individual needs of those whose activity has produced the world.

What does this tell us about the possibility of AI? If the data which are to be stored and accessed are normally organized in terms of specific goals, then it would seem that the large data base problem confronting AI could be solved if one just constructed a list of objectives and their priorities—what computer workers dealing with decision-making programs call a utility function—and programmed it into the computer along with the facts.

We have seen, however, that explicit objectives do not work, even for organizing simple problem-solving programs. The difficulties of simple means-ends analysis suggest that in order for the computer to solve even well-structured problems, it is not sufficient for the machine to have an objective and to measure its progress toward this preset end. Planning requires finding the essential operations, so "pragmatic considerations," for example, the relative importance of logical operations had to be surreptitiously supplied by the programmers themselves before the logic program could begin. We must now try to describe in more detail how this pragmatic structuring differs from means-ends analysis, ultimately asking, of course, whether this human capacity for purposive organization is in principle programmable on digital machines.

The difference between human goals and machine ends or objectives has been noted by one scientist who has himself been working on pattern recognition. Satosi Watanabe describes this difference as follows:

> For man, an evaluation is made according to a system of values which is non-specific and quasi-emotive, while an evaluation for a robot could only be made according to a table or a specific criterion. . . . This difference is subtle but profound. [One might say] that a man has values while a machine has objectives. Certainly men too have objectives, but these are derived from a system of values and are not the final arbiter of his actions, as they would be for a robot. . . . As soon as the objective is set the machine can pursue it just as the man can. Likewise human utilitarian behavior can be easily simulated by a machine if the quantitative utility and the probability of each alternative event is fixed and given to the machine. But a machine can never get at the source from which this utility is derived.[1]

Watanabe claims that these values are essential to intelligent behavior. For one thing, as Watanabe points out, "there are infinitely many possible hypotheses that are supported by experience. Limitation of these hypotheses to a smaller subset is often done by a vaguely conceived criterion, such as the principle of simplicity, or the principle of elegance."[2] More specifically, Watanabe argues that it can be demonstrated that any two objects have the same number of predicates in common. If this does not seem to us to be the case, it is because we consider certain predicates more important than others. This decision as to what is important depends on our system of values.[3]

But why on our system of values and not on a list of objectives? How does what Watanabe calls a system of values differ from having a utility function? So far the only difference seems to be that values are vaguer. But throughout Watanabe's analysis there is no argument showing why these values are not just vague objectives which could be represented by a region on a quantitative scale. To understand this important difference, which Watanabe has noted, but not explained, one must first abandon his way of posing the problem. To speak of values already gives away the game. For values are a product of the same philosophical tradition which has laid down the conceptual basis of artificial intelligence. Although talk of values is rather new in philosophy, it represents a final stage of objectification in which the pragmatic considerations which pervade experience and determine what counts as an object are conceived of as just further characteristics of independent objects, such as their hardness or color. A value is one more property that can be added to or subtracted from an object. Once he has adopted this terminology and the philosophical position it embodies, Watanabe is unable to explain how values differ from somewhat vague properties, and thus cannot explain why he feels they cannot be programmed. To understand the fundamental difficulty Watanabe is trying to get at, we must be able to distinguish between objects, and the field or situation which makes our experience of objects possible. For what Watanabe misleadingly calls values belongs to the structure of the *field* of experience, not the objects in it.

We have seen that experience itself is organized in terms of our tasks. Like the pattern of a chess game, the world is a field in which there are areas of attraction and repulsion, paths of accessibility, regions of activity and of repose. In our own perceptual world we are all master players. Objects are already located and recognized in a general way in terms of the characteristics of the field they are in before we zero in on them and concern ourselves with their details. It is only because our interests are *not* objects in our experience that they can play this fundamental role of organizing our experience into meaningful patterns or regions.

Heidegger has described the way human concerns order experiences into places and regions:

Equipment has its *place* or else it 'lies around': this must be distinguished in principle from just occurring at random in some spacial position. . . . The kind of place which is constituted by direction and remoteness (and closeness is only a mode of the latter) is already oriented towards a region and oriented within it. . . . Thus anything constantly ready-to-hand of which circumspective Being-in-the-World takes account beforehand has its place. The 'where' of its readiness-to-hand is put to account as a matter for concern. . . .[4]

Heidegger is also the first to have called attention to the way philosophy has from its inception been dedicated to trying to turn the concerns in terms of which we live into objects which we could contemplate and control. Socrates was dedicated to trying to make his and other people's commitments explicit so that they could be compared, evaluated, and justified. But it is a fundamental and strange characteristic of our lives that insofar as we turn our most personal concerns into objects, which we can study and choose, they no longer have a grip on us. They no longer organize a field of significant possibilities in terms of which we act but become just one more possibility we can choose or reject. Philosophers thus finally arrived at the nihilism of Nietzsche and Sartre in which personal concerns are thought of as a table of values which are arbitrarily chosen and can be equally arbitrarily abandoned or transvaluated. According to Nietzsche, "The great man is necessarily a skeptic. . . . Freedom from any kind of conviction is part of the strength of his will."[5]*

But what is missing in this picture besides a sense of being gripped by one's commitment? What difference does it make when one is trying to produce intelligent behavior that one's evaluations are based on a utility function instead of some ultimate concern? One difference, which Watanabe notes without being able to explain, is that a table of values must be specific, whereas human concerns only need to be made as specific as the situation demands. This flexibility is closely connected with the human ability to recognize the generic in terms of purposes, and to extend the use of language in a regular but nonrulelike way. Moreover, man's ultimate concern is not just to achieve some goal which is the end of a series; rather, interest in the goal is present at each moment structuring the whole of experience and guiding our activity as we constantly select what is relevant in terms of its significance to the situation at hand.[6] A machine table of objectives, on the other hand, has only an arbitrary relation to the alternatives before the machine, so that it must be explicitly appealed to at predetermined intervals to evaluate the machine's progress and direct its next choice.

Herbert Simon and Walter Reitman have seen that emotion and motivation play some role in intelligent behavior, but their way of simulating this role is to write programs where "emotions" can *interrupt* the work on one problem to introduce extraneous factors or work on some other problem.[7] They do not seem to see that emotions and concerns *accompany* and *guide* our cognitive behavior. This is again a case of not being able to see what one would not know how to program.

Heidegger tries to account for the pervasive concern organizing human experience in terms of a basic human need to understand one's being. But this analysis remains very abstract. It accounts for significance in general but not for any specific goal or specific significance. Thus Heidegger in effect assimilates all human activity to creative problem solving or artistic creation where we do not fully know what our goal was until we have achieved it. For Heidegger there can be no list of specifications which the solution must fulfill. Still, our needs are determinate enough to give things specific meaning for us, and many of our goals are quite explicit. To understand this we require a more concrete phenomenological analysis of human needs.

The philosophical and psychological tradition (with the exception of the pragmatists), however, has tried to ignore the role of these needs in intelligent behavior, and the computer model has reinforced this tendency. Thus N. S. Sutherland, Professor of Experimental Psychology at the University of Sussex, in an article "Machines and Men," writes:

Survival and self maintenance are achieved by genetically building into the human brain a series of drives or goals. Some of the obvious ones are hunger, thirst, the sexual drive and avoidance of pain. All of these drives are parochial in the sense that one could imagine complex information processing systems exhibiting intelligent behavior but totally lacking them.[8]

We have seen, however, that our concrete bodily needs directly or indirectly give us our sense of the task at hand, in terms of which our experience is structured as significant or insignificant. These needs have a very special structure, which, while more specific than Heidegger's account, does resemble artistic creation. When we experience a need we do not at first know what it is we need. We must search to discover what allays our restlessness or discomfort. This is not found by comparing various objects and activities with some objective, determinate criterion, but through what Todes calls our sense of gratification. This gratification is experienced as the discovery of what we needed all along, but it is a retroactive understanding and covers up the fact that we were unable to make our need determinate without first receiving that gratification. The original fulfillment of any need is, therefore, what Todes calls a creative discovery.[9]*

Thus human beings do not begin with a genetic table of needs or values which they reveal to themselves as they go along. Nor, when they are authentic, do they arbitrarily adopt values which are imposed by their environment. Rather, in discovering what they need they make more specific a general need which was there all along but was not determinate.

This is most obvious when dealing with less instinctual psychological needs. When a man falls in love he loves a particular woman, but it is not that particular woman he needed *before* he fell in love. However, after he is in love, that is after he has found that this particular relationship is gratifying, the need becomes specific as the need for that particular woman, and the man has made a creative discovery about himself. He has become the sort of person that needs that specific relationship and must view himself as having lacked and needed this relationship all along. In such a creative discovery the world reveals a new order of significance which is neither simply discovered nor arbitrarily chosen.

Sören Kierkegaard has a great deal to say about the way one's personality or self is redefined in such an experience, and how everything in a person's world gets a new level of meaning. Since such a change, by modifying a person's concerns, changes the whole field of interest in terms of which everything gets its significance, Kierkegaard speaks of these fundamental changes as changes in our sphere of existence. And because such a change cannot be predicted on the basis of our previous concerns, yet once it has taken place is so pervasive that we cannot imagine how it could have been otherwise, Kierkegaard speaks of a change of sphere of existence as a leap.[10]

This same sort of change of world can take place on a conceptual level. Then it is called a conceptual revolution. Thomas Kuhn in his book *The Structure of Scientific Revolutions* has studied this sort of transformation. As he puts it: "Insofar as their only recourse to that world is through what they see and do, we may want to say that after a revolution scientists are responding to a different world."[11]

The conceptual framework determines what counts as a fact. Thus during a revolution there are no facts to which scientists can appeal to decide which view is correct. "The data themselves [have] changed. This is the [sense] in which we may want to say that after a revolution scientists work in a different world."[12] The idea that knowledge consists of a large store of neutral data, taken for granted by Minsky, is inadequate to account for these moments of profound change. According to Kuhn, "there can be no scientifically or empirically neutral system of language or concepts."[13]

What occurs during a scientific revolution is not fully reducible to a reinterpretation of individual and stable data. In the first place the data are not unequivocally stable. A pendulum is not a falling stone, nor is oxygen dephlogisticated air.[14]

This leads Kuhn to a rejection of the whole philosophical tradition which has culminated in the notion of reason as based on the storage and processing of "data." On the basis of his research Kuhn sees both the inadequacy of this tradition and why it nonetheless continues to seem self-evident.

Are theories simply man-made interpretations of given data? The epistemological viewpoint that has most often guided Western philosophy for three centuries dictates an immediate and unequivocal, Yes! In the absence of a developed alternative, I find it impossible to relinquish entirely that viewpoint. Yet it no longer functions effectively, and the attempts to make it do so through the introduction of a neutral language of observations now seem to me hopeless.[15]

In suggesting an alternative view, or more exactly, in analyzing the way science actually proceeds so as to provide the elements of an alternative view, Kuhn focuses on the importance of a paradigm, that is, a specific accepted example of scientific practice, in guiding research. Here, as in the case of family resemblance studied earlier, objects are understood not in terms of general rules but rather in terms of their relation to a specific concrete case whose traits or implications cannot be completely formalized.

[Scientists can] agree in their *identification* of a paradigm without agreeing on, or even attempting to produce, a full *interpretation* or *rationalization* of it. Lack of a standard interpretation or of an agreed reduction to rules will not prevent a paradigm from guiding research. . . . Indeed, the existence of a paradigm need not even imply that any full set of rules exist.[16]

It is just this open-ended richness of paradigms which makes them important:

Paradigms may be prior to, more binding, and more complete than any set of rules for research that could be unequivocally abstracted from them.[17]

Without such paradigms scientists confront the world with the same bewilderment which we have suggested would necessarily confront an AI researcher trying to formalize the human form of life:

In the absence of a paradigm . . . all of the facts that could possibly pertain to the development of a given science are likely to seem equally relevant.[18]

Indeed, without a paradigm it is not even clear what would count as a fact, since facts are produced in terms of a particular paradigm for interpreting experience. Thus finding a new paradigm is like a Kierkegaardian leap:

Just because it is a transition between incommensurables, the transition between competing paradigms cannot be made a step at a time, forced by logic and neutral experience. Like the gestalt switch, it must occur all at once (though not necessarily in an instant) or not at all.[19]

Here it becomes clear that the idea of problem solving as simply storing and sorting through data with a specific end in view can never do justice to these fundamental conceptual changes, yet these changes determine the conceptual space in which problems can first be posed and in terms of which data get their pervasive character of relevance and significance, so that problems can be solved. The reigning conceptual framework implicitly guides research just as the perceptual field guides our perception of objects.

Finally, even more fundamental than these conceptual revolutions studied by Kuhn are cultural revolutions; for example, the beginning of Greek philosophy, as we have seen, set up a view of the nature of man and rationality on which all subsequent conceptual revolutions have rung changes. Equally radically, with the beginning of Christianity a new kind of love became possible which was not possible in Greece; heroism became suspect as a sign of pride, and goodness came to consist in the sacrifices of saints. These cultural revolutions show us, as Pascal first pointed out, that there is no sharp boundary between nature and culture —even instinctual needs can be modified and overridden in terms of paradigms—thus there is no fixed nature of man.

Man's nature is indeed so malleable that it may be on the point of changing again. If the computer paradigm becomes so strong that people begin to think of themselves as digital devices on the model of work in artificial intelligence, then, since for the reasons we have been rehearsing, machines cannot be like human beings, human beings may become progressively like machines. During the past two thousand years the importance of objectivity; the belief that actions are governed by fixed values; the notion that skills can be formalized; and in general that one can have a theory of practical activity, have gradually exerted their influence in psychology and in social science. People have begun to think of themselves as objects able to fit into the inflexible calculations of disembodied machines: machines for which the human form-of-life must be analyzed into meaningless facts, rather than a field of concern organized by sensory-motor skills. Our risk is not the advent of superintelligent computers, but of subintelligent human beings.

Conclusion

This alternative conception of man and his ability to behave intelligently is really an analysis of the way man's skillful bodily activity as he works to satisfy his needs generates the human world. And it is this world which sets up the conditions under which specific facts become accessible to man as both relevant and significant, because these facts are originally organized in terms of these needs. This enables us to see the fundamental difference between human and machine intelligence. Artificial intelligence must begin at the level of objectivity and rationality where the facts have already been produced. It abstracts these facts[1]* from the situation in which they are organized and attempts to use the results to simulate intelligent behavior. But these facts taken out of context are an unwieldy mass of neutral data with which artificial intelligence workers have thus far been unable to cope. All programs so far "bog down inexorably as the information files grow."[2]

No other data-processing techniques exist at present besides the accumulation of facts, and once the traditional philosophical assumptions underlying work in artificial intelligence have been called into question there is no reason to suppose that digital data storage and retrieval techniques will ever be powerful enough to cope with the amount of data generated when we try to make explicit our knowledge of the world. Since the data about the world may well be infinite and the formalization of our form-of-life may well be impossible, it would be more reasonable to suppose that digital storage techniques can never be up to the task.

Moreover, if this phenomenological description of human intelligence is correct, there are in principle reasons why artificial intelligence can never be completely realized. Besides the technological problem posed by storing a great number of bits of neutral data, there are in the last analysis no fixed facts, be they a million or ten million, as Minsky would like to believe. Since human beings produce facts, the facts themselves are changed by conceptual revolutions.

Finally, if the philosopher or artificial intelligence researcher proposes to meet this objection by formalizing the human needs which generate this changing context, he is faced with the source of this same difficulty. Indeterminate needs and goals and the experience of gratification which guides their determination cannot be simulated on a digital machine whose only mode of existence is a series of determinate states. Yet, it is just because these needs are never completely determined for the individual and for mankind as a whole that they are capable of being made more determinate, and human nature can be retroactively changed by individual and cultural revolutions.

CONCLUSION: THE SCOPE AND

LIMITS OF ARTIFICIAL REASON

10

The Limits of Artificial Intelligence

We are now in a position to draw together the various strands of our philosophical argument concerning the limits of artificial intelligence. The division of the field of artificial intelligence into two subfields, Cognitive Simulation (CS) and Artificial Intelligence (AI), has led to the treatment of two separate but interrelated questions: (1) Does a human being in "processing information" actually follow formal rules like a digital computer?, and (2) Can human behavior, no matter how generated, be described in a formalism which can be manipulated by a digital machine?

In discussing each of these questions we found, first, that the descriptive or phenomenological evidence, considered apart from traditional philosophical prejudices, suggests that nonprogrammable human capacities are involved in all forms of intelligent behavior. Moreover, we saw that no contrary empirical evidence stands up to methodological scrutiny. Thus, insofar as the question whether artificial intelligence is possible is an empirical question, the answer seems to be that further significant progress in Cognitive Simulation or in Artificial Intelligence is extremely unlikely.

If in the face of these difficulties workers in artificial intelligence still wish to justify their optimism, the burden of proof is henceforth on them. They must show that despite the empirical difficulties artificial intelligence *must be* possible. But the *a priori* case for artificial intelligence is even weaker here than the empirical one. The very arguments which are supposed to show that formalization must be possible turn out to be either incoherent or self-contradictory and show, on the contrary, that barring certain highly unlikely empirical assumptions which have been ruled out by common agreement, formalization is impossible. The *a priori* arguments *for* formalization thus turn into conditional in principle arguments *against* the possibility of CS and AI.

Let us review these arguments in more detail. In discussing CS we found that in playing games such as chess, in solving complex problems, in recognizing similarities and family resemblances, and in using language metaphorically and in ways we feel to be odd or ungrammatical, human beings do not seem to themselves or to observers to be following strict rules. On the contrary, they seem to be using global perceptual organization, making pragmatic distinctions between essential and inessential operations, appealing to paradigm cases, and using a shared sense of the situation to get their meanings across.

Of course, all this orderly but apparently nonrulelike activity might nonetheless be the result of unconsciously followed rules. But when one tries to understand this as a philosophical proposal that *all* behavior *must* be understood as following from a set of instructions, one finds a regress of rules for applying rules. This regress cannot be terminated by an appeal to ordinary facts for, according to the original claim, the facts must themselves always be recognized and interpreted by rule.

One way to avoid this regress would be to claim that the ultimate data are inputs of physical energy and that such inputs can always be digitalized and processed according to rule. This seems to be Fodor's view. The claim that these inputs are processed in a sequence of operations like a digital program is not unintelligible, but would, as Fodor admits, demand an incredibly complex formalism which no one has been able to discover or invent. In the absence of any empirical or *a priori* argument that such a formalism for processing physical inputs does or must exist, and given the empirical evidence that the brain functions like an analogue computer, there is no reason to suppose and every reason to doubt that the processing of physical inputs in the human brain takes the form of a digital computer program.

The only other way to avoid the regress of rules is to modify the thesis and claim that on the lowest level rules are automatically applied without instructions. But this leads to trouble in two ways: (1) Once the *a priori* thesis that all behavior must follow instructions is thus weakened, we might as well claim that skilled behavior need not be based on unconsciously followed instructions at *any* level, so the argument that in spite of the phenomenological evidence subjects *must* be following rules must be abandoned.

(2) If one nonetheless insists that there *must be* an ultimate level of uninterpreted givens, and that the givens are neither physical inputs nor ordinary objects, one is left with the view that these givens must be impoverished bits of information about the human world. This gives us the notion of "stimulus information," the sense data or snapshots introduced by Neisser. But this *a priori* notion of stimulus information turns out to be incomprehensible. All that is given empirically are continuous physical inputs to the organism, on the one hand, and the world of ordinary objects given to the perceiving subject, on the other. No cognitive psychologist has succeeded in defining another sort of input between these two which would provide the ultimate bits of information to which the rules are to be applied. All accounts offered thus far turn out to be an incoherent mixture of physical description in terms of energy, and phenomenalist description in terms of crudely defined sense data.

Thus the psychological claim that, appearances notwithstanding, intelligent behavior is produced by following fixed formal rules like a digital computer is stuck with a regress of rules for applying rules. It can not extricate itself from this regress by appeal to a notion of physical input which it cannot use or stimulus input which it cannot define.

Although there is no empirical evidence either from psychology or from the success of current work, AI workers, like workers in CS, are confident that a formalization of intelligent behavior must be possible. Their argument is never explicitly stated, but it seems to be based on an ontological assumption that the world can be analyzed into independent logical elements and an epistemological assumption that our understanding of the world can then be reconstructed by combining these elements according to heuristic rules. The first claim is safe enough. Since he is not committed to describing human beings, the AI worker, unlike the cognitive psychologist, has no trouble identifying the ultimate bits to which the rules must be applied—they are digitalized sound waves and the elements in the mosaic of a TV tube. These can be recognized without appeal to further rules. But the second claim, that these elements can be reassembled, when put forward as an *a priori* necessity, runs into a regress of higher and higher order rules, the converse of the regress of rules for applying rules faced by those in Cognitive Simulation.

Since each of the logical elements is assumed to be independent of all the others, it has no significance until related to the other elements. But once these elements have been taken out of context and stripped of all significance it is not so easy to give it back. The significance to be given to each logical element depends on other logical elements, so that in order to be recognized as forming patterns and ultimately forming objects and meaningful utterances each input must be related to other inputs by rules. But the elements are subject to several interpretations according to different rules and which rule to apply depends on the context. For a computer, however, the context itself can only be recognized according to a rule.

Here again, too, this computer-dictated analysis conflicts with our experience. A phenomenological description of our experience of being-in-a-situation suggests that we are always already in a context or situation which we carry over from the immediate past and update in terms of events that in the light of this past situation are seen to be significant. We never encounter meaningless bits in terms of which we have to identify contexts, but only facts which are already interpreted and which reciprocally define the situation we are in. Human experience is only intelligible when organized in terms of a situation in which relevance and significance are already given. This need for prior organization reappears in AI as the need for a hierarchy of contexts in which a higher or broader context is used to determine the relevance and significance of elements in a narrower or lower context.

Thus, for example, to pick out two dots in a picture as eyes one must have already recognized the context as a face. To recognize this context as a face one must have distinguished *its* relevant features such as shape and hair from the shadows and highlights, and these, in turn, can be picked out as relevant only in a broader context, for example, a domestic situation in which the program can expect to find faces. This context too will have to be recognized by its relevant features, as social rather than, say, meteorological, so that the program selects as significant the people rather than the clouds. But if each context can be recognized only in terms of features selected as relevant and interpreted in terms of a broader context, the AI worker is faced with a regress of contexts.

As in the case of Cognitive Simulation, there might have been an empirical way out of the regress. Just as for CS the ultimate uninterpreted bits might have been digitalized physical inputs, here the ultimate context or set of contexts might have been recognizable in terms of certain patterns or objects which had a fixed significance and could be used to switch the program to the appropriate subcontext of objects or discourse. But again as in CS the evidence is against this empirical possibility. There do not seem to be any words or objects which are always relevant and always have the same significance the way the red spot of a female stickleback always means mating time to the male.

There remains only one possible "solution." The computer programmer can make up a hierarchy of contexts and general rules for how to organize them for the computer. He does this by appealing to his general sense of what is generally relevant and significant for a human being. In *some* situations, however, any fact may become important. To formalize this so that the computer could exhibit human flexibility, the programmer would have to be able to make explicit all that he normally takes for granted in being a human being. However, once he tries to treat his own situation as if he were a computer looking at it from the outside, the computer programmer is himself faced with an infinity of meaningless facts whose relevance and significance could only be determined in a broader context.

Thus it turns out that a logical atomist ontology does not entail a logical atomist epistemology. Even if the world is scanned into the computer in terms of logically independent bits, this does not mean that one can argue *a priori* that it can be reassembled. In fact the attempt to argue *a priori* that because the world can be resolved into bits it can be interpreted by formal rules ends up showing just the opposite.

These considerations are supported by a general theory of human experience as being-already-in-a-situation in which the facts are always already interpreted. This theory also suggests that the ultimate situation in which human beings find themselves depends on their purposes, which are in turn a function of their body and their needs, and that these needs are not fixed once and for all but are interpreted and made determinate by acculturation and thus by changes in human self-interpretation. Thus in the last analysis we can understand why there are no facts with built-in significance and no fixed human forms of life which one could ever hope to program.

This is not to say that children do not begin with certain fixed responses—in fact, if they did not, learning could never get started—but rather that these responses are outgrown or overridden in the process of maturation. Thus no fixed responses remain in an adult human being which are not under the control of the significance of the situation.

Could we then program computers to behave like children and bootstrap their way to intelligence? This question takes us beyond present psychological understanding and present computer techniques. In this book I have only been concerned to argue that the current attempt to program computers with fully formed Athene-like intelligence runs into empirical difficulties and fundamental conceptual inconsistencies. Whether a child computer could begin with situation-free responses and gradually learn depends on the role indeterminate needs and ability to respond to the global context play in learning. What work has been done on learning by Piaget, for example, suggests that the same forms of "information processing" are required for learning which are required for mature intelligent behavior, and that intelligence develops by "conceptual revolutions." This should not surprise us. Computers can only deal with facts, but man—the source of facts—is not a fact or set of facts, but a being who creates himself and the world of facts in the process of living in the world. This human world with its recognizable objects is organized by human beings using their embodied capacities to satisfy their embodied needs. There is no reason to suppose that a world organized in terms of these fundamental human capacities should be accessible by any other means.

The Future of Artificial Intelligence

But these difficulties give us no idea of the future of artificial intelligence. Even if the attempt to program isolated intelligent activities always ultimately requires the programming of the whole mature human form of life, and even if an Athene-like digital computer is impossible in principle—that is, even if mature human intelligence is organized in terms of a field which is reciprocally determined by the objects in it and capable of radical revision—the question still remains to what extent workers in artificial intelligence can use their piecemeal techniques to approximate intelligent human behavior. In order to complete our analysis of the scope and limits of artificial reason we must now draw out the practical implications of the foregoing arguments.

Before drawing our practical conclusions, however, it will be helpful to distinguish four areas of intelligent activity. We can then determine to what extent intelligent behavior in each area presupposes the four human forms of "information processing" we distinguished in Part I. This will enable us to account for what success has been attained and predict what further progress can be expected.

One can distinguish four types of intelligent activity (see Table 1). We have seen that the first two types are amenable to digital computer simulation, while the third is only partially programmable and the fourth is totally intractable.

Area I is where the S–R psychologists are most at home. It includes all forms of elementary associationistic behavior where meaning and context are irrelevant to the activity concerned. Rote learning of nonsense syllables is the most perfect example of such behavior so far programmed, although any form of conditioned reflex would serve as well.

Table 1

CLASSIFICATION OF INTELLIGENT ACTIVITIES

I. Associationistic	II. Simple-Formal	III. Complex-Formal	IV. Nonformal

Characteristics of Activity

I. Associationistic	II. Simple-Formal	III. Complex-Formal	IV. Nonformal
Irrelevance of meaning and situation.	Meanings completely explicit and situation independent.	In principle, same as II; in practice, internally situation-dependent, independent of external situation.	Dependent on meaning and situation which are not explicit.
Innate or learned by repetition.	Learned by rule.	Learned by rule and practice.	Learned by perspicuous examples.

Field of Activity (and Appropriate Procedure)

I. Associationistic	II. Simple-Formal	III. Complex-Formal	IV. Nonformal
Memory games, e.g., "Geography" (association).	Computable or quasi-computable games, e.g., nim or tic-tac-toe (seek algorithm or count out).	Uncomputable games, e.g., chess or go (global intuition and detailed counting out).	Ill-defined games, e.g., riddles (perceptive guess).
Maze problems (trial and error).	Combinatorial problems (nonheuristic means/ends analysis).	Complex combinatorial problems (planning and maze calculation).	Open-structured problems (insight).
Word-by-word translation (mechanical dictionary).	Proof of theorems using mechanical proof procedures (seek algorithm).	Proof of theorems where no mechanical proof procedure exists (intuition and calculation).	Translating a natural language (understanding in context of use).
Response to rigid patterns (innate releasers and classical conditioning).	Recognition of simple rigid patterns, e.g., reading typed page (search for traits whose conjunction defines class membership).	Recognition of complex patterns in noise (search for regularities).	Recognition of varied and distorted patterns (recognition of generic or use of paradigm case).

Kinds of Program

I. Associationistic	II. Simple-Formal	III. Complex-Formal	IV. Nonformal
Decision tree, list search, template.	Algorithm.	Search-pruning heuristics.	None.

Also some games, such as the game sometimes called Geography (which simply consists of finding a country whose name begins with the last letter of the previously named country), belong in this area. In language translating, this is the level of the mechanical dictionary; in problem solving, that of pure trial-and-error search routines; in pattern recognition, matching pattern against fixed templates.

Area II is the domain of Pascal's *esprit de géométrie*—the terrain most favorable for artificial intelligence. It encompasses the conceptual rather than the perceptual world. Problems are completely formalized and completely calculable. For this reason, it might best be called the area of the simple-formal. Here artificial intelligence is possible in principle and in fact.

In Area II, natural language is replaced by a formal language, of which the best example is logic. Games have precise rules and can be calculated out completely, as in the case of nim or tic-tac-toe. Pattern recognition on this level takes place according to determinate types, which are defined by a list of traits characterizing the individuals which belong to the class in question. Problem solving takes the form of reducing the distance between means and ends by repeated application of formal rules. The formal systems in this area are simple enough to be manipulated by algorithms which require no search procedure at all (for example, Wang's logic program). Heuristics are not only unnecessary here, they are a positive handicap, as the superiority of Wang's algorithmic logic program over Newell, Shaw, and Simon's heuristic logic program demonstrates. In this area, artificial intelligence has had its only unqualified successes.

Area III, complex-formal systems, is the most difficult to define and has generated most of the misunderstandings and difficulties in the field. It contains behavior which is in principle formalizable but in fact intractable. As the number of elements increases, the number of transformations required grows exponentially with the number of elements involved. As used here, "complex-formal" includes those systems which in practice cannot be dealt with by exhaustive enumeration algorithms (chess, go, etc.), and thus require heuristic programs.[1]*

Area IV might be called the area of nonformal behavior. This includes all those everyday activities in our human world which are regular but not rule governed. The most striking example of this controlled imprecision is our disambiguation of natural languages. This area also includes games in which the rules are not definite, such as guessing riddles. Pattern recognition in this domain is based on recognition of the generic, or of the typical, by means of a paradigm case. Problems on this level are open-structured, requiring a determination of what is relevant and insight into which operations are essential, before the problem can be attacked.[2]* Techniques on this level are usually taught by generalizing from examples and are followed intuitively without appeal to rules. We might adopt Pascal's terminology and call Area IV the home of the *esprit de finesse*. Since in this area a sense of the global situation is necessary to avoid storing an infinity of facts, it is impossible in principle to use discrete techniques to reproduce directly adult behavior. Even to order the four as in Table 1 is misleadingly encouraging, since it suggests that Area IV differs from Area III simply by introducing a further level of complexity, whereas Area IV is of an entirely different order than Area III. Far from being more complex, it is really more primitive, being evolutionarily, ontogenetically, and phenomenologically prior to Areas II and III, just as natural language is prior to mathematics.

The literature of artificial intelligence generally fails to distinguish these four areas. For example, Newell, Shaw, and Simon announce that their logic theorist "was devised to learn how it is possible to solve difficult problems such as proving mathematical theorems [II or III], discovering scientific laws from data [III and IV], playing chess [III], or understanding the meaning of English prose [IV]."[3] The assumption, made explicitly by Paul Armer of the RAND Corporation, that all intelligent behavior is of the same general type, has encouraged workers to generalize from success in the two promising areas to unfounded expectation of success in the other two.

This confusion has two dangerous consequences. First there is the tendency, typified by Simon, to think that heuristics discovered in one field of intelligent activity, such as theorem proving, must tell us something about the "information processing" in another area, such as the understanding of a natural language. Thus, certain simple forms of information processing applicable to Areas I and II are imposed on Area IV, while the unique form of "information processing" in this area, namely that "data" are not being "processed" at all, is overlooked. The result is that the same problem of exponential growth that causes trouble when the techniques of Areas I and II are extended to Area III shows up in attempts to reproduce the behavior characteristic of Area IV.[4*]

Second, there is the converse danger. The success of artificial intelligence in Area II depends upon avoiding anything but discrete, determinate, situation-free operations. The fact that, like the simple systems in Area II, the complex systems in Area III are formalizable leads the simulator to suppose the activities in Area III can be reproduced on a digital computer. When the difference in degree between simple and complex systems turns out in practice, however, to be a difference in kind —exponential growth becoming a serious problem—the programmer, unaware of the differences between the two areas, tries to introduce procedures borrowed from the observation of how human beings perform the activities in Area IV—for example, position evaluation in chess, means-ends analysis in problem solving, semantic considerations in theorem proving—into Area III. These procedures, however, when used by human beings depend upon one or more of the specifically human forms of "information processing"—for human beings at least, the use of chess heuristics presupposes fringe consciousness of a field of strength and weakness; the introduction of means-ends analysis eventually requires planning and thus a distinction between essential and inessential operations; semantic considerations require a sense of the context.

The programmer confidently notes that Area III is in principle formalizable just like Area II. He is not aware that in transplanting the techniques of Area IV into Area III he is introducing into the continuity between Areas II and III the discontinuity which exists between Areas III and IV and thus introducing all the difficulties confronting the formalization of nonformal behavior. Thus the problems which in principle should only arise in trying to program the "ill-structured," that is, open-ended activities of daily life, arise in practice for complex-formal systems. Since what counts as relevant data in Area III is completely explicit, heuristics can work to some extent (as in Samuel's Checker

Program), but since Area IV is just that area of intelligent behavior in which the attempt to program digital computers to exhibit fully formed adult intelligence must fail, the unavoidable recourse in Area III to heuristics which presuppose the abilities of Area IV is bound, sooner or later, to run into difficulties. Just how far heuristic programming can go in Area III before it runs up against the need for fringe consciousness, ambiguity tolerance, essential/inessential discrimination, and so forth, is an empirical question. However, we have seen ample evidence of trouble in the failure to produce a chess champion, to prove any interesting theorems, to translate languages, and in the abandonment of GPS.

Still there are some techniques for approximating some of the Area IV short-cuts necessary for progress in Area III, without presupposing the foregoing human forms of "information processing" which cannot be reproduced in any Athena-like program.

To surmount present stagnation in Area III the following improved techniques seem to be required:

1. Since current computers, even primitive hand-eye coordinating robots, do not have bodies in the sense described in Chapter 7, and since no one understands or has any idea how to program the global organization and indeterminacy which is characteristic of perception and embodied skills, the best that can be hoped for at this time is some sort of crude, wholistic, first-level processing, which approximates the human ability to zero in on a segment of a field of experience before beginning explicit rule-governed manipulation or counting out. This cannot mean adding still further explicit ways of picking out what area is worth exploring further. In chess programs, for example, it is beginning to be clear that adding more and more specific bits of chess knowledge to plausible move generators, finally bogs down in too many *ad hoc* subroutines. (Samuel thinks this is why there has been no further progress reported for the Greenblatt chess program.[5]) What is needed is something which corresponds to the master's way of seeing the board as having promising and threatening areas.

Just what such wholistic processing could be is hard to determine, given the discrete nature of all computer calculations. There seem to be two different claims in the air. When Minsky and Papert talk of finding "global features," they seem to mean finding certain isolable, and determinate, features of a pattern (for example, certain angles of intersection of two lines) which allow the program to make reliable guesses about the whole. This just introduces further heuristics and is not wholistic in any interesting sense. Neisser, however, in discussing the problem of segmenting shapes for pattern recognition before analyzing them in detail makes a more ambitious proposal.

Since the processes of focal attention cannot operate on the whole visual field simultaneously, they can come into play only after preliminary operations have already segregated the figural units involved. These preliminary operations are of great interest in their own right. They correspond in part to what the Gestalt psychologists called "autochthonous forces," and they produce what Hebb called "primitive unity." I will call them the *preattentive processes* to emphasize that they produce the objects which later mechanisms are to flesh out and interpret.

The requirements of this task mean that the preattentive processes must be genuinely "global" and "wholistic." Each figure or object must be separated from the others in its entirety, as a potential framework for the subsequent and more detailed analyses of attention.[6]

But Neisser is disappointing when it comes to explaining how this crude, first approximation is to be accomplished by a digital computer. He seems to have in mind simply cleaning-up heuristics which, as Neisser implicitly admits, only work where the patterns are already fairly clearly demarcated. "Very simple operations can separate units, *provided they have continuous contours or empty spaces between them.* Computer programs which follow lines or detect gaps, for example, are as easily written as those which fill holes and wipe out local irregularities."[7] But such techniques fail, for example, in the case of cursive script.

Of course, it is hard to propose anything else. What is being asked for is a way of dealing with the field of experience before it has been broken up into determinate objects, but such preobjective experience is, by definition, out of bounds for a digital computer. Computers must apply specific rules to determinate data; if the problem is one of first carving out the determinate data, the programmer is left with the problem of applying determinate rules to a blur.

The best that can be hoped in trying to circumvent the techniques of

Area IV, therefore, may well be the sort of clever heuristics Minsky and Papert propose to enable a first-pass program to pick out certain specific features which will be useful in directing the program in filling in more details. But such *ad hoc* techniques risk becoming unmanageable and in any case can never provide the generality and flexibility of a partially determinate global response.

2. A second difficulty shows up in connection with *representing* the problem in a problem-solving system. It reflects the need for essential/inessential discrimination. Feigenbaum, in discussing problems facing artificial intelligence research in the second decade, calls this problem "the most important though not the most immediately tractable."[8] He explains the problem as follows:

In heuristic problem solving programs, the search for solutions within a problem space is conducted and controlled by heuristic rules. The representation that defines the problem space is the problem solver's "way of looking at" the problem and also specifies the form of solutions. Choosing a representation that is right for a problem can improve spectacularly the efficiency of the solution-finding process. The choice of problem representation is the job of the human programmer and is a creative act.[9]

This is the activity we called finding the deep structure or insight. Since current computers, even current primitive robots, do not have needs in the sense we have discussed in Chapter 9, and since no one has any idea how to program needs into a machine, there is no present hope of dispensing with this "creative act." The best that can be expected at this time is the development of programs with specific objectives which take an active part in organizing data rather than passively receiving them. Programmers have noticed that, in the analysis of complex scenes, it is useful to have the program formulate an hypothesis about what it would expect to find on the basis of data it already has, and look for that. This should not be confused with the way the human being organizes *what counts as data* in terms of his field of purposes. All that can be expected is fixed rules to apply to fixed data; that is, there will be a programmed set of alternatives, and the program can, on the basis of present data, select one of these alternatives as the most probable and look for further data on the basis of this prediction.

Thus, specific long-range objectives or a set of alternative long-range objectives might be built into game-playing and problem-solving programs, so that in certain situations certain strategies would be tried by the computer (and predicted for the opponent). This technique, of course, would not remove the restriction that all these alternatives must be explicitly stored beforehand and explicitly consulted at certain points in the program, whereas human purposes implicitly organize and direct human activity moment by moment. Thus even with these breakthroughs the computer could not exhibit the flexibility of a human being solving an open-structured problem (Area IV), but these techniques could help with complex-formal problems such as strategy in games and long-range planning in organizing means-ends analysis.

3. Since computers are not in a situation, and since no one understands how to begin to program primitive robots, even those which move around, to have a world, computer workers are faced with a final problem: how to program a representation of the computer's environment. We have seen that the present attempt to store all the facts about the environment in an internal model of the world runs up against the problem of how to store and access this very large, perhaps infinite amount of data. This is sometimes called the large data base problem. Minsky's book, as we have seen, presents several *ad hoc* ways of trying to get around this problem, but so far none has proved to be generalizable.

In spite of Minsky's claims to have made a first step in solving the problem, C. A. Rosen in discussing current robot projects after the work reported in Minsky's book acknowledges new techniques are still required:

We can foresee an ultimate capability of storing an encyclopedic quantity of facts about specific environments of interest, but new methods of organization are badly needed which permit both rapid search and logical deductions to be made efficiently.[10]

In Feigenbaum's report, there is at last a recognition of the seriousness of this problem and even a suggestion of a different way to proceed. In discussing the mobile robot project at the Stanford Research Institute, Feigenbaum notes:

It is felt by the SRI group that the most unsatisfactory part of their simulation effort was the simulation of the environment. Yet, they say that 90% of the effort of the simulation team went into this part of the simulation. It turned out to be very difficult to reproduce in an internal representation for a computer the necessary richness of environment that would give rise to interesting behavior by the highly adaptive robot.[11]

We have seen that this problem is avoided by human beings because their model of the world is the world itself. It is interesting to find work at SRI moving in this direction.

It is easier and cheaper to build a hardware robot to extract what information it needs from the real world than to organize and store a useful model. Crudely put, the SRI group's argument is that the most economic and efficient store of information about the real world is the real world itself.[12]

This attempt to get around the large data base problem by recalculating much of the data when needed is an interesting idea, although how far it can go is not yet clear. It presupposes some solution to the wholistic problem discussed in 1 above, so that it can segment areas to be recognized. It also would require some way to distinguish essential from inessential facts. Most fundamentally, it is of course limited by having to treat the real world, whether stored in the robot memory or read off a TV screen, as a set of facts; whereas human beings organize the world in terms of their interests so that facts need be made explicit only insofar as they are relevant.

What can we expect while waiting for the development and application of these improved techniques? Progress can evidently be expected in Area II. As Wang points out, "we are in possession of slaves which are . . . persistent plodders."[13] We can make good use of them in the area of simple-formal systems. Moreover, the protocols collected by Newell, Shaw, and Simon suggest that human beings sometimes operate like digital computers, within the context of more global processes. Since digital machines have symbol-manipulating powers superior to those of humans, they should, so far as possible, take over the digital aspects of human "information processing."

To use computers in Areas III and IV we must couple their capacity for fast and accurate calculation with the short-cut processing made possible by fringe-consciousness, insight, and ambiguity tolerance. Leibniz already claimed that a computer "could enhance the capabilities of the mind to a far greater extent than optical instruments strengthen the eyes." But microscopes and telescopes are useless without the selecting and interpreting eye itself. Thus a chess player who could call on a machine to count out alternatives once he had zeroed in on an interesting area would be a formidable opponent. Likewise, in problem solving, once the problem is structured and an attack planned, a machine could take over to work out the details (as in the case of machine-shop allocation or investment banking). A mechanical dictionary which could display meanings on a scope ranked as to their probable relevance would be useful in translation. In pattern recognition, machines are able to recognize certain complex patterns that the natural prominences in our experience lead us to ignore. Bar-Hillel, Oettinger, and John Pierce have each proposed that work be done on systems which promote a symbiosis between computers and human beings. As Walter Rosenblith put it at a recent symposium, "Man *and* computer is capable of accomplishing things that neither of them can do alone."[14]

Indeed, the first successful use of computers to augment rather than replace human intelligence has recently been reported. A theorem-proving program called SAM (Semi-Automated Mathematics) has solved an open problem in lattice theory. According to its developers:

Semi-automated mathematics is an approach to theorem-proving which seeks to combine automatic logic routines with ordinary proof procedures in such a manner that the resulting procedure is both efficient and subject to human intervention in the form of control and guidance. Because it makes the mathematician an essential factor in the quest to establish theorems, this approach is a departure from the usual theorem-proving attempts in which the computer *unaided* seeks to establish proofs.[15]

One would expect the mathematician, with his sense of relevance, to assist the computer in zeroing in on an area worth counting out. And this is exactly what happens.

The user may intervene in the process of proof in a number of ways. His selection of the initial formulas is of course an important factor in determining the course AUTO-LOGIC will take. Overly large or ill-chosen sets of initial formulas tend to divert AUTO-LOGIC to the proving of trivial and uninteresting results so that it never gets to the interesting formulas. Provided with a good set of initial formulas, however, AUTO-LOGIC will produce useful and interesting results. As the user sees that AUTO-LOGIC is running out of useful ways in which to use the original formulas, he can halt the process and insert additional axioms or other material. He can also guide the process by deleting formulas which seem unimportant or distracting. This real-time interplay between man and machine has been found to be an exciting and rewarding mode of operation.[16]

Instead of trying to make use of the special capacities of computers, however, workers in artificial intelligence—blinded by their early success and hypnotized by the assumption that thinking is a continuum—will settle for nothing short of unaided intelligence. Feigenbaum and Feldman's anthology opens with the baldest statement of this dubious principle:

In terms of the continuum of intelligence suggested by Armer, the computer programs we have been able to construct are still at the low end. What is important is that we continue to strike out in the direction of the milestone that represents the capabilities of human intelligence. Is there any reason to suppose that we shall never get there? None whatever. Not a single piece of evidence, no logical argument, no proof or theorem has ever been advanced which demonstrates an insurmountable hurdle along the continuum.[17]

Armer prudently suggests a boundary, but he is still optimistic:

It is irrelevant whether or not there may exist some upper bound above which machines cannot go in this continuum. Even if such a boundary exists, there is no evidence that it is located close to the position occupied by today's machines.[18]

Current difficulties, once they are interpreted independently of optimistic *a priori* assumptions, however, suggest that the areas of intelligent behavior are *discontinuous* and that *the boundary is near.* The stagnation of each of the specific efforts in artificial intelligence suggests that there can be no piecemeal breakthrough to fully formed adult intelligent behavior for any isolated kind of human performance. Game playing, language translation, problem solving, and pattern recognition, each depends on specific forms of human "information processing," which are in turn based on the human way of being in the world. And this way of being-in-a-situation turns out to be unprogrammable in principle using presently conceivable techniques.

Alchemists were so successful in distilling quicksilver from what seemed to be dirt that, after several hundred years of fruitless efforts to convert lead into gold, they still refused to believe that on the chemical level one cannot transmute metals. They did, however, produce—as by-products—ovens, retorts, crucibles, and so forth, just as computer workers, while failing to produce artificial intelligence, have developed assembly programs, debugging programs, program-editing programs, and so on, and the M.I.T. robot project has built a very elegant mechanical arm.

To avoid the fate of the alchemists, it is time we asked where we stand. Now, before we invest more time and money on the information-processing level, we should ask whether the protocols of human subjects and the programs so far produced suggest that computer language is appropriate for analyzing human behavior: Is an exhaustive analysis of human reason into rule-governed operations on discrete, determinate, context-free elements possible? Is an approximation to this goal of artificial reason even probable? The answer to both these questions appears to be, No.

Does this mean that all the work and money put into artificial intelligence have been wasted? Not at all, if instead of trying to minimize our difficulties, we try to understand what they show. The success and subsequent stagnation of Cognitive Simulation and of AI, plus the omnipresent problems of pattern recognition and natural language understanding and their surprising difficulty, should lead us to focus research on the four human forms of "information processing" which they reveal and the situational character of embodied human reason which underlies them all. These human abilities are not necessary in those areas of intelligent activity in which artificial intelligence has had its early success, but they are essential in just those areas of intelligent behavior in which artificial intelligence has experienced consistent failure. We can then view recent work in artificial intelligence as a crucial experiment disconfirming the traditional assumption that human reason can be analyzed into rule-governed operations on situation-free discrete elements—the most important disconfirmation of this metaphysical demand that has ever been produced. This technique of turning our philosophical assumptions into technology until they reveal their limits suggests fascinating new areas for basic research.

C. E. Shannon, the inventor of information theory, sees, to some extent, how different potentially intelligent machines would have to be. In his discussion of "What Computers Should be Doing," he observes:

Efficient machines for such problems as pattern recognition, language translation, and so on, may require a different type of computer than any we have today. It is my feeling that this will be a computer whose natural operation is in terms of patterns, concepts, and vague similarities, rather than sequential operations on ten-digit numbers.[19]

We have seen that, as far as we can tell from the only being that can deal with such "vagueness," a "machine" which could use a natural language and recognize complex patterns would have to have a body so that it could be at home in the world.

But if robots for processing nonformal information must be, as Shannon suggests, entirely different from present digital computers, what can now be done? Nothing directly toward programming present machines to behave with human intelligence. We must think in the short run of cooperation between men and digital computers, and only in the long run of nondigital automata which, if they were in a situation, would exhibit the forms of "information processing" essential in dealing with our nonformal world. Artificial Intelligence workers who feel that some concrete results are better than none, and that we should not abandon work on artificial intelligence until the day we are in a position to construct such artificial men, cannot be refuted. The long reign of alchemy has shown that any research which has had an early success can always be justified and continued by those who prefer adventure to patience.[20]* If researchers insist on *a priori* proof of the impossibility of success, one can at best use formal methods such as Gödel's to prove the limitations of formal systems, but such proofs are irrelevant to AI.[21]*

Researchers could in any case respond that at least the goal can be approached. If, however, one accepts empirical evidence as to whether the effort has been misdirected, he has only to look at the predictions and the results. Even if there had been no predictions, only hopes, as in language translation, the results are sufficiently disappointing to be self-incriminating.

If the alchemist had stopped poring over his retorts and pentagrams and had spent his time looking for the deeper structure of the problem, as primitive man took his eyes off the moon, came out of the trees, and discovered fire and the wheel, things would have been set moving in a more promising direction. After all, three hundred years after the alchemists we did get gold from lead (and we have landed on the moon), but only after we abandoned work on the alchemic level, and worked to understand the chemical level and the even deeper nuclear level instead.

Notes

Introduction to the Revised Edition

1. SIGART Newsletter, No. 57 (April 1976), p. 4. Unfortunately, Herbert Simon does not seem to have accepted McDermott's good advice. In a talk on "Artificial Intelligence Systems That Understand," given at the 5th International Joint Conference on Artificial Intelligence—1977, he introduced a new system called, of all things, UNDERSTAND! (IJCAI-77, *Proceedings*), p. 1059.
2. *Ibid.*
3. Hubert L. Dreyfus, "Alchemy and Artificial Intelligence," The RAND Corporation (December 1965), P. 3244.
4. Terry Winograd, "On Some Contested Suppositions of Generative Linguistics about the Scientific Study of Language," *Cognition,* Vol. 5 (1977), pp. 151–179.
5. SIGART Newsletter, No. 57 (April 1976), p. 4.
6. This horror of criticism is very real. When I was invited to review two recent publications of Minsky, Papert, and Winston for *Creative Computing,* the book review editor at the same time invited Seymour Papert to review my book, so as to balance the presentation. According to the book review editor, Papert replied by threatening that if *Creative Computing* published my critique there would be disapproval from the AI community and reprisals from M.I.T. Press. Moreover, he promised that if *Creative Computing* rejected my review, he would submit an article which the editor had been trying in vain to get from him, as well as furnish additional articles by his students.
7. Pamela McCorduck, *Machines Who Think: A Personal Inquiry into the History and Prospects of Artificial Intelligence* (San Francisco: W. H. Freeman Press, forthcoming).
8. B. G. Buchanan, *Computing Reviews* (January 1973), p. 20.
9. Edward A. Feigenbaum, "The Art of Artificial Intelligence" (IJCAI-77, *Proceedings*), p. 1014.
10. Buchanan, *op. cit.,* p. 20, cited in note 8 above.
11. Marvin Minsky and Seymour Papert, M.I.T. Artificial Intelligence Laboratory Memo (November 29, 1971), p. 120.

12. Terry Winograd, "A Procedural Model of Language Understanding," *Computer Models of Thought and Language,* Roger Schank and Kenneth Colby, eds. (San Francisco: W. H. Freeman Press, 1973). (SHRDLU is an anti-acronym whose letters don't stand for anything. It was picked up by Winograd from *Mad Magazine,* which uses this frequent typesetter's error as the name of mythical monsters and the like.)

13. Terry Winograd, "Understanding Natural Language," *Cognitive Psychology* No. 3 (New York: Academic Press, 1972), pp. 8–11.

14. Winograd, "A Procedural Model of Language Understanding," p. 167, cited in note 12 above.

15. Marvin Minsky and Seymour Papert, Draft, July 1970, of a Proposal to ARPA for Research on Artificial Intelligence at M.I.T., 1970–1971, p. 39.

16. *Ibid.*

17. *Ibid.,* pp. 42–44.

18. *Ibid.,* p. 48.

19. *Ibid.,* pp. 50–52.

20. Ibid., p. 52.

21. Terry Winograd, "Artificial Intelligence and Language Comprehension," in *Artificial Intelligence and Language Comprehension* (Washington, D.C.: National Institute of Education, 1976), p. 9.

22. Winograd, "Understanding Natural Language," p. 26, cited in note 13 above.

23. Herbert A. Simon, "Artificial Intelligence Systems That Understand" (IJCAI-77, *Proceedings*), p. 1062.

24. *Ibid.,* p. 1063.

25. *Ibid.,* p. 1064.

26. Terry Winograd, *Five Lectures on Artificial Intelligence,* AI Laboratory Memo No. 246, Computer Science Department Report, Stanford University (1974), p. 20.

27. This view is worked out by Martin Heidegger in *Being and Time* (New York: Harper & Row, 1962). See especially p. 93 and all of section 18.

28. M.I.T. Artificial Intelligence Laboratory, Memo No. 299 (September 1973), p. 95. (My italics.)

29. *Ibid.,* p. 95.

30. *Ibid.,* p. 96.

31. Patrick H. Winston and the Staff of the M.I.T. AI Laboratory, AI Memo No. 366 (May 1976), p. 22.

32. Winograd, "Artificial Intelligence and Language Comprehension," p. 17, cited in note 21 above.

33. Patrick H. Winston, *The Psychology of Computer Vision,* P. H. Winston, ed. (New York: McGraw Hill, 1975), p. 7.

34. Winston and the Staff of the M.I.T. AI Laboratory, pp. 77–78, cited in note 31 above.

35. Winston, *The Psychology of Computer Vision,* p. 8, cited in note 33 above.

36. Winston and the Staff of the M.I.T. AI Laboratory, p. 79, cited in note 31 above.

37. Winston, *The Psychology of Computer Vision,* p. 2, cited in note 33 above.

38. Winograd, "Artificial Intelligence and Language Comprehension," p. 3, cited in note 21 above.

39. Marvin Minsky, ed., *Semantic Information Processing* (Cambridge, Mass.: M.I.T. Press, 1969), p. 7.

40. Marvin Minsky and Seymour Papert, *Artificial Intelligence* (Condon Lectures, Oregon State System of Higher Education, Eugene, Oregon, 1973).

41. *Ibid.,* p. 11.

42. *Ibid.,* p. 34.

43. Erich Goldmeier, *Similarity in Visually Perceived Forms* (New York: International Universities Press, 1972), p. 1.

44. *Ibid.,* p. 128.

45. John Haugeland, "The Plausibility of Cognitive Psychology," *The Behavioral and Brain Sciences,* Vol. 1, No. 2 (preprint).

46. *Ibid.*

47. Reprinted in *The Psychology of Computer Vision,* P. H. Winston, ed. (New York: McGraw Hill, 1975), Chapter 5.

48. *Ibid.,* p. 185.

49. Minsky and Papert, *Artificial Intelligence,* p. 54, cited in note 40 above.

50. Winston, *The Psychology of Computer Vision,* p. 158, cited in note 47 above.

51. *Ibid.,* p. 194.

52. *Ibid.,* p. 193.

53. *Ibid.,* pp. 193–194.

54. *Ibid.,* p. 160.

55. Minsky and Papert, *Artificial Intelligence,* p. 56, cited in note 40 above.

56. *Ibid.*

57. Winston, *The Psychology of Computer Vision,* p. 157, cited in note 47 above.

58. Eleanor Rosch, "Human Categorization," in *Advances in Cross-Cultural Psychology,* Vol. 1, N. Warren, ed. (London: Academic Press, 1977), p. 30.

59. Minsky and Papert, *Artificial Intelligence,* p. 25, cited in note 40 above.

60. *Ibid.*

61. M.I.T., Project MAC, Progress Report VI, July 1968 to July 1969, p. 50.

62. *Ibid.* (My italics.)

63. *Ibid.*

64. Bertram Raphael, *Computer and People,* Vol. 25, No. 10, October 1976 (Newtonville, Mass.: Berkeley Enterprises, Inc.), pp. 7, 8.

65. *Ibid.*

66. Bertram Raphael, *The Thinking Computer* (San Francisco: W. H. Freeman Press, 1976), p. 284.

67. Edward A. Feigenbaum, "The Art of Artificial Intelligence: Themes and Case Studies of Knowledge Engineering" (IJCAI-77, *Proceedings*), p. 1014.

68. In the first issue of a journal entitled *Cognitive Science,* Allan Collins defines the field as follows:

"Cognitive science is defined principally by the set of problems it addresses and the set of tools it uses. The most immediate problem areas are representation of knowledge, language understanding, image understanding, question answering, inference, learning, problem solving, and planning. . . . The tools of cognitive science consist of a set of analysis techniques and a set of theoretical formalisms. The analysis techniques include such things as protocol analysis, discourse analysis, and a variety of experimental techniques developed by cognitive psychologists in recent years. The theoretical formalisms include such notions as means-ends analysis, discrimination nets, semantic nets, goal-oriented languages, production systems, ATN grammars, frames, etc."

69. Winston and the Staff of the M.I.T. AI Laboratory, p. 48, cited in note 31 above.
70. Shortliffe's MYCIN program example in Feigenbaum, "The Art of Artificial Intelligence," p. 1022, cited in note 67 above.
71. *Ibid.*, p. 1023. Before being overly impressed by these statistics, however, the reader should realize that to achieve this performance the program requires the aid of human experts. Feigenbaum does not mention that in order to know when to prescribe powerful but dangerous drugs the program must be given an evaluation of the seriousness of the patient's illness. This judgment cannot be computed from a battery of medical tests but must be arrived at by an experienced phsyician with a holistic grasp of the patient's overall condition. The knowledge engineers have wisely not even tried to reduce this intuitive aspect of the diagnosis to heuristics rules.
72. *Ibid.*, p. 1016.
73. *Ibid.*, p. 1017.
74. *Ibid.*
75. SIGART Newsletter, No. 60 (November 1976), p. 12.
76. Michael Polanyi, *Personal Knowledge* (London: Routledge and Kegan Paul, 1962), p. 31.
77. A ply is one total set of possible moves starting from a given position, plus the total set of possible responses to each of these moves.
78. Winston and the Staff of the M.I.T. AI Laboratory, p. 74, cited in note 31 above.
79. Roger C. Schank et al., Panel on Natural Language Processing (IJCAI-77, *Proceedings*), pp. 1007 and 1008.
80. Ira Goldstein and Seymour Papert, M.I.T. AI Laboratory, AI Memo No. 337 (July 1975, revised March 1976), "Artificial Intelligence, Language and the Study of Knowledge," p. 7.
81. M.I.T. AI Laboratory, Memo No. 299, p. 77, cited in note 28 above.
82. Edmund Husserl, *Cartesian Meditations* (The Hague: Martinus Nijhoff, 1960), p. 53. Husserl is unclear, and so was I in the first edition of this book, as to whether his noemata were meant to be formalizable. On p. 249 I note that the noemata are abstract, but on the same page and on p. 339 in note 10 I claim that noemata are supposed to have a kind of indeterminacy not expressible in a formal symbol structure. I now think that to be abstractible is to be formalizable and, although Husserl seems to hold elsewhere that some sort of nonformal abstraction is possible, it seems clear that Husserl thought of the noema as a "system of predicates" (see E. Husserl, *Ideas* [New York: Collier, 1931], p. 337), i.e., as a formal symbolic description of stereotypical objects, and that it was his goal to "explicate systematically . . . this set of structural types" (*Cartesian Meditations,* p. 51).
83. Husserl, *Cartesian Meditations,* p. 51, cited in preceding note.

84. Marvin Minsky, "A Framework for Representing Knowledge" in *The Psychology of Computer Vision,* P. H. Winston, ed. (New York: McGraw-Hill, 1975), p. 212.

85. Winston, *The Psychology of Computer Vision,* p. 16, cited in note 33 above.

86. Husserl, *Cartesian Meditations,* pp. 54–55, cited in note 82 above.

87. Marvin Minsky, unpublished draft of the frame paper, February 27, 1974, p. 68.

88. Minsky, "A Framework for Representing Knowledge," p. 240, cited in note 84 above.

89. *Ibid.,* p. 255. (My italics.)

90. *Ibid.*

91. *Ibid.* (My italics.)

92. *Ibid.,* p. 213.

93. Thomas Kuhn, *The Structure of Scientific Revolutions,* 2nd edition (Chicago: University of Chicago Press, 1970), p. 15.

94. Minsky, "A Framework for Representing Knowledge," p. 261, cited in note 84 above. (My italics.)

95. Kuhn, *The Structure of Scientific Revolutions,* p. 200, cited in note 93 above.

96. *Ibid.,* p. 192.

97. *Ibid.,* p. 11. (My italics.)

98. Roger C. Schank, "The Primitive Acts of Conceptual Dependency," *Theoretical Issues in Natural Language Processing* (Cambridge, Mass., June 10–13, 1975), p. 39.

99. Roger C. Schank, "Using Knowledge to Understand," *Theoretical Issues in Natural Language Processing* (Cambridge, Mass., June 10–13, 1975), p. 131. (My italics.)

100. *Ibid.*

101. Roger C. Schank and Robert P. Abelson, *Scripts, Plans, Goals and Understanding* (Hillsdale, N.J.: Lawrence Erlbaum Associates, 1970), p. 51.

102. This is John Searle's way of formulating this important point. In a talk at the University of California at Berkeley (October 19, 1977), Schank agreed with Searle that to understand a visit to a restaurant the computer needs more than a script; it needs to know everything that people know. He added that he is unhappy that as it stands his program cannot distinguish "degrees of weirdness." Indeed, for the program it is equally "weird" for the restaurant to be out of food as it is for the customer to respond by devouring the chef. Thus Schank seems to agree that without some understanding of degree of deviation from the norm, the program does not understand a story even when in that story events follow a completely normal stereotyped script. It follows that although scripts capture a necessary condition of everyday understanding, they do not provide a sufficient condition.

103. Schank, "Using Knowledge to Understand," p. 132, cited in note 99 above.

104. Society for the Interdisciplinary Study of the Mind, Symposium for Philosophy and Computer Technology, State University College, New Paltz, New York, March 1977.

105. Schank and Abelson, *Scripts, Plans, Goals and Understanding,* p. 50, cited in note 101 above.

106. *Ibid.,* p. 74.

107. *Ibid.,* p. 97. (My italics.)

108. *Ibid.,* p. 138.

109. *Ibid.,* p. 145.

110. *Ibid.,* p. 149.

111. Roger C. Schank, "Conceptual Dependency: A Theory of Natural Language Understanding," *Cognitive Psychology,* No. 3 (New York: Academic Press, 1972), pp. 553–554.

112. Terry Winograd, "Towards a Procedural Understanding of Semantics," *Revue Internationale de Philosophie,* No. 117–118 (Foundation Universitaire de Belgique, 1976), p. 262.

113. *Ibid.,* p. 268.

114. Daniel G. Bobrow and Terry Winograd, "An Overview of KRL, a Knowledge Representation Language," *Cognitive Science,* Vol. 1, No. 1 (1977), p. 7.

115. Winograd, "Towards a Procedural Understanding of Semantics," pp. 276–278, cited in note 112 above.

116. *Ibid.,* pp. 281–282. (My italics.)

117. *Ibid.,* p. 280.

118. Bobrow and Winograd, "An Overview of KRL," p. 8, cited in note 114 above.

119. Winograd, *Five Lectures on Artificial Intelligence,* p. 80, cited in note 26 above.

120. Bobrow and Winograd, "An Overview of KRL," p. 32, cited in note 114 above.

121. Winograd, "Towards a Procedural Understanding of Semantics," p. 283, cited in note 112 above.

122. *Ibid.,* pp. 287–288.

123. *Ibid.,* p. 282.

124. Panel on Natural Language Processing (IJCAI-77, *Proceedings*), p. 1008, cited in note 79 above.

This notion of a physical symbol system is Newell and Simon's refinement of what Papert and Minsky called a "symbolic description" (see p. 18 above).

"A physical symbol system consists of a set of entities, called symbols, which are physical patterns that can occur as components of another type of entity called an expression (or symbol structure). Thus, a symbol structure is composed of a number of instances (or tokens) of symbols related in some physical way (such as one token being next to another). At any instant of time the system will contain a collection of these symbol structures. Besides these structures, the system also contains a collection of processes that operate on expressions to produce other expressions. . . . An expression designates an object if, given the expression, the system can either affect the object itself or behave in ways dependent on the object." (A. Newell and H. Simon, "Computer Science as Empirical Inquiry: Symbols and Search," in *Communications of the ACM,* Vol. 19, No. 3 [March 1976], p. 116.)

When spelled out in further detail this definition enables Newell and Simon to state with new precision the fundamental assumption of cognitive science—an assumption which they now (unlike in their earlier papers) clearly recognize as an hypothesis:

"The Physical Symbol System Hypothesis [states:] A physical symbol system has the necessary and sufficient means for general intelligent action." *(Ibid.)*

125. Winograd, "Towards a Procedural Understanding of Semantics," p. 264, cited in note 112 above.

126. *Ibid.,* p. 297.

127. Bobrow and Winograd, "An Overview of KRL," p. 43, cited in note 114 above.

128. Ludwig Wittgenstein, *Philosophical Investigations* (Oxford, Eng.: Basil Blackwell, 1953). This particular way of putting the argument also owes a great deal to discussions with John Searle.

129. Goldstein and Papert, M.I.T. AI Laboratory, pp. 29–31, cited in note 80 above.

130. *Ibid.,* p. 33.

131. *Ibid.,* p. 34.

132. *Ibid.*

133. *Ibid.,* pp. 30–31. (My italics.)

134. Not to mention its *prima facie* implausibility, noted by, of all people, that arch-formalizer, John McCarthy:

> "Minsky . . . confused matters by using the word 'frame' for patterns into which situations may fit. His hypothesis seems to have been that almost all situations encountered in human problem solving fit into a small number of previously known patterns of situation and goal. I regard this as unlikely. . . ." (John McCarthy, "Epistemological Problems of Artificial Intelligence" [IJCAI-77, *Proceedings*], p. 1040).

135. Schank and Abelson, *Scripts, Plans, Goals and Understanding,* p. 144, cited in note 101 above.

136. Panel on Natural Language Processing (IJCAI-77, *Proceedings*), p. 1009, cited in note 79 above.

137. McCarthy, "Epistemological Problems of Artificial Intelligence," p. 1038, cited in note 134 above.

138. *Ibid.,* p. 1038.

139. Joseph Weizenbaum, *Computer Power and Human Reason* (San Francisco: W. H. Freeman and Co., 1976).

140. *Ibid.,* p. 200. Or, as Weizenbaum puts the same point on p. 222:

> "We are capable of listening with the third ear, of sensing truth that is truth beyond any standards of provability. It is *that* kind of understanding, and the kind of intelligence that is derived from it, which I claim is beyond the abilities of computers to simulate."

141. *Ibid.,* p. 200.

142. Cited in Chapter 6, note 30, of this book.

143. Weizenbaum, *Computer Power and Human Reason,* p. 226, cited in note 139 above.

144. *Ibid.,* p. 225. This strong thesis, however, conflicts with Weizenbaum's use of AI terminology to describe the background as "a conceptual framework" (p. 190), and, even more misleadingly as a "belief structure" (p. 198). Both these terms presuppose the possibility of explicit descriptions.

145. *Ibid.,* p. 210.

146. *Ibid.,* p. 207.

147. *Ibid.,* p. 160. In this connection Weizenbaum asserts that cognitive science, because it merely seeks to give a mechanical account of how the mind works rather than some

sort of general theory on the model of physics or Chomskian linguistics, cannot be taken seriously as a contribution to our understanding of the mind. If the mind *is* even in part an information-processing mechanism, which Weizenbaum assumes and I doubt, then an explanation of its capacities in terms of its functional components and their interactions would, indeed, be just the kind of understanding one would hope to obtain. For a detailed account of this sort of understanding, see John Haugeland's "The Plausibility of Cognitive Psychology," cited in note 45 above.

148. *Ibid.*, p. 214. (My italics.)
149. Cited in note 142 above.
150. Weizenbaum, *Computer Power and Human Reason,* p. 13, cited in note 139 above. It is ironic that Weizenbaum, who is generally sensitive to the cues provided by a writer's vocabulary, adopts the jargon of the technologists he abhors in speaking of human beings as "humans," thus taking one step more down the path of assimilating human beings to objects like tables and computers.
151. *Ibid.*, p. 227. What makes an account of Weizenbaum's book difficult is that he also advances a strong in-principle argument inconsistent with the weak "moral" argument we have been following. He asserts that "human becoming" (what I call man's capacity to redefine himself and his world, see p. 277) does, indeed, play an essential and unformalizable role in human behavior so that very little of our everyday intelligence can be formalized:

"[S]ince *the domain of human intelligence is, except for a small set of formal problems, determined by man's humanity,* every other intelligence, however great, must necessarily be alien to the human domain." (p. 223, my italics.)

But here Weizenbaum's commitment to the technologists' dichotomy between intelligence and wisdom shows up along different lines. Rather than distinguishing unformalizable wisdom from everyday formalizable intelligence, Weizenbaum now distinguishes informal everyday intelligence concerned with what matters to human beings from formalizable intelligence "absolutely alien to any and all authentic human concerns" (p. 226). But this notion of an alien intelligence, frequently appealed to by those in AI who see that without a body and culture a computer may well not be able to interact with human beings on their own terms, is just another version of the philosopher's illusion of a pure intellect. Once we accept that our idea of intelligence is essentially connected with knowing what is important in particular contexts, it becomes impossible to say what such an absolutely alien intelligence would be. We can attribute inferior intelligence to bees and bats, and superior intelligences to figures like Landru in *Star Trek,* because we suppose they still share our needs for food, company, etc. and have purposes similar to ours such as seeking food, protecting their young, etc. It is these needs and purposes which make their activity intelligent and intelligible. There are, indeed, artifacts with completely arbitrary goals, which we refer to metaphorically as "intelligent," as when we speak, for example, of sophisticated goal-directed missiles as "smart bombs," but if it weren't for Plato and Aristotle, who so disconnected intelligence from human activity that they thought of the planets as governed by "intelligences," no one would suppose that devices which shared none of our human concerns could literally be characterized as having an alien intelligence.

152. Herman Melville, *Moby Dick* (New York: Modern Library College Editions, 1952), p. 477.

INTRODUCTION

1. Plato, *Euthyphro,* VII, trans. F. J. Church (New York: Library of Liberal Arts), 1948, p. 7.
2. Marvin Minsky, *Computation: Finite and Infinite Machines* (Englewood Cliffs, N.J.: Prentice-Hall, 1967), p. 106. Of course, Minsky is thinking of computation and not moral action.
3. *Ibid.*
4. Aristotle, *Nicomachean Ethics,* trans. J. A. K. Thomson as *The Ethics of Aristotle* (New York: Penguin Books, 1953), p. 75.
5. Hobbes, *Leviathan* (New York: Library of Liberal Arts, 1958), p. 45.
6. Leibniz, *Selections,* ed. Philip Wiener (New York: Scribner, 1951), p. 18.
7. *Ibid.,* p. 25
8. *Ibid.,* p. 15.
9. *Ibid.,* p. 23.
10. *Ibid.,* p. 48. (My italics.)
11. George Boole, *Laws of Thought,* Collected Logical Works (Chicago: Open Court, 1940), Vol. II, p. 1.
12. A. M. Turing, "Computing Machinery and Intelligence," reprinted in *Minds and Machines,* ed. Alan Ross Anderson (Englewood Cliffs, N.J.: Prentice-Hall, 1964), p. 11.
13. *Ibid.,* p. 13.
14. In Chapter 5 we shall have occasion to see how this principle gives strong but unwarranted confidence to those working to simulate human thought process with digital machines.
15. Martin Heidegger, "The End of Philosophy and the Task of Thinking," in *Basic Writings* (New York: Harper & Row, 1977), p. 376. "Philosophy is ending in the present age. It has found its place in the scientific attitude. . . . [T]he fundamental characteristic of this scientific attitude is its cybernetic, that is, technological character."

16. Turing, *op. cit.*, p. 7.
17. *Ibid.*, p. 5.
18. See, for example, the critical articles by Kieth Gunderson and Michael Scriven in *Minds and Machines*, cited in note 12 above.
19. Turing, *op. cit.*, p. 30.
20. Claude E. Shannon, "A Chess-Playing Machine," reprinted in *World of Mathematics*, ed. James R. Newman (New York: Simon and Schuster, 1956), p. 2129.
21. *Ibid.*
22. Allen Newell, "The Chess Machine," in *The Modeling of Mind*, Kenneth M. Sayre and Frederick J. Crosson, eds. (South Bend, Ind.: Notre Dame University Press, 1963), p. 89.
23. Allen Newell, J. C. Shaw, and H. A. Simon, "Chess-Playing Programs and the Problem of Complexity," in *Computers and Thought*, Edward A. Feigenbaum and Julian Feldman, eds. (New York: McGraw-Hill, 1963), p. 48.
24. *Ibid.*, p. 45.
25. Allen Newell, J. C. Shaw, and H. A. Simon, "Empirical Explorations with the Logic Theory Machine: A Case Study in Heuristics," in *Computers and Thought*, p. 109.
26. Allen Newell, J. C. Shaw, and H. A. Simon, "Report on a General Problem-Solving Program," *Proc. Int. Conf. on Information Processing* (Paris: UNESCO, 1960), p. 257.
27. *Ibid.*, p. 259.
28. Herbert A. Simon and Allen Newell, "Heuristic Problem Solving: The Next Advance in Operations Research," *Operations Research*, Vol. 6 (January–February 1958), p. 6.
29. Noam Chomsky, *Language and Mind* (New York: Harcourt, Brace & World, 1968), p. v.
30. Turing, *op. cit.*, p. 14, cited in note 12 above.
31. Marvin Minsky, "Machines Are More Than They Seem," *Science Journal* (October 1968), p. 3.
32. Herbert A. Simon and Allen Newell, "Heuristic Problem Solving: The Next Advance in Operations Research," cited in note 28 above.
33. W. Ross Ashby, "Review of Feigenbaum's *Computers and Thought*," *Journal of Nervous and Mental Diseases*.
34. D. E. Smith, *History of Mathematics* (Boston: Ginn, 1925), Vol. II, p. 284.
35. Newell, Shaw, and Simon, "Chess-Playing Programs and the Problem of Complexity," p. 60.
36. *Ibid.*, p. 45.
37. Allen Newell, J. C. Shaw, and H. A. Simon, *The Processes of Creative Thinking*, The RAND Corporation, P–1320 (September 16, 1958), p. 6.
38. *Ibid.*, p. 78.
39. Norbert Wiener, "The Brain and the Machine (Summary)," in *Dimensions of Mind*, Sidney Hook, ed. (New York: Collier, 1961), p. 110.

40. Michael Scriven, "The Complete Robot: A Prolegomena to Androidology," in *Dimensions of Mind,* p. 122.

41. H. A. Simon and Peter A. Simon, "Trial and Error Search in Solving Difficult Problems: Evidence from the Game of Chess," *Behavioral Science,* Vol. 7 (October 1962), p. 429.

42. For example, the abstract of the Simon and Simon article (note 41 above) makes no mention of the forced mates but rather concludes: "This paper attempts to clear away some of the mythology which surrounds the game of chess by showing that successful problem solving is based on a highly selective, heuristic 'program' rather than on prodigies of memory and insight" (p. 425). And the article itself concludes with the unjustified generalization: "The evidence suggests strongly that expert chess players discover combinations because their programs incorporate powerful selective heuristics and not because they think faster or memorize better than other people" (p. 429). The evidence honestly evaluated suggests that at best this is the case only in specific situations in the end game.

43. Paul Armer, "Attitudes Toward Intelligent Machines," in *Computers and Thought,* p. 405.

44. Fred Gruenberger, *Benchmarks in Artificial Intelligence,* The RAND Corporation, P–2586 (June 1962), p. 6.

45. The glee with which this victory was announced to the computer community, as if the prior claims about what computers could do had thereby been vindicated, is echoed by Alvin Toffler on p. 187 of *Future Shock* (New York: Random House, 1971). The author interprets me as saying that no computer would *ever* play even amateur chess. From the full quotation it is clear that this is a distortion. My assertion was simply a correct report of the state of the art at the time (1965): "According to Newell, Shaw, and Simon themselves, evaluating the Los Alamos, the IBM, and the NSS programs: 'All three programs play roughly the same quality of chess (mediocre) with roughly the same amount of computing time.' Still no chess program can play even amateur chess, and the world championship is only two years away."

46. Seymour Papert, 9th RAND Symposium (November 7, 1966), p. 116.

47. Donald Michie, *Science Journal,* Vol. 4, No. 10 (October 1968), p. 1.

48. Eliot Hearst, "Psychology Across the Chessboard," *Psychology Today* (June 1967), p. 32.

49. The third prediction—that most psychological theories would take the form of computer programs—has indeed been partially fulfilled, although there are still plenty of behaviorists. But the important question here is not whether a certain task, impressive in itself like master play or original theorem proving, has been achieved, but whether what is predicted would be an achievement even if it came to pass. The substitution in psychology of computer models for behaviorist models is by no means obviously a step forward. The issue is complicated and requires detailed discussion (see Chapter 4).

50. Papert, *op. cit.,* p. 117.

Part I. Ten Years of Research in Artificial Intelligence (1957–1967)

CHAPTER 1. PHASE I (1957–1962) COGNITIVE SIMULATION

1. Anthony G. Oettinger, "The State of the Art of Automatic Language Translation: An Appraisal," in *Beitraege zur Sprachkunde und Informations Verarbeitung,* ed. Herbert Marchl, Vol. 1, Heft 2 (Munich: Oldenbourg Verlage, 1963), p. 18.

2. Yehoshua Bar-Hillel, "The Present Status of Automatic Translation of Languages," in *Advances in Computers,* F. L. Alt, ed. (New York: Academic Press, 1960), Vol. 1, p. 94.

3. National Academy of Sciences, *Language and Machines* (Washington, D.C., 1966), p. 29.

4. Oettinger, *op. cit.,* p. 21.

5. *Ibid.,* p. 27. Such critical evaluations of machine translation often end with the comforting conclusion that at least the work added to our knowledge of the structure of language. But even this justification is questionable. Chomsky takes a dim view of this "spin-off": ". . . an appreciable investment of time, energy, and money in the use of computers for linguistic research —appreciable by the standards of a small field like linguistics—has not provided any significant advance in our understanding of the use or nature of language. These judgments are harsh, but I think they are defensible. They are, furthermore, hardly debated by active linguistic or psycholinguistic researchers." (Noam Chomsky, *Language and Mind* [New York: Harcourt, Brace & World, 1968], p. 4.)

6. *Language and Machines, op. cit.,* p. 32.

7. The most important papers reporting work done during this period have been collected in Edward A. Feigenbaum and Julian Feldman, eds., *Computers and Thought* (New York: McGraw-Hill, 1963).

8. A protocol is a verbal report of a subject in the process of solving a problem. Here is a typical protocol from a subject trying to solve a logic problem: "Well, looking at the left hand side of the equation, first we want to eliminate one of the sides by using rule 8. It appears too complicated to work with first. Now—no,—no, I can't do that because I will be eliminating either the Q or the P in that total expression. I won't do that at first. Now I'm looking for a way to get rid of the horseshoe inside the two brackets that appear on the left and right sides of the equation. And I don't see it. Yeh, if you apply rule 6 to both sides of the equation, from there I'm going to see if I can apply rule 7." (*Computers and Thought,* p. 282.)

9. H. A. Simon, *Modeling Human Mental Processes,* The RAND Corporation, P–2221 (February 20, 1961), p. 15. Not that these problems were unsolved. Several routine, nonheuristic, mathematical algorithms have been published which solve these and more complex routing problems.

10. Allen Newell and H. A. Simon, *Computer Simulation of Human Thinking,* The RAND Corporation, P–2276 (April 20, 1961); also published in *Science,* Vol. 134 (December 22, 1961), p. 19. (My italics.)
11. H. A. Simon, *op. cit.,* p. 12.
12. Marvin Minsky, "Descriptive Languages and Problem Solving," *Proceedings of the 1961 Western Joint Computer Conference;* reprinted in *Semantic Information Processing,* Minsky, ed. (Cambridge, Mass.: M.I.T. Press, 1969), p. 420.
13. *Ibid.*
14. Allen Newell, *Some Problems of Basic Organization in Problem-Solving Programs,* The RAND Corporation, RM–3283–PR (December 1962), p. 4.
15. G. W. Ernst and A. Newell, *Generality and GPS,* Carnegie Institute of Technology, January 1967, p. i.
16. *Ibid.,* p. 45.
17. H. Gelernter, J. R. Hansen, and D. W. Loveland, "Empirical Explorations of the Geometry-Theorem Proving Machine," in *Computers and Thought,* p. 160.
18. Oliver G. Selfridge and Ulric Neisser, "Pattern Recognition by Machine," in *Computers and Thought,* p. 238.
19. Murray Eden, "Other Pattern-Recognition Problems and Some Generalizations," in *Recognizing Patterns: Studies in Living and Automatic Systems,* Paul A. Kolers and Murray Eden, eds. (Cambridge, Mass.: M.I.T. Press, 1968), p. 196.
20. Selfridge and Neisser, *op. cit.,* p. 244.
21. *Ibid.,* p. 250.
22. Leonard Uhr and Charles Vossler, "A Pattern-Recognition Program that Generates, Evaluates, and Adjusts its own Operations:" in *Computers and Thought,* p. 251.
23. Laveen Kanal and B. Chandrasekaran, "Recognition, Machine Recognition and Statistical Approaches," *Methodologies of Pattern Recognition* (New York: Academic Press, 1969), pp. 318, 319.
24. Vincent E. Giuliano, "How We Find Patterns," *International Science and Technology* (February 1967), p. 40.
25. Feigenbaum and Feldman, *Computers and Thought,* p. 276.
26. *Ibid.,* p. vi.
27. Allen Newell, "The Chess Machine," in *The Modeling of Mind,* Kenneth M. Sayre and Frederick J. Crosson, eds. (South Bend, Ind.: Notre Dame University Press, 1963), p. 80.
28. *Ibid.*
29. Allen Newell and H. A. Simon, *Computer Simulation of Human Thinking,* The RAND Corporation, P–2276 (April 20, 1961), p. 15.
30. Newell, Shaw, and Simon, "Chess-Playing Programs and the Problem of Complexity," in *Computers and Thought,* p. 47.
31. Michael Polanyi, "Experience and Perception of Pattern," in *The Modeling of Mind,* p. 214. As far as I know, Frederick Crosson was the first to see

the relevance of this gestaltist analysis to work in artificial intelligence. In the Preface to *The Modeling of Mind* he writes: ". . . Some human functions are at times performed by utilizing information or clues which are not explicitly or focally attended to, and this seems to mark a fundamental difference between such functions and the processes by which they are simulated by automata. The reason for this difference is that the operations of the digital computers which are employed as models are binary in nature. Consequently, the function which the machine can perform . . . must be, at each stage, all-or-none, i.e., sufficiently specific and explicit to be answered 'yes' or 'no' " (p. 21). Crosson, however, does not spell out the peculiarities and function of this nonfocal form of awareness, so it remains unclear whether on his view all implicit cues could in principle be made explicit and what, if anything, would be lost in a model which dealt only with explicit cues.

32. Newell and Simon, *An Example of Human Chess Play in the Light of Chess Playing Programs,* Carnegie Institute of Technology, August 1964, pp. 10–11.

33. *Ibid.,* p. 13. (My italics.)

34. *Ibid.,* p. 11. Newell and Simon go on: "More generally, psychology has had little to say about how global concepts organize behavior." This is, of course, incredibly provincial. Gestalt psychology talks of little else. What Newell and Simon mean is that the kind of psychology they prefer, i.e., the kind of psychology that uses a computer program as its model of explanation, has no way of dealing with such global processes.

35. *Ibid.,* p. 14.

36. Eliot Hearst, "Psychology Across the Chessboard," *Psychology Today* (June 1967), p. 35.

37. *Ibid.,* p. 37.

38. Minsky notes this difficulty, but on sheer faith he supposes that there must be a heuristic solution: "This might be done through some heuristic technique that can assess relevancy, or through a logic which takes such consequences into account. The trouble with the latter is that the antecedents of all the propositions must contain a condition about the state of the system, and for complex systems this becomes overwhelmingly cumbersome. Other systematic solutions to the problem seem about equally repellent. It is a problem that seems urgently to require a heuristic solution." (*Semantic Information Processing,* p. 422.)

39. Newell, Shaw, and Simon, "Chess-Playing Programs and the Problem of Complexity," in *Computers and Thought,* p. 65.

40. Oettinger, *op. cit.,* p. 26, cited in note 1 above.

41. *Ibid.*

42. In serial processing the program consists of a series of operations, each one depending on the results of the previous ones. In parallel processing several such series of computation are performed simultaneously. Parallel processing can be simulated by a serial program, but the important logical difference

remains that in a serial program each step depends on the previous ones, while in a parallel program, the operations in each series are independent of the operations in any other series.

43. Ludwig Wittgenstein, *The Blue and Brown Books* (Oxford, Eng.: Basil Blackwell, 1960), p. 25. The participants in The RAND symposium on "Computers and Comprehension" suggest the psychological basis and advantage of this nonrulelike character of natural languages. "It is crucial that language is a combinatory repertoire with unlimited possible combinations whose meanings can be inferred from a finite set of 'rules' governing the components' meaning. (The so-called 'rules' are learned as response sets and are only partly formalizable.)" (M. Kochen, D. M. MacKay, M. E. Maron, M. Scriven, and L. Uhr, *Computers and Comprehension*, The RAND Corporation, RM–4065–PR [April 1964], p. 12.)

44. Bar-Hillel, *op. cit.*, pp. 105, 106, cited in note 2 above.

45. Edward Feigenbaum, "The Simulation of Verbal Learning Behavior," in *Computers and Thought*, p. 298.

46. Marvin Minsky, "Steps Toward Artificial Intelligence," in *Computers and Thought*, p. 447.

47. Michael Scriven, *Primary Philosophy* (New York: McGraw-Hill, 1966), p. 186.

48. Wittgenstein, *Philosophical Investigations* (Oxford, Eng.: Basil Blackwell, 1953), p. 227. Wittgenstein is here talking about how we learn to judge an expression of feeling, but his point is more general.

49. Allen Newell and H. A. Simon, "GPS: A Program That Simulates Human Thought," in *Computers and Thought*, p. 288.

50. *Ibid.*, p. 289.

51. *Ibid.*, p. 290. The arbitrary nature of this *ad hoc* explanation is evident from the context. Moreover, when questioned on this point at his 1968 Mellon Lecture at M.I.T., Simon answered that he did not believe that parallel processing played a role in cognitive processes, and did not remember ever having held that it did.

52. *Ibid.*, p. 291.

53. *Ibid.*, p. 292.

54. *Ibid.*

55. Max Wertheimer, *Productive Thinking* (New York: Harper & Bros., 1945), p. 202.

56. Marvin Minsky, "Descriptive Languages and Problem Solving," in *Semantic Information Processing*, p. 421, cited in note 12 above.

57. Newell, Shaw, and Simon, *The Processes of Creative Thinking*, The RAND Corporation, P–1320 (September 16, 1958), pp. 43–44.

58. George Miller, Eugene Galanter, and Karl H. Pribram, *Plans and the Structure of Behavior* (New York: Holt, Rinehart and Winston, 1960), pp. 179–180.

59. *Ibid.*, p. 180.

60. *Ibid.*, p. 191.

61. *Ibid.,* p. 190. (My italics.)
62. Wertheimer, *op. cit.,* p. 195, cited in note 55 above.
63. Hearst, *op. cit.,* p. 32, cited in note 36 above.
64. Minsky, "Descriptive Languages and Problem Solving," in *Semantic Information Processing,* p. 420, cited in note 12 above.
65. *Ibid.,* p. 123.
66. Edward Feigenbaum, "Artificial Intelligence: Themes in the Second Decade," IFIP Congress 1968, Supplement, p. J–15.
67. Whatever information processing the human brain employs to pick out patterns, this work is no doubt aided by the organization of human receptors. But even if organization of the input into perceptual prominences (figure and ground) could be built into the receptors of a digital machine, such selective receptors would amount to introducing a stage of analogue processing, which workers in artificial intelligence are committed to avoid.
68. Oliver G. Selfridge and Ulric Neisser, "Pattern Recognition by Machine," in *Computers and Thought,* p. 238.
69. Earl Hunt, *Computer Simulation: Artificial Intelligence Studies and their Relevance to Psychology* (Brown and Farber, 1968), p. 145.
70. Selfridge and Neisser, "Pattern Recognition by Machine," in *Computers and Thought,* p. 238.
71. Aron Gurwitsch, "On the Conceptual Consciousness," in *The Modeling of Mind,* p. 203.
72. *Ibid.,* pp. 204–205.
73. Maurice Merleau-Ponty, *Phenomenology of Perception* (London: Routledge & Kegan Paul, 1962), pp. 128 ff.
74. Wittgenstein, *The Blue and Brown Books,* p. 25.
75. Of course, it only looks like "narrowing down" or "*dis*-ambiguation" to someone who approaches the problem from the computer's point of view. We shall see later that for a human being the situation is structured in terms of interrelated meanings so that the other possible meanings of a word or utterance never even have to be eliminated. They simply do not arise.
76. Cited in Merleau-Ponty, *Sense and Non-Sense,* (Evanston, Ill.: Northwestern University Press, 1964), p. 54.
77. Wittgenstein, *Philosophical Investigations,* p. 583.
78. Wittgenstein, *Philosophical Investigations,* p. 32.
79. Since typicality, unlike classification, depends on comparison with specific cases, such resemblance must be fairly concrete. Thus we can speak of a typical Indian, but not a typical man.
80. An interesting attempt to overcome this all-or-nothing character of class membership has been made by L. A. Zadeh. (See, for example, "Fuzzy Sets," *Information and Control,* Vol. 8, No. 3 [June 1965].) But Zadeh's work, although interesting, still defines classes in terms of specific traits, merely allowing class members to be defined in terms of *degree* of membership in the class. "A fuzzy set is a class of objects with a continuum of grades of membership" (p. 338). Moreover, as Zadeh uses it, fuzziness is itself a fuzzy

concept. Under fuzziness, Zadeh indiscriminately lumps five different pattern recognition problems: vagueness of boundary, context-dependence, purpose-dependence, dependence on subjective evaluation, and family resemblance. Thus it is never clear just which problem, if any, the formalization of fuzziness is supposed to solve.

81. Wittgenstein, *Philosophical Investigations*, p. 32.
82. This analysis is worked out in detail by Renford Bambrough, cf. "Universals and Family Resemblances," in *Wittgenstein: The Philosophical Investigations* (New York: Anchor, 1966).
83. *Ibid.*, p. 49.
84. Alvin Toffler's *Future Shock* provides an excellent illustration of this first step fallacy. (See note 2 of Chapter 2.)
85. Herbert Simon, *The Shape of Automation for Men and Management* (New York: Harper & Row, 1965), p. 96.

CHAPTER 2. PHASE II (1962–1967) SEMANTIC INFORMATION PROCESSING

1. Marvin Minsky, ed., *Semantic Information Processing* (Cambridge, Mass.: M.I.T. Press, 1969), pp. 6, 7.
2. For example, the following report in the *Chicago Tribune* of June 7, 1963: "The development of a machine that can listen to any conversation and type out the remarks just like an office secretary was announced yesterday by a Cornell University expert on learning machines. The device is expected to be in operation by fall [*sic*]. Frank Rosenblatt, director of Cornell's cognitive systems research, said the machine will be the largest 'thinking' device built to date. Rosenblatt made his announcement at a meeting on learning machines at Northwestern University's Technological Institute."

In their mathematical study, *Perceptrons* (Cambridge, Massachusetts: M.I.T. Press, 1969), Minsky and Papert arrive at a much less optimistic evaluation of perceptron work: "Perceptrons have been widely publicized as 'pattern recognition' or 'learning' machines and as such have been discussed in a large number of books, journal articles, and voluminous 'reports.' Most of this writing . . . is without scientific value. . . . [p. 4].

"Rosenblatt's [1958] schemes quickly took root, and soon there were perhaps as many as a hundred groups, large and small, experimenting with the model either as a 'learning machine' or in the guise of 'adaptive' or 'self-organizing' networks or 'automatic control' systems. The results of these hundreds of projects and experiments were generally disappointing, and the explanations inconclusive. The machines usually work quite well on very simple problems but deteriorate very rapidly as the tasks assigned to them get harder" [p. 9].

In the light of these practical difficulties and the theoretical limitations Minsky and Papert demonstrate, enthusiasm about the future of Perceptrons is a perfect illustration of the first step fallacy. (See note 84 above.) Typical of this falacious extrapolation is Toffler's claim (*Future Shock*, p. 186) that:

"Experiments by . . . Frank Rosenblatt and others demonstrate that machines can learn from their mistakes, improve their performance, and in certain limited kinds of learning, outstrip human students." Toffler gives no indication of the seriousness of these limitations.

3. Minsky, *Semantic Information Processing*, p. 7.

4. *Ibid.*, p. 8.

5. Minsky, "Descriptive Languages and Problem Solving," in *Semantic Information Processing*, p. 419.

6. Minsky, *Semantic Information Processing*, pp. 7–8.

7. *Ibid.*, p. 5.

8. Minsky, "Artificial Intelligence," *Scientific American*, Vol. 215, No. 3 (September 1966), p. 257.

9. Daniel G. Bobrow, "Natural Language Input for a Computer Problem Solving System" in *Semantic Information Processing*, p. 135.

10. *Ibid.*, p. 137.

11. Minsky, *Semantic Information Processing*, p. 18.

12. *Ibid.*, p. 20.

13. Bobrow, *op. cit.*, p. 183.

14. Daniel Bobrow, "Natural Language Input for a Computer Problem Solving Program," MAC–TR–1, M.I.T., abstract of thesis, p. 3. (My italics.)

15. Bobrow, "Natural Language Input for a Computer Problem Solving System," in *Semantic Information Processing*, p. 135.

16. *Ibid.*, p. 144.

17. *Ibid.*, p. 191.

18. *Ibid.*, p. 135. In the sense of "understands" and "English" used by Bobrow, a machine which did nothing more than, when told, "You are on," answered the question "Are you on?" with "Yes," would "understand English."

19. *Ibid.*, p. 194.

20. Minsky, *Semantic Information Processing*, p. 14.

21. Bobrow, *op. cit.*, in *Semantic Information Processing*, p. 192.

22. Minsky, "Artificial Intelligence," p. 260, cited in note 8 above.

23. Bobrow, *Semantic Information Processing*, p. 194.

24. Bobrow, *Natural Language Input*, p. 3, cited in note 14 above.

25. In his *Scientific American* article (p. 258), Minsky asks: "Why are the programs not more intelligent than they are?" and responds, ". . . until recently resources—in people, time and computer capacity—have been quite limited. A number of the more careful and serious attempts have come close to their goal . . . others have been limited by core memory capacity; still others encountered programming difficulties."

26. Thomas G. Evans, "A Program for the Solution of a Class of Geometric-Analogy Intelligence Test Questions," in *Semantic Information Processing*, pp. 346–347.

27. *Ibid.*, p. 349.

28. *Ibid.*, p. 350.

29. *Ibid.*

30. Minsky, *Semantic Information Processing,* p. 16. (My italics.)
31. Minsky, *"Artificial Intelligence,"* p. 250. (My italics.)
32. Evans, *op. cit.,* p. 280. (My italics.)
33. Rudolf Arnheim, "Intelligence Simulated," *Midway,* University of Chicago (June 1967), pp. 85–87.
34. *Ibid.*
35. Unlike Minsky, Simon, although one of the faithful, does not seem to require a public profession of faith on the part of his Ph.D. students.
36. Ross Quillian, "Semantic Memory," in *Semantic Information Processing,* p. 262.
37. Ross Quillian, *Semantic Memory,* Bolt, Beranek and Newman, Inc., paper AFCRL–66–189 (October 1966), p. 54. (Omitted in Minsky's condensed version of the thesis.)
38. Quillian, "Semantic Memory," in *Semantic Information Processing,* pp. 230–231.
39. *Ibid.,* p. 221.
40. *Ibid.,* p. 222.
41. *Ibid.,* p. 216.
42. *Ibid.,* p. 247.
43. Quillian, *Semantic Memory,* p. 113, cited in note 37 above.
44. Quillian, "Semantic Memory," in *Semantic Information Processing,* p. 236
45. *Ibid.,* p. 235.
46. *Ibid.,* p. 235.
47. *Ibid.,* p. 241.
48. Minsky, *Semantic Information Processing,* p. 1.
49. *Ibid.,* p. 26.
50. *Ibid.,* p. 18.
51. Marvin Minsky, *Computation: Finite and Infinite Machines* (Englewood Cliffs, N.J.: Prentice-Hall, 1967), p. 2.
52. Minsky, *Semantic Information Processing,* p. 13.
53. *Ibid.*
54. *Ibid.* (My italics.)
55. *Ibid.,* p. 26.
56. Bar-Hillel, "Critique of June 1966 Meeting," SIGART *Newsletter,* p. 1.

CONCLUSION

1. Minsky, *"Artificial Intelligence,"* p. 258, cited in note 8 above.
2. R. J. Solomonoff, "Some Recent Work in Artificial Intelligence," *Proceedings of the IEEE,* Vol. 54, No. 12 (December 1966), p. 1689.
3. *Ibid.,* p. 1691.
4. *Ibid.,* p. 1693.
5. *Ibid.*
6. Fred M. Tonge, "A View of Artificial Intelligence," *Proceedings, A.C.M. National Meeting* (1966), p. 379.
7. P. E. Greenwood, *Computing Reviews* (January–February 1967), p. 31.

Part II. Assumptions Underlying Persistent Optimism

INTRODUCTION

1. Allen Newell and H. A. Simon, *Computer Simulation of Human Thinking,* The RAND Corporation, P–2276 (April 20, 1961), p. 9. (My italics.)

CHAPTER 3. THE BIOLOGICAL ASSUMPTION

1. It should be noted, for the discussion at hand, that even if restricted types of perceptrons can be shown to be incapable of recognition and learning (See note 2 of Chapter 2.) the theoretical possibility that a neural net of sufficient complexity could learn is not excluded. This possibility must constantly be borne in mind in evaluating the arguments for the biological and psychological assumptions that the brain or mind must function like a *heuristically programmed* digital computer.
2. John von Neumann, *Probabilistic Logics and the Synthesis of Reliable Organisms from Unreliable Components, Collected Works,* A. H. Taub, ed. (New York: Pergamon Press, 1963), Vol. 5, p. 372. (My italics.)
3. John von Neumann, "The General and Logical Theory of Automata," reprinted in *The World of Mathematics* (New York: Simon and Schuster, 1956), p. 2077.
4. I am grateful to Walter M. Elsasser and R. L. Gregory for having helped me formulate this distinction.
5. Theodore H. Bullock, "Evolution of Neurophysiological Mechanisms," in *Behavior and Evolution*, Anne Roe and George Gaylord Simpson, eds. (New Haven, Conn.: Yale University Press, 1958), p. 172.
6. Jerome Lettvin, lecture at the University of California, Berkeley, November 1969.
7. Walter A. Rosenblith, "On Cybernetics and the Human Brain," *The American Scholar* (Spring 1966), p. 247.

CHAPTER 4. THE PSYCHOLOGICAL ASSUMPTION

1. Ulric Neisser, *Cognitive Psychology* (New York: Appleton-Century-Crofts, 1967), p. 6.
2. Miller, Galanter, and Pribram, *Plans and the Structure of Behavior* (New York: Holt, Rinehart and Winston, 1960), p. 57.
3. Claude E. Shannon, "The Mathematical Theory of Communication," in *The Mathematical Theory of Communication*, Claude E. Shannon and Warren Weaver (Urbana: University of Illinois Press, 1962), p. 3.
4. Warren Weaver, "Recent Contributions to the Mathematical Theory of Communication," in *The Mathematical Theory of Communication*, p. 99, cited in note 3 above.

5. In this context, Newell, Shaw, and Simon's claim to have synthesized the contributions of behaviorists and Gestaltists by, on the one hand, accepting behavioral measures, and, on the other, recognizing that "a human being is a tremendously complex, organized system" ("GPS: A Program that Simulates Human Thought," pp. 280, 293) shows either a will to obscure the issues or a total misunderstanding of the contribution of each of these schools.

6. See Part III.

7. Jerry A. Fodor, "The Appeal to Tacit Knowledge in Psychological Explanation," *The Journal of Philosophy*, Vol. No. 20 (October 24, 1968), p. 632.

8. *Ibid.*, p. 629.

9. *Ibid.*, p. 637.

10. Jerry Fodor, *Psychological Explanation* (New York: Random House, 1968), p. 138.

11. The other reading of the simulability claim, the reading which is relevant to the mentalist's purposes but, unfortunately, lacks the immediate credibility of the first, is that any analog processor can also be represented. The flaw in this alternative, however, is difficult to grasp until a few examples have clarified the distinction between simulation and representation. The division function of a slide rule is simulated by any algorithm which yields appropriate quotients; but it is represented only if the quotients are obtained in a *sliderulelike manner* in which the steps correspond to comparing lengths. On a computer this would amount to assigning (colinear) spatial coordinates to the mantissas of two log tables, and effecting a "translation" by subtracting. To treat a more general case, one can simulate any multiply coupled harmonic system (such as most commercial analogue computers) by solving their characteristic differential equations. On the other hand, a representation, roughly a simulation of the inner operation as well as the end result, would require a simulation of each electronic component (resistors, capacitors, wires, etc.), their effects on one another, and thence their variations iterated through time.

Each of these analogues happens to be both simulable and representable, but this is not always the case. Some analogues are not composed of identifiable parts, e.g., a soap film "computing" the minimum surface which is bounded by an irregularly shaped wire, and hence are not representable in anything like the above fashion.

Now it might be claimed that since a soap bubble (or any other material object) is made of atoms it can still always be represented in principle by working out an immense (!) amount of quantum mechanics. But it is at best very dubious that such a mountain of equations would or could amount to an explanation of how something works, or in the case of the brain, have any relevance at all to psychology. If this needs to be any more obvious than it is, think of an ordinary adding machine that works with wheels and cogs; our conviction that it works mechanically and can be represented in every interesting sense is not in the least based on the fact that it is made of atoms. In fact, it could be made of some totally mysterious, indivisible substance and everyone would remain confident that insofar as it worked with the wheels, cogs, and all, it would still be a mechanism, and any representation in terms of the wheels and cogs would count as an explanation. Essentially the same point could be made about electronic analogue computers, slide rules, and so on.

Thus, the plausibility of the *a priori* position that an analogue can always be digitally represented is illegitimate, only borrowed, so to speak, from the plausibility of the much weaker and irrelevant claim of mere simulability.

12. Miller, Galanter, and Pribram, *op. cit.*, p. 16. (My italics.)
13. Newell and Simon, "GPS: A Program that Simulates Human Thought," p. 293.
14. Newell and Simon, *Computer Simulation of Human Thinking*, p. 9.
15. *Ibid.*, p. 292.
16. Thomas Kuhn, *The Structure of Scientific Revolutions* (Chicago: University of Chicago Press, 1962), p. 81.
17. *Ibid.*, p. 17.
18. *Ibid.*, p. 81.
19. Newell and Simon, *Computer Simulation of Human Thinking*, p. 9.
20. Herbert Simon and Alan Newell, "Information Processing in Computer and Man," *American Scientist*, Vol. 52 (September 1964), p. 282.
21. Miller, Galanter, and Pribram, *op. cit.*, p. 16. (My italics.)
22. See Plato, *Meno.*
23. Introduction, Section I.
24. Miller et al., *op. cit.*, p. 17. Or compare Minsky in his article "Artificial Intelligence," *Scientific American*, Vol. 215, No. 3 (September 1966): "Evans began his work . . . by proposing a theory of the steps or processes a human brain might use in dealing with such a situation" (p. 250). Again, Minsky and Papert direct their book *Perceptrons* (M.I.T. Press, 1969) to "psychologists and biologists who would like to know how the brain computes thoughts" (p. 1). Quillian in his thesis, *Semantic Memory*, says, ". . . to understand such meaning is either to find or to create in the brain of the understander some configuration of symbols. . . ." (p. 70).
25. Jerry Fodor, *Psychological Explanation*, p. 30.
26. *Ibid.*, p. 22.
27. Neisser, *op. cit.*, p. 3.
28. Of course, phenomenologically, it is objects, not light waves we have direct access to.
29. Neisser, *op. cit.*, p. 3.
30. *Ibid.* (My italics.)
31. Unless one adopts the identity theory of sensations and brain states which Neisser does not seem to hold, since it would require a further justification which Neisser nowhere gives.
32. Neisser, *op. cit.*, p. 4. (My italics.)
33. *Ibid.*, p. 5. "Our knowledge of the world *must* be somehow developed from the stimulus input. . . ."

34. *Ibid.*, p. 22.
35. Neisser, *op. cit.*, p. 8.
36. *Ibid.*, p. 10.
37. *Ibid.*, p. 140.
38. Rather than revive the Humean notion of sense data and then find oneself forced to introduce Kantian rules to account for their combination into the perception of objects, it would be more illuminating, and presumably a better guide to research, to determine what psychologists such as Neisser actually *do*, regardless of their mistaken conceptualization. Such work involves trying to find those cues in the perceptual field which are significant in various areas of perception; for example, those cues which are essential in our perception of depth. One can find out which cues are necessary by systematically excluding various factors such as binocular vision, displacement, texture gradient, etc. One can even determine the order of dependence of these cues and the number of cues that can be taken account of in a given time. The results, it is hoped, will resemble the sequential steps diagrammed in the flow chart of a computer program. If so, one can formalize the laws which relate input to output at each stage.

    Such work requires no talk of "unconscious rules" organizing fragmentary elements into perceptions. It should never lead us to say that "we have no immediate access to the world nor to any of its properties." What would be psychologically real in such a theory would not be fragments and rules, but just those cues in our normal perception of objects which play a role in the theory.

    Although we are most often not explicitly aware of them, these cues are not unconscious. We can become explicitly aware of them by focusing our attention on them, whereas we cannot become aware of neural events or even the "snapshots" of objects Neisser tells us we actually perceive. Sometimes the cues may be so slight that we would never discover them by simply looking. For example, one cannot see the slight displacement of each dot of a Julesz pattern which produces the illusion of depth. But if told what to look for we could presumably find the displacement with a suitable measuring device. Thus these cues can be said to be psychologically real in the straightforward sense that we can become aware of them.

    The "flow chart" too has psychological reality in those restricted cases in which it expresses the order of dependence of the cues. It is surely in some rough way correlated with the physical processes going on in the brain, but even in these cases this does not justify talking of unconscious processing as if the brain were a digital computer operating according to a program.

    Interestingly enough, when psychologists actually undertake this sort of research, they find that no individual cues are necessary and sufficient but that different collections of cues are sufficient under specific restricted conditions. Also the order of dependence of the cues varies from situation to situation. The results, then, resemble a flow chart in only a very limited way in very sharply restricted cases. To fully formalize their theory in terms of their computer model the experimenters would either have to specify the input in terms of abstract situation-independent variables, or find metarules for recognizing specific situations and correlating these situations with specific orders of dependence. So far no such abstract variables and rules have been found. (See my article, "Phenomenology and Mechanism," *NOUS*, Vol. V, No. 1, Feb., 1971.)

39. Fodor, *Psychological Explanation*, p. 26, cited in note 23 above.
40. *Ibid.*, p. 29.
41. *Ibid.*, p. 26.
42. *Ibid.*, p. 28.
43. *Ibid.*
44. *Ibid.*, p. 140. (My italics.)
45. *Ibid.*, p. 141.
46. *Ibid.*, p. 83.
47. *Ibid.*, p. 85. (My italics.)
48. *Ibid.*, p. 146.

CHAPTER 5. THE EPISTEMOLOGICAL ASSUMPTION

1. By "reproduction" I mean the production of essential features of the behavior in question. I do not mean an exact copy, any more than a photographic reproduction of the Eiffel Tower is made of steel. Since computers are not expected to move and exhibit behavior in the normal sense, we are not concerned with using the formal theory of a kind of performance to exactly copy that performance. The production of essential characteristics of a certain performance without imitating the performance in detail would normally be called "simulation." Thus a computer can simulate an election without casting any votes—but the term "simulation" is already preempted by the cognitive simulationists who wish to include in their model not just the critical behavior but the steps by which that behavior was produced.

2. This bicycle example is taken from Michael Polanyi's *Personal Knowledge* (London: Routledge & Kegan Paul), p. 49. Polanyi's analysis of the example is worth quoting at length:

"From my interrogations of physicists, engineers, and bicycle manufacturers, I have come to the conclusion that the principle by which the cyclist keeps his balance is not generally known. The rule observed by the cyclist is this. When he starts falling to the right he turns the handlebars to the right, so that the course of the bicycle is deflected along a curve towards the right. This results in a centrifugal force pushing the cyclist to the left and offsets the gravitational force dragging him down to the right. This maneuver presently throws the cyclist out of balance to the left, which he counteracts by turning the handlebars to the left; and so he continues to keep himself in balance by winding along a series of appropriate curvatures. A simple analysis shows that for a given angle of unbalance the curvature of each winding is inversely proportional to the square of the speed at which the cyclist is proceeding.

"But does this tell us exactly how to ride a bicycle? No. You obviously cannot adjust the curvature of your bicycle's path in proportion to the ratio of your unbalance over the square of your speed; and if you could you would fall off the machine, for there are a number of other factors to be taken account in practice which are left out of in the formulation of this rule."

In spite of this important insight—that the formalism cannot account for the performance—Polanyi blurs the significance of this example by referring to "hidden rules" (p. 53). This reference to hidden rules shows that Polanyi, like Plato, fails to distinguish between performance and competence, between explanation and understanding, between the rule one is following and the rule which can be used to describe what is happening. It is just such a confusion which gives rise to the optimism of those in Cognitive Simulation.

Polanyi does have an objection of his own to CS. He holds that "in an important sense" we do know the rules, but claims that "one cannot deal with this as if it were unconscious knowledge, for the point is that it is a (more or less unconscious) knowledge *with a bearing* on an end. It is this quality of the subsidiary awareness, its *functionally performing quality,* that the machine cannot duplicate, because the machine operates throughout on one single level of awareness." (Personal communication.) This is an interesting intermediate position, but one still wonders why, granted this second kind of awareness, Polanyi feels it necessary to assume that we are following rules in any sense at all.

3. Minsky, *Computation: Finite and Infinite Machines* (Englewood Cliffs, N.J.: Prentice-Hall, 1967), p. vii.
4. A. M. Turing, "Computing Machinery and Intelligence," in *Minds and Machines,* ed. Alan Ross Anderson (Englewood Cliffs, N.J.: Prentice-Hall, 1964), p. 8.
5. Minsky, *Computation: Finite and Infinite Machines,* p. 107.
6. *Ibid.*
7. Turing, *op. cit.,* pp. 22–23.
8. *Ibid.*
9. James T. Culbertson, "Some Uneconomical Robots," *Automata Studies,* C. E. Shannon and J. McCarthy, eds. (Princeton, N.J.: Princeton University Press, 1956), p. 100.
10. *Ibid.,* p. 114.
11. Why no such isolable inputs and outputs can be found will only become clear when we have described the relation of the human subject to his world. See Chapter 9, especially p. 266.
12. Minsky, "Matter, Mind, and Models," in *Semantic Information Processing,* p. 429.
13. H. J. Bremermann, "Optimization Through Evolution and Recombination," in *Self-Organizing Systems* (Washington, D.C., 1962), p. 1.

14. *Ibid.,* p. 2.
15. Minsky, *Computation,* p. 107.
16. John McCarthy, "Programs with Common Sense," in *Semantic Information Processing,* p. 410.
17. Chomsky sometimes defines competence and performance so as to preserve this separation and to make the relation of a theory of competence to a theory of performance an empirical question. For example: "To avoid what has been a continuing misunderstanding, it is perhaps worthwhile to reiterate that a generative grammar is not a model for a speaker or a hearer. It attempts to characterize *in the most neutral possible terms* the knowledge of the language that provides the basis for actual use of a language by a speaker-hearer. When we speak of a grammar as generating a sentence with a certain structural description, we mean simply that the grammar assigns this structural description to the sentence." (*Aspects of the Theory of Syntax* [Cambridge, Mass.: M.I.T. Press, 1965], p. 9.) (My italics.)

This straightforward definition, however, leaves some doubt as to how Chomsky understands the competence/performance distinction he has introduced. If competence is what one knows when one knows a language, it would be an empirical question whether the rules which describe competence play any role at all in producing the performance. Yet at times Chomsky seems to hold that competence necessarily plays a role in performance and builds this into the very definition of performance and competence and their relation: "By a 'generative grammar' I mean a description of the *tacit competence* of the speaker-hearer that *underlies* his actual performance in production and perception (understanding) of speech. A generative grammar, ideally, specifies a pairing of phonetic and semantic representations over an infinite range; it thus constitutes a hypothesis as to how the speaker-hearer interprets utterances, abstracting away from many factors that interweave with tacit competence to determine actual performance." (*Cartesian Linguistics* [New York: Harper & Row, 1966], p. 75.) (My italics.)

Or see also ". . . We must abstract for separate and independent study a cognitive system, *a system of knowledge and belief,* that *develops* in early childhood and that *interacts* with many other factors to determine the kinds of behavior that we observe; to introduce a technical term, we must isolate and study the system of *linguistic competence* that *underlies* behavior but that is not realized in any direct or simple way in behavior." (*Language and Mind* [New York: Harcourt, Brace and World, 1968], p. 4.) (My italics.)

When Chomsky speaks of "tacit competence" which "underlies . . . actual performance" and which "determines . . . behavior," we find the same tendency we found in Polanyi when he assumed that the rule he suggests for describing bicycle-riding competence is involved in bicycle-riding performance. On this reading, the role of the formalism expressing the competence is no longer neutral. Whatever the correct formalism is, it is necessarily involved in producing the performance.

. Yet if the competence/performance distinction is to have the effect of separating a formal theory from a psychological theory, the relation of a theory of competence to a theory of performance cannot be built in by definition; or to put it the other way around, if it belongs to the definition of competence to underlie performance, then competence cannot mean simply a formal theory which "pairs phonetic and semantic representations over an infinite range." It would have to mean an idealized psychological theory of how language is produced, and the competence/performance distinction would only call attention to the fact that other factors such as fatigue and learning had been disregarded.

At times Chomsky seems to hold this view. "We do not interpret what is said in our presence *simply* by application of the linguistic principles that determine the phonetic and semantic properties of an utterance. Extralinguistic beliefs concerning the speaker and the situation play a fundamental role in determining how speech is produced, identified, and understood. Linguistic performance is, furthermore, governed by principles of cognitive structure (for example, by memory restrictions) that are not, properly speaking, aspects of language.

"To study a language, then, we must attempt to disassociate a variety of factors that *interact* with *underlying competence* to determine actual performance; the technical term 'competence' refers to the ability of the idealized speaker-hearer to associate sounds and meanings strictly in accordance with the rules of his language." ("The Formal Nature of Language," appendix to *Biological Foundations of Language,* Eric Lenneberg, [New York: Wiley, 1967], p. 398.) (My italics.)

What, then, is the relation between competence and performance? If one discovered in psycholinguistics that language is *produced* in a way which does not involve the rules postulated by Chomsky's linguistic formalism at all, as the latest research seems to suggest (See T. G. Bever, *The Cognitive Basis for Linguistic Structures,* chapter entitled "The Non-Distinction Between Linguistic Competence and Performance in the Adult": ". . . behavioral processes manipulate linguistically-defined internal and external *structures* but do not mirror or directly simulate the grammatical processes that relate those structures within a grammar. Such a conclusion invalidates any model for speech recognition which attempts directly to incorporate grammatical rules as an isolable component of the recognition processes." Preprint p. 101), would Chomsky give up his formal description? Chomsky seems to want to have it both ways: to make the role of his formalism for competence independent of psychology so he would not have to give it up no matter what experiments showed and yet to make its role in performance a matter of definition. On the one hand, he says: "When we say that a sentence has a certain derivation with respect to a particular generative grammar, *we say nothing about how the speaker or hearer might proceed,* in some practical or efficient way, to construct such a derivation. These questions belong to the theory of language use—the theory of performance."

(*Aspects of the Theory of Syntax,* p. 9. [My italics.]) Yet in *Language and Mind* Chomsky says: "The problem of determining the character of such grammars and the principles that govern them is a typical problem of science, perhaps very difficult, but in principle admitting of definite answers that are right or wrong as they *do or do not correspond to the mental reality*" (p. 16). (My italics.)

Underlying this uncertainty as to the status of the formal grammatical structure characterizing the speaker's intuitions concerning grammaticality is the powerful conjunction of the Platonic assumption that the formalism which enables us to *understand* behavior is also involved in *producing* that behavior, and the Kantian assumption that all orderly behavior is governed by rules, both reinforced by the idea of a computer program. Chomsky does not question the assumption that "the person who has acquired knowledge of a language has internalized a system of rules . . ." (*Language and Mind,* p. 23), nor that these rules function as a "mechanism" for "generating" sentences. These convictions taken together lead to Chomsky's Cartesian theory of innate ideas, which even he admits is difficult to accept: "It is not easy to accept the view that a child is capable of constructing an extremely complex mechanism for generating a set of sentences, some of which he has heard, or that an adult can instantaneously determine whether (and if so, how) a particular item is generated by this mechanism, which has many of the properties of an abstract deductive theory. Yet this appears to be a fair description of the performance of the speaker, listener, and learner." ("A Review of B. F. Skinner's *Verbal Behavior,*" *The Structure of Language* [Englewood Cliffs, N.J.: Prentice-Hall, 1964], p. 577.)

This view, however implausible, seems acceptable thanks to the presence of the computer: ". . . there is no difficulty in principle in programming a computer with a schematism that sharply restricts the form of a generative grammar, with an evaluation procedure for grammars of the given form, with a technique for determining whether given data is compatible with a grammar of the given form, with a fixed substructure of entities (such as distinctive features), rules, and principles, and so on—in short, with a universal grammar of the sort that has been proposed in recent years." (*Language and Mind,* p. 73.)

Chomsky goes on to connect this computer model with the classical tradition: "For reasons that I have already mentioned, I believe that these proposals can be properly regarded as a further development of classical rationalist doctrine, as an elaboration of some of its main ideas regarding language and mind." (*Language and Mind,* p. 73.) He concludes: "By pursuing the kinds of research that now seem feasible and by focusing attention on certain problems that are now accessible to study, we may be able to spell out in some detail the elaborate and abstract computations that determine, in part, the nature of percepts and the character of the knowledge that we can acquire—the highly specific ways of interpreting phenomena that are, in large measure, beyond our consciousness and control and that may be unique to man." (*Language and Mind,* pp. 84–85.) In this neo-Cartesianism the traditional philosophical assumption that man's unique attribute may be to be a highly sophisticated computer becomes fully explicit, perhaps for the first time since Hobbes prematurely drew the same conclusion on the basis of Newtonean physics.

18. Sören Kierkegaard, *Concluding Unscientific Postscript* (Princeton, N.J.: Princeton University Press, 1944), pp. 108 and 311.

19. This attitude is forcefully and naïvely expressed in Sayre's introduction to *The Modeling of Mind,* Kenneth M. Sayre, and J. Crosson, eds. (South Bend, Ind.: Notre Dame University Press, 1962):

"Any mental function which is such that (1) its input and output can be specified with precision, and (2) the transformation it performs can be approximated by equations which express a determinate relationship between input and output, can for these reasons alone be simulated with some degree of adequacy. If, on the other hand, we do not have a clear understanding of either the input, the output, or the transformation, we will be unable to achieve an adequate simulation of that function. Our inability in such a case, however, is a discredit to the human mind, and not a symptom of any 'transcendence' of mental functions" (p. 14).

20. Ludwig Wittgenstein, *The Blue and Brown Books* (Oxford, Eng.: Basil Blackwell, 1960), p. 25.

21. See, for example, Wittgenstein, *Philosophical Investigations* (Oxford, Eng.: Basil Blackwell, 1953), pp. 39, 40, 41, 42.

"A rule stands like a sign-post.—Does the sign-post leave no doubt open about the way I have to go? Does it show which direction I am to take when I have passed it; whether along the road on the footpath or cross-country? But where is it said which way I am to follow it; whether in the direction of its finger or (e.g.) in the opposite one?—And if there were, not a single sign-post, but a chain of adjacent ones or of chalk marks on the ground— is there any *one* way of interpreting them?—So I can say, the sign-post does after all leave no room for doubt. Or rather: it sometimes leaves room for doubt and sometimes not. And now this is no longer a philosophical proposition, but an empirical one" (pp. 39, 40).

CHAPTER 6. THE ONTOLOGICAL ASSUMPTION

1. Minsky, *Semantic Information Processing,* p. 11.

2. *Ibid.*

3. A digital computer is composed of flip/flops which perform logical operations, but this does not limit the computer to instantiating information-processing models. The same flip/flops could be organized to represent neural sets, or the interference patterns making up holograms. The information-processing approach, however, uses the computer to instantiate symbolic descriptions so that combinations of flip/flops represent discrete

facts. If one assumes that these symbolic descriptions are composed of primitives which correspond to isolable features of the world, one makes the ontological assumption.

4. Allen Newell, *Learning, Generality and Problem-Solving,* The RAND Corporation, RM–3285–1–PR (February 1963), p. 17.

5. Murray Eden, "Other Pattern Recognition Problems and Some Generalizations," in *Recognizing Patterns: Studies in Living and Automatic Systems,* ed. Kolers and Eden (Cambridge, Mass.: M.I.T. Press, 1968), p. 153. (My italics.)

6. Minsky, *Semantic Information Processing,* p. 25.

7. *Ibid.,* pp. 25, 26.

8. *Ibid.,* pp. 26, 27.

9. *Ibid.,* p. 27.

10. Not that we know what it means to make our situation *completely* explicit and cannot do it. We only know what it means to make a situation sufficiently explicit for a *specific purpose.*

11. See note 17.

12. Leibniz, *Selections,* ed. Philip Wiener (New York: Scribner, 1951), p. 20.

13. *Ibid.,* p. 10.

14. Merleau-Ponty, *Phenomenology of Perception* (London: Routledge & Kegan Paul, 1962), pp. 5, 58 ff.

15. Martin Heidegger, *Der Satz vom Grund* (Pfullingen: Günther Neske, 1957), p. 42.

16. Heidegger, p. 203. In *Der Satz vom Grund,* Heidegger remarks: ". . . the determination of language as information originally supplies the basis for the construction of thinking machines, and for the construction of large-scale computer installations," and "information theory is, as pronouncement, already the arrangement whereby all objects are put in such form as to assure man's domination over the entire earth and even the planets." (My translation.)

17. Wittgenstein, *Philosophical Investigations,* p. 21. "What lies behind the idea that names really signify simples?—Socrates says in the Theaetetus: 'If I make no mistake, I have heard some people say this: there is no definition of the primary elements—so to speak—out of which we and everything else are composed. . . . But just as what consists of these primary elements is itself complex, so the names of the elements become descriptive language by being compounded together.' Both Russell's 'individuals' and my 'objects' *(Tractatus Logico-Philosophicus)* were such primary elements. But what are the simple constituent parts of which reality is composed? . . . It makes no sense at all to speak absolutely of the 'simple parts of a chair.' "

18. John McCarthy, "Programs with Common Sense," in *Semantic Processing Information,* p. 403.

19. *Ibid.,* p. 410.

20. *Ibid.,* p. 411.

21. *Ibid.,* p. 413.

22. *Ibid.*, p. 411.
23. Bar-Hillel, "The Present Status of Automatic Translation of Language," in *Advances in Computers,* ed. F. L. Alt (New York: Academic Press, 1964), Vol. 1, p. 94.
24. *Ibid.*, pp. 158, 159. It might seem from Bar-Hillel's example that the computer need only check the immediate verbal context for words such as "toy" to determine that "playpen" is the relevant reading. But, as John Haugeland has suggested, a little modification of the example will show that contextual analysis cannot get around Bar-Hillel's objection: "Little Johnny was playing on the floor beside his pen. He was drawing a picture with a red pen on some green paper. When the drawing was finished, he looked for his toy box, and found it inside the pen." It is conceivable that the first two occurrences of "pen" could be disambiguated with information from the surrounding words. But it is clear that since the clues to both meanings of pen are in the immediate verbal context of the last sentence (indeed, in the sentence itself), the disambiguation of the last occurrence of "pen" requires the "common knowledge" that Bar-Hillel has in mind.
25. *Ibid.*, p. 160.
26. Minsky, *Semantic Information Processing,* p. 23. It might also seem that Bar-Hillel's argument rests on accidental ambiguities which might be eliminated by subscripting the various meanings of "pen." John Haugeland, however, has advanced an interesting argument to show that such ambiguity, at least in translating between natural languages, is inevitable:

> "Imagine constructing a language Eng* which is like English except that the different senses of words are separated by subscripts (i.e., $pen_1 =$ writing instrument, $pen_2 =$ baby's enclosure, etc.). Even though this would disambiguate the Bar-Hillel example, it is clear that it is really not going to be any easier to translate Eng* into an arbitrary target language (or into Tar*). Translating brother, sister, and cousin into Polynesian languages is a good example: In the following two tables, the columns specify the possible permutations of boy and girl for a pair of children, the rows specify genealogical connections between them, and the boxes name their relationship under the various conditions. Thus, in English, a is the brother of b just in case a is a boy and a and b have the same parents. The problem is that $brother_1$, which has only one meaning in Eng*, is ambiguous to a Tongan because it has the two distinct senses 'brother of a boy', and 'brother of a girl'.
>
> "There are two things to be seen from this example. First, ambiguity in the meanings of words is a relative concept. Thus, the word 'brother' is unambiguous relative to some languages (e.g., German), ambiguous in the above way to other languages, and probably ambiguous in still different ways relative to other languages again. Second, it would be impossible to have any language (say Lang*) which is unambiguous relative to all possible natural

	English				Tongan (Polynesian)			
Sex of a	boy	boy	girl	girl	boy	boy	girl	girl
Sex of b	girl	boy	girl	boy	girl	boy	girl	boy
a and b have the same parents	brother	brother	sister	sister	tu'anga'ane	tokoua	tokoua	tu'afefine
a and b do not have the same parents, but the same maternal or paternal grandparents	cousin	cousin	cousin	cousin	tu'anga'ane	tokoua	tokoua	tu'afefine

languages. For if any noun of Lang* is not a proper noun then it must refer to at least two distinguishable states of the universe. But then it is possible that there exists a natural language in which two common nouns are distinguished by the same criterion which separates two of the referents of the one common noun of Lang*. Since this contradicts the hypothesis, it follows that Lang* can have only proper nouns (one for each distinguishable state of the universe), which I take to be a reduction to absurdity." (Private communication.)

27. Jerrold Katz and Jerry Fodor, "The Structure of a Semantic Theory," in *The Structure of Language*, Jerrold Katz and Jerry Fodor (Englewood Cliffs, N.J.: Prentice-Hall, 1964), p. 487.
28. *Ibid.*, p. 489.
29. *Ibid.*, pp. 489–490.
30. Joseph Weizenbaum, "Contextual Understanding by Computers," in *Recognizing Patterns*, p. 181, cited in note 5 above.
31. *Ibid.*
32. *Ibid.*, p. 189.
33. *Ibid.*, pp. 181–182.
34. *Ibid.*, p. 182.
35. Wittgenstein, *Philosophical Investigations*, p. 226.
36. The only exception seems to be Thomas L. Jones' MAC memo no. 195, "A Computer Model of Simple Forms of Learning."
   If this isolated thesis had set a trend, it would have meant a complete shift in the goal and methods of artificial intelligence research, but it was apparently a dead end.
37. Except for the alternative of facts with context-free fixed significance which we have seen AI workers such as Weizenbaum implicitly reject.

Part III. Alternatives to the Traditional Assumptions

INTRODUCTION

1. There is, however, a new interest in what might be called "experimental phenomenology." Eleanor Rosch, for example, has shown that subjects consistently classify objects not in terms of necessary and sufficient features, but as more or less distant from a typical example or prototype. See "Principles of Categorization" in *Cognition & Categorization,* E. Rosch, ed. (Hillsdale, N.J.: Erlbaum Press, 1977). There is also much interest in the work of R. N. Shepard showing that subjects rotate mental images at constant speeds. See R. N. Shepard and B. Metzler, "Mental Rotation of Three-Dimensional Objects," *Science,* Vol. 178, No. 3972 (February 1971), pp. 701–703. Such experimental work with images is an embarrassment to workers in AI, since all agree that insofar as images are different from symbolic descriptions they cannot be accounted for in an information-processing model.
2. Chomsky, *Language and Mind,* pp. 18–19.

CHAPTER 7. THE ROLE OF THE BODY IN INTELLIGENT BEHAVIOR

1. Descartes, *Discourses,* Library of Liberal Arts, p. 36.
2. Herbert Simon, *The Shape of Automation for Men and Management* (New York: Harper & Row, 1965), p. 96.
3. *Ibid.,* p. 40.
4. Anthony Oettinger, "Language and Information," *American Documentation,* Vol. 19, No. 3 (July 1968), p. 297.
5. Oettinger, "The Semantic Wall," in *Human Communication: A Unified View,* E. David and P. Denes, eds. (New York: McGraw-Hill, 1972), p. 5.
6. Oettinger, "Language and Information," p. 298, cited in note 4 above.
7. Neisser, *Cognitive Psychology,* p. 90.
8. Maurice Merleau-Ponty, *Phenomonology of Perception* (London: Routledge & Kegan Paul, 1962), p. 4.
9. *Ibid.,* p. 68.
10. This phenomenon lies at the basis of Husserl's whole theory of perception. For Husserl argued that, in recognizing an object, we give a somewhat determinate global meaning—a noema—to an otherwise indeterminate but determinable sensuous matter. We then proceed to make this open global meaning more determinate. (See E. Husserl, *Ideas* [New York: Collier, 1931], Part Three. Also, my forthcoming book, *Husserl's Phenomenology of*
11. John McCarthy, "Information," *Scientific American,* Vol. 215, No. 3 (September 1966), p. 65.
12. Neisser, *op. cit.,* p. 86.
13. Minsky, "Artificial Intelligence," *Scientific American,* Vol. 215, No. 3 (September 1966), p. 257.

14. Neisser, *op. cit.*, p. 235.
15. *Ibid.*, p. 244.
16. *Ibid.*, p. 245.
17. *Ibid.*, p. 235. (My italics.)
18. *Ibid.*, p. 246.
19. Of course, these field effects, like any other physical phenomenon, can be simulated by solving the differential equations describing the forces involved, but this in no way affects the Gestaltists' point which is that one could only simulate human behavior indirectly by simulating the physical analogue (the brain) not directly by programming a digital computer.
20. Neisser, *op. cit.*, p. 247.
21. Donald MacKay, "A Mind's Eye View of the Brain," in *Progress in Brain Research, 17: Cybernetics of the Nervous System* (a memorial volume honoring Norbert Wiener) (Amsterdam, Holland: Elsevier Publishing Company, 1965), p. 16.
22. J. Piaget, *Psychology of Intelligence* (New York: Humanities Press, 1966), p. 82.
23. Merleau-Ponty, *Phenomenology of Perception*, p. 142.
24. *Ibid.*, p. 234.
25. *Ibid.*, p. 235.
26. *Ibid.*, p. 318.
27. Edward Feigenbaum, "Artificial Intelligence: Themes in the Second Decade," IFIP Congress '68, Supplement, p. J–13.
28. Michael Polanyi, *Personal Knowledge: Towards a Post-Critical Philosophy* (New York: Harper & Row, 1964), p. 59.
29. Merleau-Ponty, *op. cit.*, p. 106.
30. Piaget, *op. cit.*, p. 35. These motor schemata must have their muscular and neural basis, but there is no reason to suppose that these physical correlates go through a rule-governed sequence of independent operations. Both the global and underdetermined character of the motor schemata argue against this possibility.
31. Michael Polanyi, "The Logic of Tacit Inference," in *Knowing and Being* (Chicago: University of Chicago Press, 1969), p. 148. Polanyi again defeats his own point by adding in a later account of language learning: "To the question, how a child can learn to perform [according to] a vast set of complex rules, intelligible only to a handful of experts, we can reply that the striving imagination has the power to implement its aim by the subsidiary practice of ingenious rules of which the subject remains focally ignorant." ("Sense-giving and Sense Reading," *Knowing and Being*, p. 200.)
32. Oettinger, "The Semantic Wall," p. 11, cited in note 5 above.

CHAPTER 8. THE SITUATION: ORDERLY BEHAVIOR WITHOUT RECOURSE TO RULES

1. Minsky, "Matter, Mind, and Models," *Semantic Information Processing*, p. 431.
2. Real creativity is too much to ask. Minsky has pointed out that a minimum condition for problem solving is that the computer have a criterion for an acceptable solution: "To begin with we have to replace our intuitive require-

ments by reasonably well-defined technical questions. . . . A minimal requirement is that one have a method of discerning a satisfactory solution should
one appear. If we cannot do this then the problem must be replaced by one
which is well defined in that sense, and we must hope that solution of the
substitute problem will turn out to be useful." ("Some Methods of Artificial
Intelligence and Heuristic Programming," in *Proc. Symposium on the
Mechanization of Intelligence* [London: HMSO], p. 7.) In creative work,
however, as Newell, Shaw, and Simon note, part of the agent's task is to
define the problem and what would count as a solution. (Newell, Shaw, and
Simon, *The Processes of Creative Thinking,* The RAND Corporation, P–
1320 [September 16, 1958], p. 4.) An artist, for example, does not have a
criterion of what counts as a solution to his artistic problem. He invents the
problem and the solution as he goes along. His work may later determine
standards of success, but his success is prior to the canons later introduced
by the critics. If the *program* is to be creative, the task of defining the
problem and the rules for recognizing a satisfactory solution cannot be taken
over by the programmer. But it is impossible to imagine how a computer
program, which needs a definite criterion for what its problem is and when
it has been solved, could creatively solve a problem, or know that it had done
so.

3. This and the following quotations elaborating my racing example are ex-
cerpts from a letter from Charles Taylor, growing out of a seminar he gave
on this book while it was still in manuscript.

4. Minsky, *Semantic Information Processing,* p. 27.

5. Taylor.

6. Martin Heidegger, *Being and Time* (New York: Harper & Row, 1962),
p. 109.

7. Wittgenstein, *Philosophical Investigations,* p. 50.

8. Samuel Todes, *The Human Body as the Material Subject of the World.*
Harvard doctoral dissertation, 1963. See also "Comparative Phenomenology
of Perception and Imagination, Part I: Perception," *Journal of Existential-
ism* (Spring 1966). Todes' thesis also contains interesting suggestions as to
some very pervasive features of our experience and their function. He describes certain characteristics of the body, e.g., that it moves forward more
easily than backward, that it generates a right/left field, that it must balance
itself in a gravitational field in which it can be upside down; and he shows
the role these experiences play in our knowledge of objects.

9. Taylor.

10. Feigenbaum, *An Information Processing Theory of Verbal Learning,* P–1817
(Santa Monica: The RAND Corporation, 1959). "In the EPAM models
such a classification structure, termed a 'discrimination net' is the primary
information structure. It is the product of discrimination learning, and it
embodies at any moment all the discrimination learning that has taken place
up to a given time. EPAM's discrimination net is a *tree* structure, since only
one branch leads to any given node from above: only one pathway leads from
the top node, or *root,* to any other node in the net. A stimulus object
presented to EPAM may be *classified* by being sorted to a terminal node in
the net." (William Wynn, *An Information-Processing Model of Certain Aspects of Paired-Associate Learning,* p. 5.)

11. Wynn, *op. cit.,* p. 9.
12. Minsky, *Semantic Information Processing,* pp. 425–426.
13. *Ibid.,* p. 426.
14. *Ibid.,* p. 427.
15. *Ibid.,* p. 428.
16. Neisser, *Cognitive Psychology,* p. 3.
17. *Ibid.*
18. *Ibid.*
19. Oettinger, "Language and Information," p. 296.
20. *Ibid.*
21. Ludwig Wittgenstein, *Zettel* (Berkeley: University of California Press, 1967), p. 78.

Chapter 9. The Situation as a Function of Human Needs

1. Satosi Watanabe, "La Simulation mutuelle de l'homme et la machine," *Compte Rendu du Symposium sur La Technologie et l'humanité* (Lausanne, 1965), p. 6. (My translation.)
2. Watanabe, "Comments on Key Issues," in *Dimensions of Mind,* ed. Sidney Hook (New York: Collier, 1961), p. 135.
3. Watanabe, "Mathematical Explication of Classification of Objects," in *Information and Prediction in Science,* S. Dockx and P. Bernays, eds. (New York: Academic Press, 1965), p. 39.
4. Heidegger, *Being and Time,* pp. 136–137.
5. Friedrich Nietzsche, *The Will to Power,* ed. Walter Kaufmann (New York: Vintage), p. 505. For Sartre *all* specific values are the product of a completely arbitrary choice, although the demand for values is grounded in the human condition understood as a lack. (See *Being and Nothingness,* Part II, ch. 1, "The For-Itself and the Being of Value.")
6. See Heidegger's analysis of being-unto-death in *Being and Time,* Section 48.
7. Herbert Simon, "Motivation and Emotional Controls of Cognition," *Psychological Review,* Vol. 74, No. 1 (1967), pp. 29–39. See also, Walter R. Reitman, *Cognition and Thought* (New York: Wiley, 1965).
8. N. S. Sutherland, *Science Journal* (October 1968), p. 48.
9. See Samuel Todes, *The Human Body as the Material Subject of the World,* doctoral dissertation, Harvard University, 1963. The only philosopher who has begun to notice the difficulty the biological basis of human behavior poses for artificial intelligence is Keith Gunderson, who, in a recent paper "Philosophy and Computer Simulation" notes: "At this point the area of research known as biosimulation takes on far greater importance than CS." *(Ryle, A Collection of Critical Essays,* Oscar P. Wood and George Pitcher, eds. [New York: Anchor, 1970] p. 339.)

10. See Sören Kierkegaard, *Fear and Trembling* (Garden City, N.Y.: Anchor) pp. 52–55. Also *Concluding Unscientific Postscript,* (Princeton, N.J.: Princeton University Press), p. 231 or p. 379, where the leap is called "the absolute venture."
11. Thomas Kuhn, *The Structure of Scientific Revolutions* (Chicago: University of Chicago Press, 1962), p. 110.
12. *Ibid.,* p. 134.
13. *Ibid.,* p. 145.
14. *Ibid.,* p. 120.
15. *Ibid.,* p. 125.
16. *Ibid.,* p. 44.
17. *Ibid.,* p. 46.
18. *Ibid.,* p. 15.
19. *Ibid.,* p. 149.

CONCLUSION

1. Facts like "A man has two hands," rather than like "Z flip/flop is on." The difference is the same as the difference between a fact about the content of a picture and a fact about one of the dots composing the picture. It is clearly these real-world facts which are at stake, since Minsky suggests we have to deal with millions of *them,* not millions of bits.
2. Minsky, *Semantic Information Processing,* p. 18.

Conclusion: The Scope and Limits of Artificial Reason

1. It is difficult to classify and evaluate the various one-purpose programs that have been developed for motor design, line balancing, integrating, and so forth. These programs are relevant to work in artificial intelligence, but they are not clearly successful programs, until (a) like the chess and checker programs they are tested against human professionals; and (b) the problems attacked by these programs have, if possible, been formalized so that these heuristic programs can be compared with nonheuristic programs designed for the same purpose. (Wherever such a comparison has been made—in checkers, logic, pattern recognition, chess—the nonheuristic programs have proved either equal or superior to their heuristic counterparts.)

On the other hand, programs which simulate investment banking procedures and the like have no bearing on Cognitive Simulation or Artificial Intelligence at all. They merely show that certain forms of human activity are sufficiently simple and stereotyped to be formalized. Intelligence was surely involved in *formulating* the rules which investors now follow in making up a portfolio of stocks, but the *formalization* of these rules only reveals them to be explicable and unambiguous, and casts no light on the intelligence involved in discovering them or in their judicious application.

The challenge for artificial intelligence does not lie in such *ex post facto* formalizations of specific tasks, but rather in Area II where the system is sufficiently complex to require elegant techniques in order to reach a solution, in Area III where the formal system is so complex that no decision procedure exists and one has to resort to heuristics, and in Area IV in which behavior is flexible and not strictly formalizable.

2. The activities found in Area IV can be thought of as the sort of "milestones" asked for by Paul Armer in his article, "Attitudes toward Intelligent Machines": "A clearly defined task is required which is, at present, in the exclusive domain of humans (and therefore incontestably 'thinking') but which may eventually yield to accomplishment by machines," in Feigenbaum and Feldman, eds., *Computers and Thought,* p. 397.

3. Allen Newell, J. C. Shaw, and H. A. Simon, "Empirical Explorations with the Logic Theory Machine: A Case Study in Heuristics," in *Computers and Thought,* p. 109.

4. "The . . . obstacle to the expansion of a semantic information retrieval system is the same one which occurs in programs for theorem proving, game playing, and other areas of artificial intelligence: the problem of searching through an exponentially growing space of possible solutions. Here there is no basic transformation that can be made to avoid the mathematical fact that the number of possible interconnections between elements is an exponential function of the number of elements involved." (Raphael, "SIR: Semantic Information Retrieval," in *Semantic Information Processing,* p. 114.)

5. Lecture at the University of California at Berkeley, March 1970.

6. Neisser, *Cognitive Psychology,* p. 89.

7. *Ibid.* (My italics.)

8. Edward Feigenbaum, "Artificial Intelligence: Themes in the Second Decade," IFIP Congress '68, Final Supplement, p. J–19.

9. *Ibid.*

10. C. A. Rosen, "Machines That Act Intelligently," *Science Journal,* (October 1968), p. 114.

11. Feigenbaum, *op. cit.,* p. J–13.

12. *Ibid.*

13. Hao Wang, "Toward Mechanical Mathematics," in *The Modeling of Mind,* Kenneth M. Sayre and Frederick J. Crosson, eds. (South Bend, Ind.: Notre Dame University Press, 1963), p. 93.

14. Walter Rosenblith, in *Computers and the World of the Future,* Martin Greenberger, ed. (Cambridge, Mass.: MIT Press, 1962), p. 309.

15. J. R. Guard, F. C. Oglesby, J. H. Bennett, and L. G. Settle, "Semi-Automated Mathematics," *Journal of the Association for Computing Machinery,* Vol. 16, No. 1 (January 1969), p. 49.

16. *Ibid.,* p. 57.

17. Feigenbaum and Feldman, *Computers and Thought,* p. 8.

18. Paul Armer, "Attitudes Toward Intelligent Machines," in *Computers and Thought,* p. 392.

19. Shannon, in *Computers and the World of the Future,* pp. 309-310, cited in note 14 above.

20. Enthusiasts might find it sobering to imagine a fifteenth-century version of Feigenbaum and Feldman's exhortation: "In terms of the continuum of substances suggested by Paracelsus, the transformations we have been able to perform on baser metals are still at a low level. What is important is that we continue to strike out in the direction of the milestone, the philosopher's stone which can transform any element into any other. Is there any reason to suppose that we will never find it? None whatever. Not a single piece of evidence, no logical argument, no proof or theorem has ever been advanced which demonstrates an insurmountable hurdle along this continuum."

21. There has been much debate concerning this question. For the classical presentation of each side see John Lucas's "Minds, Machines and Gödel," *Philosophy,* Vol. XXXVI (April/July 1961), and Paul Benacerraf's "God, the Devil, and Gödel," *Monist* Vol. 51 (January 1967). The question turns on whether the fact that a human mathematician can always recognize as true propositions that cannot be proven to be true within a given formal system, shows that human beings cannot be modeled by an information-processing model which is necessarily a formal system. But such an argument misses the point that even if AI did produce an information-processing model of a mathematician, that model would be able to see that a specific formula was true by means of calculations based on its *heuristic rules.* Of course, the heuristic calculation could itself be viewed as a proof that certain conclusions follow from certain premises, but these "premises" would be formulae describing what the mathematician perceived, believed, remembered, etc., and the "conclusions" would be what he would say or surmise, etc.—obviously not the premises and conclusions of an acceptable formal proof of the original formula.

Index